Forest Primeval

FOREST PRIMEVAL

*The Natural History of
an Ancient Forest*

Chris Maser

Sierra Club Books · San Francisco

The Sierra Club, founded in 1892 by John Muir, has devoted itself
to the study and protection of the earth's scenic and ecological resources—
mountains, wetlands, woodlands, wild shores and rivers, deserts and plains.
The publishing program of the Sierra Club offers books to the public
as a nonprofit educational service in the hope that they may enlarge
the public's understanding of the Club's basic concerns. The point of view
expressed in each book, however, does not necessarily represent that of the Club.
The Sierra Club has some sixty chapters coast to coast, in Canada, Hawaii,
and Alaska. For information about how you may participate in its programs to
preserve wilderness and the quality of life, please address inquiries to
Sierra Club, 730 Polk Street, San Francisco, CA 94109.

Library of Congress Cataloging in Publication Data
Maser, Chris.
Forest primeval : the natural history of an ancient forest / by Chris Maser.
p.   cm.
Includes index.
Bibliography: p.
ISBN 0-87156-683-4
1. Forest ecology.   2. Forest ecology—History.   3. Forest conservation.
4. Forest conservation—History.   I. Title.
QH541.5.F6M37   1989
574.5'2642—dc20   89-31775
CIP

Production by Felicity Gorden
Jacket design by Paul Gamarello
Book design by Abigail Johnston

Printed in the United States of America

10 9 8 7 6 5 4 3 2 1

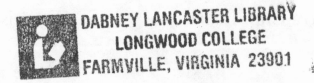

To Mother Earth,
who allowed me to make mistakes without
judgment and who taught me to observe and to question.
To the memory of Kenneth L. Gordon, my friend and my mentor
in graduate school, who had the wisdom to let me struggle,
the patience to answer my questions when I tired of struggling,
and the good humor and the gentleness to allow me
to bumble my way along the path of growth.
And to the memory of Cliff, my father,
from whom I learned much
in spite of myself.

Contents

Ancient Forest · 98

1237   1247   1252   1274   1287   1337   1412
1429–1430   1451   1492   1513   1526   1555   1620
1621   1691   1787   1803–1806   1812–1815
1832–1834   1840–1849   1850–1869   1870–1899   1900–1929
1930–1949   1950–1957   1958   1960   1963–1964
1965   1966–1967   1969–1973   1974–1987   1988

Preface

Friendship is one of the rare, beautiful gifts of life. I am fortunate to have you as a friend. Although I know the richness that your friendship gives to me, I can only guess what richness my friendship may give to you. But if I could, I know what I would give you to make your life as beautiful as mine.

I would give you the excitement of each sunrise—the birth of each new day.

I would give you the seasons in all their splendor. I would give you the May perfume of a high desert morning as the sun dries the dew from sagebrush, bitterbrush, and juniper. I would give you the July scent of ponderosa pine, the August fragrance of warm ripe blackberries, and the October aroma of a thicket of mountain-mahogany. I would give you the sharp, clean odor of spruce in the cold, thin air of a high-mountain winter.

I would give you the colors of flowers and the songs of birds. I would give you the symphony of canyon winds, the orchestration of thunderstorms, the eternal tempo of the sea.

I would give you the coolness of clear mountain streams, the tenderness of new grass. I would give you the freshness of summer rains, the silence of winter snows. I would give you the wonder of rainbows and of northern lights, and I would give you the majesty of snow-clad mountains. I would give you the sun, the moon, the stars, the wind, the rain, the snow. I would give you the fertility of the earth, the wisdom of eons entombed in rocks.

And I would give you the peace of each sunset—the reflective beauty of the land at day's end.

But I cannot give you these things. They are not mine to give. So, I offer you my hand. Take it and come back in time with me that I may paint for you with words the beauty and dignity of the land as I have seen it.

Acknowledgments

❧➤➤❦❦❦

I have never written a scientific paper or a book by myself, and this book is no exception. I have many coauthors—people with whom I have worked over the years who have shared their ideas with me, people who have fully given of their time to read the entire manuscript of this book and improve it, and people who have generously allowed me to use their photographs.

Many of the ideas that form part of the story within these pages have been gleaned over the years from colleagues: Steve Cline, Kermit Cromack, Ted Dyrness, Jerry Franklin, Ken Gordon, Don Grayson, Everett Hansen, Murry Johnson, C. Y. Li, Peter Morrison, Dave Perry, Jim Sedell, Tom Spies, Bob Storm, Fred Swanson, Bob Tarrant, Jack Ward Thomas, Jim Trappe, and Doug Ure.

The following people graciously accepted my request to read and improve the text as the story unfolded: Sue Borchers, Angeline Cromack, Jean Matthews, Zane Maser, Will Moir, Daniel Moses, and Mary Anne Stewart. My wife, Zane, had the most difficult task: she read my first draft of the manuscript and helped to make it intelligible enough to share with the others. Will Moir and Daniel Moses helped me to clarify the context of the story. Sue Borchers, Angeline Cromack, and Jean Matthews helped me to smooth out many of the details of my English. Mary Anne Stewart did one of the most thorough editing jobs I have ever had the privilege of working with.

There are three people not mentioned above whose help was invaluable in the creation of this book: Mike Castellano, Dan Luoma, and Sheila Till, the wizards who helped me learn how to use my new word processor, on which the manuscript was crafted.

Each of these people has shared his or her gift with me; I in turn have shared their gifts with you and added a touch of my own. No one's gift is any greater than anyone's else's; they are only different. I am deeply grateful for gifts that have been shared with me, for together they make the story you are about to read.

Credit for photographs:
page 14: USDA Forest Service, James Trappe; 16 & 17: USDA Forest Service, Douglas Ure; 19: USDA Forest Service, C.P.P. Reid; 20: USDA Forest Service, courtesy C.Y. Li; 23: Oregon Dept. of Fish and Wildlife, Ronald Rohweder; 29: Oregon Dept. of Fish and Wildlife, M. Millen; 31: Oregon Dept. of Fish and Wildlife, Walter Van Dyke; 37: Robert Storm; 50 & 52: Oregon Dept. of Fish and Wildlife, Charles Bruce; 72 & 74: USDA Forest Service, Jim Grace; 79: USDA Forest Service, James Trappe; 101: Oregon Dept. of Fish and Wildlife; 116: Oregon Cooperative Wildlife Research Unit, Gary Miller; 132: Oregon Dept. of Fish and Wildlife, Ronald Rohweder; 141: USDA Forest Service, Jerry Franklin; 145: Robert Storm; 173: Robert Smith and Chris Maser; 177 & 198: Oregon Dept. of Fish and Wildlife, Charles Bruce; 207: Patricia Benner; 221 & 223: USDA Forest Service, Thomas Spies; All other photographs are by Chris Maser.

Introduction

I always write the introduction to a book at least three times: first, before I write the text so I know what it is that I think I'm going to write about; then again while I'm writing the text, so that the introduction more closely reflects what it is that I think I'm writing about; and finally, when I've finished the text, so that the introduction most closely reflects what it is that I think I wrote about. In this way, I watch not only a book evolve but also myself, and it occurs to me that each book is an autobiography of my own inner journey.

Forest Primeval is no different. Writing this book has forever changed my sense of the forest, my sense of humanity, my sense of history, my sense of the humanity of history, and my sense of the history of humanity. We, the human species—whether we think so or not, whether we like it or not—are active participants in the creation of the world and the Universe. We are writer-actors on the stage of change; we are editing, writing, and rewriting the course of Nature's history, and we often become entrapped into acting out our short-sighted, poorly written, poorly constructed script.

I find this to be particularly true for those of us reared in the philosophical traditions of Western civilization. I, for example, was raised according to the biblical proclamation in Genesis that we human beings are the masters of the Earth. This means, as Joseph Campbell points out, that in the Judeo-Christian religion "God is separate from nature, and nature is condemned of God," that we human beings can create a more perfect world than that of Nature. This notion carries over into the language of our European-American culture: take, for example, the words *natural* and *history* from the subtitle of this book.

The word *natural* in today's usage as an adjective connotes that which is inherently of pristine Creation. To many people this connotation means *unspoiled by human hands*, suggesting that somehow humanity is *not* a natural part of the Universe and therefore really *does not belong* here.

If, on the other hand, we could go back in time and forget our civilized selves long enough to join the primitive peoples of the earth, we would find them to have been the epitome of natural harmony with the environment in which they lived. True, primitive peoples survived largely by hunting and killing and lived in a world in which life was always balanced on an exceedingly fine line between earthly existence and nonexistence—the hunter and the hunted. To survive in such a violent world, primitive peoples reconciled themselves with Creation through their myths and rituals—their metaphors of Creation—and through their spiritual connection with the Creator, of which they were but a manifestation. Simply put, their lives *were* spiritual Creation because they lived their myths through enacted rituals that remained in harmony with their changing environment. They understood that their Universe was always in creation, always changing, and never created, never static or absolute; they accepted Creation as the constant in their lives and adapted themselves to it through the continuity of their myths. *Primitive peoples knew who they were and where they belonged in and of Creation.*

We, the "enlightened" peoples of Western civilization, on the other hand, have forgotten our place in the Universe. This is not really surprising. Our ancestors came from afar, from the pastoral scenes of Europe, and they saw not a land to be understood and nurtured but a wild, untamed continent to be conquered. Why? Because they came from civilized countries with civilized myths and rituals and felt that they were being rudely thrust into an uncivilized continent inhabited by savages and wild beasts, the conquest of which was their duty.

What our ancestors did not understand, however, was that their myths belonged to another place and another time in the evolution of humanity and were not comparable with those of the primitive peoples of the New World. The myths of the Native Americans belonged to the land they inhabited, whereas those of our ancestors belonged to a land halfway around the world. But in line with a perfectly human tendency, our ancestors' first inclination was to survive in the wild, unknown continent and then to seek that which was familiar and comfortable by trying to force their myths from an "old," known world onto a "new," unknown world.

At best, our European ancestral myths were inharmonious with the land and the native peoples; at worst they were in a collision course with human survival on Earth. And somewhere along the way, *we have forgotten who we are. We have lost our identity* and *our sense of place in and of Creation.*

Now let's consider the word *history*. History, by definition, is of the past, but it is also of the present and of the future; yet in reality, the present is all there is. Both past and future are but illusions of the present and therefore inescapable as continuing cycles in our ever-changing Universe. History, therefore, is but a glimpse into the eternal cycle of Creation, a perceived reflection of what is, a ghost of what might have been, a dream of what might yet be. Creation is that which has, is, and will inexorably draw humanity and the ancient forest into the crucible of cosmic interrelatedness where the forest will mirror for humanity the consciousness of its own evolving self.

The way we use words defines both our myth and our sense of history. Although the Native Americans and the European Americans alike depended on the health and richness of the earth for sustenance, the Native Americans worshiped the Earth as sacred, and the European Americans treated what they called *soil* as a commodity to be owned. Whereas the Native Americans revered the earth, referring to it as Mother Earth, and had no concept of ownership, the European Americans drew imaginary lines in the soil, called them boundaries, and said, "This is mine." The European Americans perceived their "ownership" of the soil not only as the surface of what was encompassed within the boundaries but also throughout its entire depth. This difference is still evident in our choice of words, as illustrated in the following story carried in the *Corvallis Gazette-Times* in 1988:

> The remains of 28 American soldiers killed in the War of 1812 were taken from Canada to their *native soil* [emphasis mine] in flag-draped caskets . . . in the first repatriation ceremony held between the two countries. . . .
>
> "This is the day these men waited 174 years for," said U.S. Army Lt. Col. Robert Trotter. "They are coming home."

Thus, after 174 years of silence, history and myth speak, and we human beings listen. But in that 174 years we have poisoned the soil of the world with chemicals—in the guise of agriculture and of war and with hidden toxic wastes. And we have all but denuded the world of its forests—those silent witnesses of our history. Will we get sufficiently beyond our arrogance and materialism to save our historical roots for all generations from the chain saws of short-term profits based on the economics of extinction?

Today, the 13th of October 1988, I have lived fifty years, one-half of a century. To me that seems like quite an accomplishment; but when I compare it to that of the General Sherman Tree (a giant sequoia about 3,800 years old) or even to a 1,200-year-old Douglas-fir tree, it does not seem like much. Yet as I begin my next fifty years, I am acutely aware that we as human beings stand at a vantage point in our history and see the imminent liquidation of most of Nature's ancient Douglas-fir forests in the Pacific Northwest through planned extinction for short-term profits. And I wonder, what will the world be like without these regal forests? What will the future lose when the irretrievable artistry of millennia falls under the chain saw? With Asia alone reaching three billion human inhabitants and a total population of eight billion people predicted for the planet by the year 2000, has humanity already exceeded the carrying capacity of its forests? How will the loss of our global forests influence the greenhouse effect, the dramatic increase in carbon dioxide in the Earth's atmosphere that, like a greenhouse, traps heat that will warm the Earth? Forests, after all, are major users of carbon dioxide—an increase of which is one of the primary causes of the greenhouse effect.

Even though it is necessary to ask these questions, I am hardly old enough or wise enough to answer them, and I have not set out to write a litany of human blunders or a book about the future of forestry. I have instead, with the help of science and years of study, set out with you on a humble journey through a forest of a thousand years so you may see that the forest primeval represents our spiritual and historical roots as human beings, not just those of the Native Americans, or the European invaders, or the African slaves brought to the New World first by the Spanish in the 1500s and then by the European Americans two centuries later. As a masterpiece by a great painter or sculptor belongs to all of humanity in all generations, not just to the individual or museum in whose privileged trust and care it momentarily rests, so the ancient forest, the masterpiece of Creation, the historical accounting of our human struggle for consciousness through the centuries, belongs to all of humanity in all generations, not just to one special group or another who would secure it for narrow interests through lack of understanding.

As we journey through the forest of a thousand years, keep in mind that as the forest is growing and changing, so is humanity, and they will ultimately converge at a time and in a way that will forever change them both. Our story opens when humanity has as yet had little effect on the forests of the New World. As we shall see, however, settlement of the eastern coast of the New World gives birth to the concept of Manifest Destiny, a concept that drives men across the vast North American continent in a frenzy of conquest never before seen as Europeans exploit the land and its resources as short-term economic commodities. Finally, the eruption of World War II sets the technological stage for the systematic alteration of, and often the destruction of, the forest—faster and more completely than at any time in history.

In short, we cannot take a journey through a forest of a thousand years in isolation from human history; yet human history begins unpretentiously somewhere backstage. By 1787, however, humanity is starting to hog the footlights; the Constitutional Convention is preparing the way for westward expansion across what is now the United States, and by 1812 human endeavors in the Pacific Northwest begin to command center stage. By 1840, human manipulation of the environment begins to change the forest in ways never before seen, and beginning in 1870 both the forest and the Native Americans of the Pacific Northwest are relegated backstage to short-term economic exploitation of the land and advancing technology.

In just 142 years, from the start of Lewis and Clark's epic travels in 1803 to the end of World War II in 1945, we in Western civilization have achieved the technological capability to disarrange and disarticulate the basic functioning of the world. Consider, for example, that the first record of logging in what is now the Willamette National Forest in western Oregon occurred in 1875, and that 90 percent of the timber cut during the first three decades of this century was readily accessible and occurred below 4,000 feet in elevation. Every increase in the technology of logging and the utilization of wood fiber has expedited the exploitation of forests; thus from 1935 through 1980 the annual volume of timber cut has increased geometrically by 4.7 percent per year, which means a doubling of the volume cut every 15 years. By the 1970s, 65 percent of the timber cut occurred above 4,000 feet in elevation, and because the average tree harvested has become progressively younger and smaller, the increase in annual acreage cut has been five times greater than the increase in volume cut during the last 40 years. Today, humanity is rapidly deforesting the world.

I have purposefully used two styles of writing in our journey as a matter of perspective. That portraying the forest is personal and dynamic, as is the ongoing process of Creation. In contrast, that chronicling human history is an impersonal record of events because these events are remote from the forest until 1935—the year timber harvest begins its geometric increase and human history begins its inexorable bid to determine the fate of the Douglas-fir forests of the Pacific Northwest.

There is more to it, however, than simply styles of writing. In the pages that follow, I am trying, as best I can, to explore the depths of, the reality and the metaphor of, two simple words—*ancient forest*. Inherent in the definition of *ancient forest* is the notion that universal Creation is open-ended, full of wonder, full of unknowns, and full of seeming digressions in our human view of history. We in Western civilization are in love with "clean," straight lines, with quantifiable results, with final products. Creation is none of these. Creation is a process, the very existence of which is Creation.

To try and understand Creation, therefore, it is necessary also to deal with the complexities of human history. Human beings are a natural part of Creation and the Universe, and the historic intrusions of our human activity into the world of Nature are as significant in the ongoing process of Creation as a volcanic eruption, a great flood, or a catastrophic fire, or all three simultaneously in one place. In fact, the latter often have a less significant effect than our historic intrusions.

The historical episodes that I have chosen are of three kinds: first, those of individual strivings and deeds to point out that, as a forest is recognized and remembered by the sum of its individual, dominant trees, so society is recognized and remembered by the sum of its individual, dominant human beings; second, those of circumstances in Europe that give a sense of the nature, the myth, of the people who will depart European shores to settle in an unexplored continent; and third, those accentuated moments in the history of what is now the United States of America, those moments that are pivotal to our human participation in Creation—our social reflection mirrored in the fate of the Native Americans and of the ancient forest.

The issue of our social reflection mirrored in the fate of the Native Americans and of the ancient forest is one of the collision of myths and the birth of new myths. The myth and rituals of our democracy, for example, are a new myth born of a blending of European and Native American myths in the 1787 Constitutional Convention. This new myth was a way of government drawing in part on the myths enacted in the legal rituals of European law—the metaphors of social justice and freedom—and in part on their Native American counterpart—the myths enacted in the legal rituals of the Five Nation Iroquois Confederacy, in existence long before Europeans landed on the new shore. A basic ingredient that shaped the final draft of the new myth, the myth under which we live today, is that whereas the Iroquois did not believe in ownership of the land because it is part of Creation, a gift of the Creator, European Americans saw the land only as a commodity to be subdued and owned. So, rather than inheriting a myth of harmony with Nature and wonder about the Divine Mystery, we have inherited a myth of human superiority over Creation.

Sometimes myths also collide when people of one culture try to adopt the ways of another, as did the trappers and mountain men of the 1830s, who often tried to adopt the ways of Native Americans. Such attempts seldom seem successful, however, perhaps because although a new lifestyle may be adopted, the underlying myth of the original culture remains, unconscious and divergent. Thus, as the mountain men sought the solitude and freedom of the mountains, they unwittingly opened the way for a fateful collision of myths. European Americans eventually dominated and effectively imprisoned Native Americans on reservations, within whose imaginary lines on the soil Native American cultures and the myths on which they are founded have been dying—slowly and agonizingly—ever since.

By far the greater portion of European American history, however, has been the expression of our particular European American myth: the exploitation of Nature's bounty. This battle has been waged in the Pacific Northwest since 1812, but it was in the 1840s, in what is now Oregon and Washington, that the truly global dimensions of the battles of exploitation began to hack and hew at Mother Earth with an unrelenting sword whose epithet is *the economics of extinction*.

Finally, I discuss some of the episodes in my personal history in an attempt to define myself as an integral part of the forest and the forest as an integral part of me. Having grown up in the Pacific Northwest and having spent the greater part of my life in and around the ancient forest, my personal myth—my metaphor of the Eternal Mystery—is as inseparable from the life of an ancient Douglas-fir tree as the tree's roots in the earth are from its crown in the heavens.

In addition, I have noticed that the events in my life seem to be much swifter and more dramatic to me than are those in the ancient forest. I find it to be the same with humanity's view of its own history. The stage of Creation—in this case the ancient forest—seems to be infinite and unchanging compared with human events: witness the progression of historic episodes in our story in the last 176 years, from 1812 to 1988. And yet we humans must recognize and accept that while our personal and social history appears to unfold more swiftly, more dramatically, and more importantly than does that of the ancient forest, or of the desert, or of the sea, in reality such appearances are only illusions of our self-centered shortsightedness due, perhaps, to our brief, frightened pilgrimage on Earth. We human beings must learn to see that our social history changes in relation to that of the stage on which it is enacted and that together actors and stage are interdependent in the great drama of Creation.

Remember as we begin our journey that time is a figment of the human mind and has no meaning to Mother Earth. Yet time, with all its limitations, gives us human beings a sense of continuity, a sense of dimension, and a sense of place in an ever-changing universe. Thus time and human history will be the context for our journey through the forest primeval.

In the Beginning

❈❈❈

In the beginning the Earth was without form and void, and darkness was on the face of the deep. And time passed, and plants took dominion of the land. And the land broke into pieces that drifted apart, and the land changed, and time passed. And forests began to appear in the Silurian period about 350 million years ago, reaching their peak during the Carboniferous period 270 to 220 million years ago, when the climate was completely free of frost between latitudes 60 degrees north and 60 degrees south. Although forests of the Carboniferous period apparently contributed nothing to the development of modern arborescent forests, the Carboniferous forests were entombed in the Earth's strata as coal, later to relieve much pressure on modern forests for fuel. And time passed, and the Permian period, about 200 million years ago, brought forth glaciation that dwarfed any of the glacial cycles of the Pleistocene epoch, resulting in widespread destruction of old forms of plant and animal life and giving birth to new. And time passed, and the Tertiary period opened some 50 million years ago, and trees as we know them today were already present. The climate was favorable for forests in the early Tertiary, but the climatic pendulum was already swinging by the mid-Tertiary, and once more the earth experienced a series of glaciations as the Tertiary faded into history. And time

The Western Cascades might have looked like this 30 million years ago.

passed, and tremendous labor pains began during the late Eocene, about 40 million years ago, bringing the Cascade Mountains of Oregon into being. And time passed.

By the early Miocene, about 23 million years ago, three to six miles of continental sedimentary and volcanic rock were laid down. Many volcanic eruptions occurred during this time, adding lava flows from fifty to one hundred feet thick as the Western Cascade Mountain Range was born, uplifted, folded, matured, and eroded by the end of the Miocene, about 7 million years ago. (A trip along the crest of the High Cascades in Oregon might give you a fairly accurate feeling of what the Western Cascades were like about 30 million years ago. They were probably somewhat lower and had different plants and animals, but the volcanic forms of today almost certainly existed 30 million years ago.)

With the advent of the Pliocene, about 7 million years ago, the High Cascade Mountain Range began to rise through the extrusion of lava from volcanoes and volcanic vents. Uplifting of the mountain range continued, and several episodes of alpine glaciation occurred, especially on the volcanoes in the higher parts of the Cascades.

As the Cascade Mountain Ranges grew and changed, the Bering-Chukchi platform (also called the trans-Bering land bridge) between North America and Eurasia was intermittently inundated and exposed. When exposed, it formed a continuation of the Eurasian continent. The most recent exposure of the Bering-Chukchi platform began about 70,000 years ago during the last glacial stage—named the Wisconsin, after the state. During the maximum glaciation of the Wisconsin, the sea was approximately 328 feet below its present level. The Bering-Chukchi platform was apparently exposed in its entirety, forming a flat isthmus about 994 miles wide between what is now northeastern Siberia and Alaska. This land bridge remained open to migrating plants and animals, including human beings, until it was inundated by rising seas at the close of the Wisconsin glacial stage, about 10,000 years ago.

During the early and middle Miocene, 12 to 8 million years ago, more than forty genera of woody plants occupied the area from Oregon northward through Alaska, across the Bering-Chukchi platform, and through Siberia to Japan. But a pure coniferous forest—mostly fir, spruce, and hemlock—existed only in the uplands above 1,625 feet in Japan and above 2,275 feet in Oregon. This widely scattered forest began to dominate large areas of the uplands by the late Miocene, 10 to 8 million years ago, when fir, spruce, and hemlock occupied intermediate elevations throughout the western United States. The coniferous forest for the first time extended continuously from the uplands of Oregon northward through British Columbia into Alaska.

A rich northern forest of spruce, pine, and hemlock, with some larch, fir, beech, oak, and elm was becoming established in northeastern Siberia during the late Miocene or early Pliocene, about 10 to 7 million years ago. Although a similar trend was occurring simultaneously in Alaska, the early Pliocene plant communities west of the Cascade Mountains in Oregon contained an impoverished deciduous forest that still had some hickory, elm, and sycamore.

The glacial cycles of the Pleistocene that began about 1.5 million years ago caused many of the genera and species characteristic of the forests in Europe to enter the catalog of extinction. But most of the floras that had been around throughout the Tertiary, which began about 50 million years earlier, seem to have recovered their lost territories worldwide with relative ease. Major parts of the original wide-spread deciduous forest can still be found in Japan, China, Europe, and parts of the eastern United States. Extinction of the deciduous forest in the Pacific Northwest probably was caused by a climatic change that favored the coniferous trees and allowed the general establishment of the Douglas-fir forests, much as they occur today, by 10,500 years ago. In some areas, however, such as Bonaparte Meadows of the Okanogan Valley of northcentral Washington, the modern forest community that includes Douglas-fir has a history of only 2,500 years.

In North America during the four prominent glacial stages of the Pleistocene Ice Age, the climate cooled and arctic ice sheets moved southward and covered the land. In between each glacial stage, the climate warmed and the ice retreated, melting under the summer sun.

As the last glacial stage, the Wisconsin, reached its maximum development, the average temperature of the world gradually dropped, ranging from a reduction of 5 degrees Fahrenheit at the equator to one of 10 degrees at 35 to 40 degrees north latitude, about the latitude of the state of Kansas, and one of 25 degrees at the edge of the ice sheet. The snow line was lowered about 3,000 feet for each 10-degree drop in average annual temperature; consequently, subarctic plants and animals occurred as far south as Virginia, Texas, and Oklahoma.

Crossing the Bering-Chukchi platform before its inundation at the close of the Wisconsin glacial stage, some of the Native Americans' ancient ancestors migrated south and east out of Alaska and arrived in the Great Plains of North America between 15,000 and 20,000 years ago. These Ancient Ones represent some of the earliest human inhabitants of North America, of whom very little specific evidence is known. They reached the southeastern United States about 15,000 years ago, the northeastern United States and southern part of southeastern Canada about 14,000 years ago, and the southern half of the Lower Peninsula of Michigan 1,000 years later. Between 14,000 and 11,000 years ago, they inhabited what is now Las Vegas, Nevada, and traveled throughout the Columbia Basin of northcentral Oregon and eastern Washington. They did not, however, cross the Cascade–Sierra Nevada mountain ranges and reach the coastal areas of northern California and Oregon until about 8,000 years ago.

The Ancient Ones who crossed the Bering-Chukchi platform were hunters of big game, and as millennia passed, they gradually became nomadic foragers who subsisted by gathering, fishing, and hunting small game animals. In more recent times, they settled into semipermanent and permanent communities and finally became agriculturalists whose economy depended on farm crops as well as on hunting with spears and bows and arrows, fishing, and gathering. They also made pottery, a sign of their evolving culture and of their commitment to a place.

While the Ancient Ones were migrating over the North American continent, the Appalachian highlands were open, treeless, grass-and-sedge tundra with permafrost. Virginia was dominated by white spruce and pine and is thought to have been a spruce parkland interspersed with ponds, marshes, and prairies. Spruce trees were also scattered throughout much of what are now grasslands, from southern Saskatchewan southward to northeastern Kansas, and from western Minnesota southward to western Missouri. Between 16,600 and 13,700 years ago, for example, both spruce and tamarack occurred in southwestern Missouri. In Texas, on the other hand, pine was predominant over spruce about 17,400 years ago.

The center of the North American continent was a grassland during the Pleistocene epoch. The borders of the grassland expanded or withdrew as temperatures waxed and waned, and with each change the grassland competed across zones of contact with coniferous forest, deciduous forest, and desert shrub. During the interglacial times and warmer parts of glacial cycles, the deciduous forest retreated eastward, and the western grassland occupied the abandoned area. With cooling temperatures and subsequent increases in precipitation, the forest reoccupied its former distribution while the grassland retreated westward. Members of two principal plant communities (northern and southern) within the grassland itself migrated, mingled, competed, and evolved. Many species were lost, while new ones may have come into existence in this time of shifting grasses.

Changes from coniferous to deciduous forest took place rapidly following the recession of the Wisconsin glaciation. Forest composition changed first in Georgia approximately 13,600 years ago. It took another 1,000 years for change to occur in the higher and more northern Appalachians. Since the initial coniferous-deciduous forest turnover, the resulting habitat has been a closed-canopy, oak-dominated forest with only minor changes in climate and composition of forest species.

The warming, drying post-Wisconsin climate saw the eastward retreat of the deciduous forest, and an eastward and presumably southward movement of the grassland. Spruce, for example, disappeared from Texas about 12,500 years ago. The eastern deciduous forests thus became isolated from the western coniferous forests soon after the end of the Wisconsin glacial stage, approximately 10,000 years ago, and the intervening area evolved into the Great Plains of the midwestern United States and southcentral Canada.

The picture is somewhat more complex along the western and northern portions of the North American grasslands. Here the grasslands were more or less mixed with trees and shrubs that followed an east-to-west climatic gradient of decreasing precipitation and humidity. The broad-leaved deciduous forest of the East gave way to open, drier coniferous forest dominated by pine and juniper in the West. As the climate continued to warm and dry, wind-driven grass fires began to play a significant role in the evolution of the grasslands. Fires burned unchecked until quenched by rain or halted by abrupt differences in topography. As fires swept repeatedly through savanna-like grasslands, the trees and shrubs died out and were replaced by grasses.

Some fire-sensitive trees survived, however, not only along rivers and streams but also on protected escarpments and rocky promontories that served as natural firebreaks. Nonriparian, scarp-restricted woodlands extended across the Central Plains in the latitude of the Prairie Peninsula—from Indiana through Illinois, Iowa, and Nebraska to Wyoming. Numerous wooded scarps also occurred throughout the flat monotony of the short-grass steppe from eastern Montana southward to New Mexico and Texas.

Recurrent drought and subsequent fires, however, prevented the scarp-restricted trees from regaining a hold on the grasslands. Although the trees originated as part of a regional forest, prairie fires helped maintain the open conditions by sweeping across great expanses of flat topography, consuming the seasonally dry grasses. Abrupt topographic features stopped the fires and protected scattered islands of trees. Thus, although climate was a factor in the evolution of the grasslands in the center of the North American continent, so too were

Fort Rock, rising more than three hundred feet, is the remnant of a tuff cone, rock formed of compacted volcanic ash. Much of the erosion was caused by wave action in a lake that covered the floor of the valley during the Pleistocene.

the vastness and flatness of the Great Plains and the annual fire-carrying dieback of the grasses.

Northern plant and animal communities of eastern North America are composed largely of post–Wisconsin glacial stage plants and animals that immigrated to terrain previously stripped of living organisms by glacial ice. Competition favored species adapted to harsh northern environments and capable of rapid dispersal. Animal communities on the southern edge of the glacier were composed of northern and temperate species. Unadaptable temperate species continued to inhabit local refugia (areas of unaltered climate), while those with greater degrees of adaptability survived in various unglaciated areas.

As the climate changed, so did habitats surrounding the glacier. Habitats on the edge of the glacier were neither created nor destroyed as rapidly as those covered by ice. The gradual changes created a continuum of microhabitats that supported a richer living community than that in previously glaciated areas. These relationships were similar to conditions in the midwestern United States, which has little topographic diversity.

During the Wisconsin glacial stage, a large lake filled the Fort Rock Basin of southcentral Oregon, east of the High Cascade Mountain Range. The habitat was a mixture of grassy plains, riparian woodlands, and water. The grassy areas of the lowland glades and upland prairies were occupied by two species of horses and three species of camels. The stream valleys, with strips or clumps of woodland, were suited for the large ground sloth, mammoth, two species of peccaries, and one of bear, while the streams themselves had beaver and muskrats. These animals were hunted by dire-wolves and by people, who are thought to have moved into the basin about 11,000 years ago. The lakes and streams also had five species of carps and suckers as well as chinook salmon. All these species, except the salmon, are extinct. Presence of the salmon indicates a stage of overflow through an outlet to the Pacific Ocean that allowed the salmon to reach Fort Rock Lake. The salmon became landlocked when the overflow ceased but persisted in the lake until the end of its existence about 10,000 years ago.

The 10,000-year interval between the end of the Wisconsin glacial stage and the beginning of historic times must have been of crucial im-

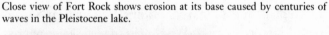

Close view of Fort Rock shows erosion at its base caused by centuries of waves in the Pleistocene lake.

Black-tailed jackrabbit (*Lepus californicus*).

portance in the establishment of modern patterns of vertebrate distribution throughout the intermountain West. For example, prior to 7,000 years ago, white-tailed jackrabbits lived in the lower elevations of the present Fort Rock Basin. The white-tailed jackrabbit is adapted to the colder climates of higher, more northerly regions and tends to occupy grassy habitats. Sage grouse, elk, and bison, each with similar habitat affinities, all lived in the Fort Rock Basin. In addition, the pika or rock rabbit lived in jumbles of broken rock.

About 7,000 years ago, two unrelated events occurred—Mount Mazama erupted, forming present-day Crater Lake, and the climate began to change. Although the tremendous eruption of Mount Mazama spread volcanic ash and pumice over a vast area, the eruption was not responsible for the climatic change. As the climate warmed and dried between 7,000 and 5,000 years ago, the plant community shifted from one that was primarily grasses and herbs to one that was primarily shrubs. This shift caused the local extinction of the white-tailed jackrabbit, sage grouse, pika, elk, and bison. The mountain cottontail and black-tailed jackrabbit, on the other hand, increased as the habitat changed because both are adapted to the warmer climates of lower, more southerly regions and tend to occupy shrubby habitats.

Between 5,000 and 4,000 years ago giant sequoias inhabited scattered areas of central California on the west side of the Sierra Nevada Mountain Range. Some of their seeds germinated and grew until these mammoths fell with age or were cut down early in this century. Although giant sequoias still live, they are not so old. One tree, however, the General Sherman Tree in Sequoia National Park, was estimated to be 3,800 years old in 1968. It would have germinated in 1832 B.C. and would have been 132 years old when, tradition says, a people called the Hyksos came from the east and conquered the Nile Delta at the end of the Thirteenth Dynasty in Egypt. The tree would have been 632 years old when the Trojan War was fought in 1200 B.C. and 1,056 years old when the first Olympic Games were held in 776 B.C. It would have been 1,617 years old when the Great Wall of China was built in 215 B.C. and 1,832 years old when Jesus was born in Bethlehem. Another ancient species, the bristlecone pine, occurs today only on high peaks from Colorado to southern Utah, central and southern Nevada, southeastern California, and northern Arizona. Some bristlecones in the White Mountains of California have been estimated to be over 4,000 years old. These trees would have germinated in 2032 B.C. and would have been 32 years old when the pyramids were built in Giza and when the Semites conquered the Third Dynasty of Ur at the northern end of the Persian Gulf, ending forever Sumerian rule. Just think what these historians of ancient times could tell us if we could talk with them and they with us.

Birth of a Forest

➤➤✕◀◀

987

It is hot and dry, very dry. The sun glides toward the Pacific Ocean. Swallows and bats mingle briefly in twilight before changing insect patrol over the top of the 700-year-old Douglas-fir forests. An owl hoots. Then another. Black clouds, like great stalking cats, devour the moon, and the night grows still and heavy.

A breeze begins to stir the treetops, like gentle probing fingers. Rain begins to polka-dot bare, parched soil on ridgetops with punctuating *plop*, *plop*, *plop*s. The wind grows strong, becomes urgent, and the rain begins to hiss as the wind scurries hither and yon through the forest canopy. Lightning flashes, thunder cracks and rolls, and the odor of ozone fills the air. Lightning slashes the darkness. Silence. Thunder. Lightning. Silence. Thunder. Lightning strikes the top of a Douglas-fir and spirals down its trunk. Lightning strikes another tree and another. Then, with a simultaneous ear-splitting crack, lightning spirals down a 250-foot-tall Douglas-fir and strikes the ground, igniting the forest floor at the base of the tree.

A small fire now casts its flickering light against the trunk of the old tree. The fire grows and spreads faster and faster across and up the slope. It finally comes to a jumble of five fallen Douglas-firs that died of root rot and blew over in a storm three years ago. Here western hemlock, the shade-tolerant tree that grows under the Douglas-fir and replaces it in old forests, forms a ladder of various ages and heights from the forest floor into the tops of the giant firs. As the flames begin to burn more intensely and leap higher from the fallen trees, they reach part of the hemlock ladder, which seems at first resistant to the heat, then explodes in flames. The flames climb the ladder into the tops of the firs. They roar through the treetops, creating their own wind and irresistibly devouring the forest before them. The irregular line of fire 250 feet above the ground throws great sheets of flame 300 feet into the air that appear to disconnect themselves from the fiery torrent in an effort to defeat the darkness. Leaping, exploding, darting forward, the flames bridge streams and open spaces and start new fires ahead of the advancing inferno. The immense shooting flames roar into the night under the twinkling light of silent stars.

In other parts of the forest, the fire creeps along the ground, burning twigs and branches and pausing occasionally to consume a snag or partly buried fallen tree. It races uphill and creeps along the contours, flares and smolders, is cool in some areas and reaches over 1,200 degrees Fahrenheit in others, kills all vegetation, and spares individual trees, small groups of trees, and whole islands. And along the big river in the valley, the great fleeces of dry moss growing on the trunks of the trees act like fuses made of the old black gunpowder up which the flames shoot into the trees, igniting their crowns like torches. Thus Nature alters her canvas that she may create a new forest.

As the pale light grows in the east on the fifth day of August 987, tall, blackened, smoking columns appear against the sky. Large fallen trees still smolder. Here and there are the charred bodies of deer that could not outrun the raging inferno, and under a large blackened tree is the body of a Native American hunter who was trapped by the flames and killed by the falling tree. A sudden, muffled *thump* punctuates the silence as a large, standing dead tree, or snag, weakened by age and the fire, crashes to earth.

The sun rises; the day becomes hot and still. Smoke hangs like a pall. By late afternoon, a light breeze off the ocean a hundred air miles away begins to blow the smoke eastward up the west flank of the Western Cascade Mountains. The breeze stirs the fire in a smoldering fallen tree, and it erupts in flame, its brightness a seeming mirror reflection of the stars as darkness settles quietly over the land.

August becomes September, then October, and on the 13th of October it becomes cloudy as the storm front off the ocean reaches the mountains. Warm, moist, blustery wind heralds the storm as falling rain magnifies the odor of burnt forest. It rains all night. Cloaked in the darkness, the surviving Douglas-fir trees begin to shed their seeds, for as the tree originally lay dormant in the seed, so the seed lies dormant in the cone of the tree. But now the blustery wind shakes the giant firs and loosens the seeds in their ripe cones hanging from boughs over 200 feet above the ground. The winged seeds whirl and spin as they ride the wind various distances to earth.

Deer mice stir in their burrows beneath the soil, some protected by pockets of wet, rotten wood from trees that fell 300 years earlier, trees that are slowly being reinvested into the soil. Some mice have already ventured out into the night, straining their large, delicate ears for sounds of danger. Well equipped for night travel, these small be-whiskered rodents lessen the darkness with large, sensitive eyes that cannot see color but can gather light.

Deer mice are the first rodents to explore the burnt-over land. They are exploratory by nature, often straying from protective cover. Whether such acts are bravery or foolishness on the part of a particular mouse is open to question; nevertheless some shorten their already-brief lives through such excursions when they are captured by owls or other predators.

A deer mouse's willingness to explore the burnt land is, however, both a help and a hindrance to the forest of the future. Being fond of the seeds of Douglas-fir, the mice eat all they find, but they don't find all of them. And not all the seeds fall at once. So, while the mice explore the ground for a banquet of seeds, especially along the protected overhang of charred fallen trees, they pause periodically in their travels to deposit fecal pellets. And it is through their fecal pellets that the mice unknowingly help prepare the soil for the next forest.

Deer mice are by nature opportunistic in their diet and have a gourmet's appreciation of the belowground fruiting bodies of fungi, called truffles. Thus, over the days and weeks since the fire, the mice have

Cross section of a truffle (*Hymenogaster parksii*) shows the inner, dark, spore-bearing tissue. Scale in millimeters.

been searching belowground for dried truffles and for those few in and near the wet, rotten wood that are still fresh. The mice have an acute sense of smell and detect the truffles by the individually distinctive odor each kind gives off at maturity.

Having found a truffle, a mouse eats it, albeit rather sloppily, and inoculates the soil with fungal spores by dropping pieces of truffle tissue with viable spores attached. The consumed portion of the truffle goes through the stomach, where fungal tissue is digested, and through the small intestine, where nutrient absorption takes place, into a pouch called the cecum, where the spores are concentrated, stored, and mixed. From the cecum, the truffle spores go into the large intestine or colon, where they are formed with other undigested material into fecal pellets, which are expelled through the rectum. Along with its reproductive spores, a truffle has one-celled plants called bacteria on its surface and inside it, as well as propagules of yeast, yet another fungus. The bacteria include a species called *Clostridium butyricum* (no common name), which is a classic nitrogen-fixing bacterium. (Nitrogen fixing means that the bacterium can take nitrogen gas out of the air and transform it into an organic compound usable by plants.)

Clostridium butyricum has a built-in survival mechanism (the endospore or internal resting stage) by which it can withstand temperatures up to 176 degrees Fahrenheit. This is an important adaptation because the surface temperature of the scorched soil can reach 160 degrees Fahrenheit during the heat of a summer's day.

Deer mice retain the spores of the truffles in their ceca for more than a month after eating the truffle. So even where the fire was hot enough to kill the existing spore inoculum in the soil, the mice reinoculate it through defecation because each fecal pellet contains live truffle spores, nitrogen-fixing bacteria, and yeast propagules. Each fecal pellet also contains all the nutrients necessary to keep the fungal spores, bacteria, and yeast in a healthy condition. And since the mice are active mainly along the fallen trees, greater numbers of pellets occur there also.

The deer mice are joined by Townsend chipmunks along the edge of the burn and the live forest. The chipmunks come out of the live forest to visit the burn by day, defecating as they go, and the mice frequent it by night, also defecating as they go. Thus the burned soil is reinoculated almost immediately by the small mammals of the forest that transport truffle spores, nitrogen-fixing bacteria, and yeast from the live forest. In addition, fungal inoculum already exists in areas where the soil was not scorched, and this inoculum is simply added to by the small mammals.

Many wind-borne seeds of annual plants, parachuted into the forest over recent years, have lain dormant in the litter of the forest floor until their release by removal of the trees. Their emergence with the rain is not the same over all acres. The greatest variety occurs where the fire was hot enough to stimulate the sleeping seeds to awaken but not hot enough to damage them. In other areas, however, the fire destroyed all or nearly all the existing seeds. In these areas, the only seeds to germinate are those of wind-borne annual plants that have been floating into the burn over the weeks since the fire. These seeds have ridden the air currents over great distances from areas that were burned up to a decade before. Many are small and barely noticeable, but others shimmer in the sun as they are carried aloft on gentle autumn breezes.

By mid-November, rains have soaked the land, and scattered

Western red-backed vole (*Clethrionomys californicus*).

sunny days have caused many seeds of the annual plants to germinate, creating a fine green mosaic over the blackened landscape. November passes and winter secures its grip in early December as snow begins to accumulate. The chipmunk is snug in its belowground nest of dry vegetation, where it will spend the winter until released by the spring sun. The deer mouse, on the other hand, will brave the winter, searching for food both below and above the blanket of snow.

Winter seems to hang on the mountain peaks as snowflakes whirl and spin and drift out of the dark sky, each adding its unique being to the growing blanket. The snow, seven feet deep by late March, covers most of the fallen trees, and the world appears lifeless as storms darken the sky and the cold, north wind blows among the blackened skeletons of yesterday's forest.

988

With the advent of April 988, the reproductive urge begins to stir in the male deer mouse as its testes descend from their winter resting places inside the lower body cavity. Once they have descended into the scrotum and cooled 2 to 3 degrees, viable sperm are produced. Then, as the female becomes receptive, she is bred, and in late pregnancy,

Creeping vole (*Microtus oregoni*).

she ushers in the warming days and melting snow of May. With these days, chipmunks awaken and their *po! po! po!* calls are heard in the forest. The deer mouse gives birth to her litter of five naked, pink babies, each of which weighs about seven one-hundredths of an ounce. Born under a large, fallen tree in a warm nest of thistledown, birds' feathers, and soft dry grasses, the young mice grow rapidly. As the first litter of mice greets the world, the chipmunk is conceiving her young.

The snow melts off the fallen trees first because the charred wood gathers and stores heat from the sun. This process also helps melt the snow along and around the fallen trees, which in turn allows young plants access to the spring sun, which in turn warms the soil and stimulates other seeds to germinate. Among them are some of the Douglas-fir seeds that fell last October; others still lie buried under snow.

Over the winter, deer mice, western red-backed voles, and creeping voles have deposited numerous fecal pellets as they traveled back and forth along a large, fallen tree a hundred yards into the burn from the edge of the forest. The tree, lying along the contour of a gentle south-facing slope, has bare, warm soil, numerous fecal pellets, and a few seeds of Douglas-fir that escaped the notice of both birds and rodents to survive the winter and be prepared for germination. All awaits in readiness for the unsurpassable miracle of life.

A slightly buried Douglas-fir seed begins to swell as it absorbs moisture from the warm soil. Its seed coat splits, and a tiny root begins to penetrate the bosom of the earth as small, green seed leaves reach toward the sun. Thus the seed of the tree becomes the seedling of the tree in its first spring of life.

As the seedling's roots spread through the soil, the new nonwoody root tip of a tiny feeder root comes in contact with a week-old fecal pellet of a deer mouse. The deer mouse had dined on a truffle the night before it deposited the pellet. The pellet thus contains between 500,000 and 800,000 truffle spores, and it only takes between 1,000 and 10,000 spores to colonize one root tip. The pellet is still soft from the moisture in the soil, and the root tip has little difficulty penetrating it.

Inside the pellet, the root tip comes in contact with the spores that have passed unscathed through the mouse's intestinal tract. Meanwhile, the yeast in the pellet is growing and producing a substance called yeast extract that is food for the nitrogen-fixing bacteria. As the root tip contacts the spores, the yeast helps stimulate the spores to germinate and grow into and around the root tip; the nitrogen-fixing bacteria and yeast become enveloped in the fungal tissues. Once inside the fungal tissue and in the absence of oxygen, the nitrogen-fixing bacteria are nurtured by the extracts of both the yeast's and the truffle's nonreproductive tissues. The bacteria in turn fix atmospheric nitrogen that may be used by both the fungus and the host tree.

The nonreproductive tissue of the truffle, called mycelia, forms a mantle around the tree's feeder root; this symbiotic association is called mycorrhiza and literally means "fungus-root." The word was coined and the fungus–host plant association described nearly a century ago. This seemingly new phenomenon dates back to the earliest-known fossils of plant rooting structures, some 400 million years ago. In fact, land plants probably originated through a symbiosis between marine fungi and photosynthesizing algae. Today, the roots of all but a few families of plants form mycorrhizae with symbiotic fungi. Woody plants in particular require mycorrhizal fungi for survival. Many herbaceous plants also depend on the fungus-root association, and most of those that do not depend on this partnership grow far better with the fungi than without them. Mycorrhizal fungi in turn depend on their green plant hosts as a source of energy and growth regulators.

Mycorrhiza, the symbiotic relationship between certain fungi and plant roots. In this case the fungus forms a mantle, a covering over the root-tip.

The host plant provides simple sugars and metabolites to the chlorophyll-lacking mycorrhizal fungi, which generally are not competent saprophytes. (Saprophytes are fungi that can live independently off decaying organic materials.) The fungus absorbs minerals, other nutrients, nitrogen, and water from the soil and transfers them to the host plant. In effect, mycorrhiza-forming fungi serve as highly efficient extensions of the host's root system. Many of the fungi produce growth regulators that induce production of new root tips and increase the useful lifespan of the host's roots. Mycorrhizal colonization also enhances the host plant's resistance to attack by pathogens. Some mycorrhizal fungi even produce compounds that prevent pathogens from contacting the root system of the host plant. At the same time, the host plant prevents mycorrhizal fungi from damaging its roots.

As the mycelia grow into and around the root tips, they also grow out into the soil, where they join billions of miles of gossamer threads from other fungi. These mycelial threads act as extensions of the seedling's root system as they wend their way through the soil, absorbing water, phosphorus, and nitrogen and sending them into the seedling's

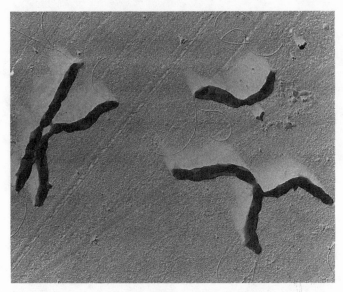

Nitrogen-fixing bacterium, *Azospirillum* spp., enlarged 3,995 times.

roots. As the seedling grows, it produces sugars that feed the fungus, which in turn expands through the soil as it is nourished by and nourishes the seedling. The tree is a product of both the sun's light and the earth's darkness; the nutrients of darkness feed the top of the tree in light, and the sugars of light feed the roots of the tree and the fungus in darkness.

Another fir seed germinates and grows, but its root tips do not contact the pellet of a deer mouse, for this seedling is growing near the edge of the forest along a fallen tree frequented by western red-backed voles. Red-backed voles deposit each night a hundred or more fecal pellets, each of which contains about 300,000 truffle spores. The seedling is growing in an area where red-backed voles have been defecating for several months. Most of the pellets have disintegrated, however, and the spores, along with the yeast and the nitrogen-fixing bacterium *Azospirillum* spp. (no common name), have formed a concentrated inoculum in the soil.

The seedling is doing well. Warmed by the spring sun and nurtured by the moist soil, its roots grow into a rich inoculum along the fallen tree. A root tip contacts a tiny pocket of 100,000 spores and is colonized by the fungus. The yeast, as before, is swept along in the process, but the nitrogen-fixing bacterium *Azospirillum* is different from that in the pellet of the deer mouse. *Azospirillum* can make its own opening into the root tip and thus enters at will. From here, the process is essentially the same as just described.

Not all seedlings fare as well, however, because some germinate in soil with a low inoculum; others germinate on scorched soil with no inoculum. Those seedlings that either are not colonized or are insufficiently colonized with mycorrhizal fungi will die of water stress during the heat of summer. Seedlings that will grow best during the summer are those that have the truffle *Rhizopogon vinicolor* (no common name) forming mycorrhizae with their roots because this truffle, a specialist with Douglas-fir, is excellent at both the uptake and transfer of water from soil and rotting wood into the seedlings' root systems.

Other seedlings, both scattered and in patches, are growing throughout the burn under an infinite variety of circumstances. Some, lacking sufficient colonization with the belowground mycorrhizal-forming fungi (truffles), are given a new lease on life as warm spring rains bring forth a bumper crop of mushrooms, many of which form mycorrhizae with the seedlings. The aboveground-fruiting mushrooms rely on wind to disseminate their spores over the landscape. If, therefore, you could catch a bit of wind and look at it under a very powerful lens, you would see beautiful microscopic spores that are borne aloft only to land on the soil and be washed belowground by rain. As the spores journey belowground, they may contact and colonize root tips, often bringing life where life was doubtful because of insufficient colonization by the spores of the truffles.

Spring matures. Here and there green plants carpet the burn, especially along fallen trees near the forest. Most of these plants, such as hawksbeard, dandelion, pearly-everlasting, and old-man-in-the-spring, came in by parachute. Others, such as California fescue, bedstraw, and beggar-ticks, came into the burn clinging to the hair of black-tailed deer, elk, and puma. Still others, such as lupine, blackcap, trailing blackberry, and wild strawberry, were deposited by birds who ate the fruits elsewhere and through defecation seeded them here.

The creeping vole has become well established in these areas of abundant green plants. Unlike the red-backed vole, who is a fungal specialist, generations of creeping voles have lived on an almost pure diet of fungi for centuries in the ancient forest but at all times have been subordinate in numbers of individuals to the generations of red-backed voles. The creeping vole is released from bondage by the fire, and its population explodes as it shifts its diet from fungi to the growing supply of grasses and herbs in the burn. The red-backed vole, on the other hand, dies out in the burned area because, with the death of the fire-injured trees, the truffles stop fruiting, and the vole is left without its specialized diet. The time shall come, however, when the roles will again be reversed.

July comes to the burn, and butterflies flit amidst flowers in the hot sun. Thistle blossoms seem to be the butterflies' favorite nectar bar. Young chipmunks join their parents and keep a watchful eye on the red-tailed hawks riding the thermals high overhead. And higher still, turkey vultures soar on cosmopolitan winds, searching always for odors of the dead animals on which they dine. Occasionally, a bright, beady-eyed creeping vole bustles into the sunlight, only to disappear immediately under the fallen tree from which it ventured. A late afternoon breeze sways the flowers. Flies buzz. A hawk screams.

The August sun warms ripe blackcaps and blackberries, and their odors attract chipmunks, who stuff their cheek pouches with the sweet fruits. Some they eat; some they bury, only to forget where, and so plant more seeds. In their eagerness to get the fruit, the chipmunks stuff so much into their cheek pouches that their forefeet and faces become purple from the juice. Deer mice trade places with the chipmunks as darkness moves westward, and they, too, enjoy the berries.

September brings spider webs floating on gentle breezes. Little gusts of wind pluck seeds from dandelions, hawksbeard, old-man-in-the-spring, and thistles and carry them aloft to join the traveling spiders. The air is filled with flying seeds and drifting spiders who have cast their lot to the wind. They know not from whence it comes or whither it goes, they are simply along for the ride.

Early October, the peak of the breeding season for elk, has warm, sunny days and cold, clear nights. Chickarees, the small tree squirrels, send their territorial chatters back and forth through the forest as they

Chickaree (*Tamiasciurus douglasi*).

busily cut and store the last Douglas-fir cones against the snows of winter. The bugling of bull elk challenging one another causes the chickarees to pause momentarily and listen.

A light blanket of snow already covers the higher elevations as October slips quietly into November. By mid-November the breeding season for black-tailed deer is in full swing. The bucks walk along the edge of the forest with swollen necks and shiny antlers in search of receptive females. On the 25th of November, dark clouds, coming northeast from the ocean, bump into the burn and rupture. It snows quietly and gently for three days and a night. The flakes, no two alike since the beginning of time, add one to the other until over two feet of snow cover the ground. When the storm is over on the 28th of November, not a deer track is to be found. Forsaking the burn until spring, the deer will complete their breeding season on the winter range at lower elevations, where the imminent danger of deep snow is lessened.

It snows off and on throughout December. The burn is covered by five feet of snow, and still the flakes fall—sometimes gently, sometimes whipped by a howling wind.

993

Seeds of herbaceous plants continue to come into the burn, and by 993 most of the burn is green. A few of the most severely scorched areas are still without vegetation, however, because the soil has yet to regain its ability to absorb water (soil that repels water is called hydrophobic soil).

As the plants grow, they gradually change the chemistry and structure of the soil; lupines, for example, contain small nodules on their roots that house nitrogen-fixing bacteria. Thus the nitrogen content of the soil is increasing dramatically where lupines grace the burn. Lupines do not grow everywhere because they have evolved to grow in nitrogen-deficient soil, and not all areas of the burn are deficient in nitrogen. In fact, the soil of the burn, like that of the forest, is a chemical and structural mosaic, ranging from fine material to coarse material, from rich in some chemicals in some places to poor in those same chemicals in other places. No two areas are the same, and each is constantly changing. So the variation in soil characteristics is infinite. As the chemistry of the soil changes, so do its structural characteristics because the soil's structure is a result of chemical interactions within its substance.

The vegetation is not only a mirror reflection of the soil's ability to grow it but also a determiner of which animals can live where. So it is not surprising that the three Mazama pocket gophers who burrowed through the snow from the high meadow just above the burn would stop in the first good patch of lupine they came to.

The gophers, who started burrowing downhill through the quarter-mile of forest in early November, finally reached the burn in late February. They are last year's young who were forced out of the lower portion of the meadow by the established adults. They arrived in the burn by chance because they had no way of knowing it was there. In a sense, they traveled blindly through the snow. They dug shallow tunnels in the upper surface of the soil and the lower surface of the snow, and they packed soil into the snow roof of their tunnels, which created a gopher subway under the snow through the forest.

Earth cores of the Mazama pocket gopher (*Thomomys mazama*).

They did not, of course, go straight downhill but spent a day or two here and a week there as they explored and hunted for food.

The spring thaw reveals their winter travels as recorded by solid cores of soil lying on the surface of the ground, going belowground in one spot and up into the snow in another. The latter is evident where one earthen core lies over another. The gophers sometimes even bumped into rocks, which they either climbed over or went around. One gopher built a nest on the surface of the soil with a toilet (a short tunnel filled with elongated fecal pellets) next to it.

The gophers, two females and a male, arrive in the burn within a few days of each other. Each establishes a burrow system while still exploring beneath the snow. The male finds one of the females on the 10th of March, and she, being receptive, conceives. The second female, exploring the surface of the snow on a quiet night in April, is caught by a great horned owl hunting along the edge of the forest.

The pregnant female gives birth to her first litter of five naked youngsters in a warm, belowground nest on the 7th of April, twenty-eight days after conception. The original population of gophers in the burn fluctuates from three, to eight, to seven.

By mid-July, the rapidly growing youngsters leave their place of

Pocket gopher nest constructed under the cover of snow. Note the earth core (entrance and exit tunnel in the snow) at lower right and the round, grass-lined nest. The fecal chamber is the entire core at left.

birth and establish their own burrow systems. They are about two-thirds grown and resemble their parents. They have stout bodies, tiny ears, and almost no visible necks. They are adapted to their subterranean lifestyle by small eyes that are cleansed of soil by a thick fluid from the tear glands, and by lips that can be closed behind their protruding, curved front teeth, allowing them to gnaw their way through the earth without any of it getting into their throats. The softness and laxness of the gophers' pelage allows them to move both forward and backward in their tunnels. In fact, they can run backward almost as fast as they can run forward.

Two kinds of tunnels are dug: shallow ones for gathering food, such as roots and tubers, and deep ones for shelter. The deep tunnels include chambers for nesting, food storage, and toilets. The burrow systems are marked by a series of earthen mounds on the surface of the ground; the gophers expel the excess earth through inclined lateral shafts that result in fan-shaped mounds. These deep burrows cause the gophers to bring subsurface soil to the surface. Because the subsurface soil contains few spores of mycorrhizal fungi compared with the surface soil, gopher mounds of subsurface soil are often bare of plants because the spores of the necessary mycorrhizal fungi in this deep soil are not plentiful enough to inoculate the roots of plants and allow them to become established. In turn, however, this bare soil is vital to the Cascade tiger beetle, whose survival depends on a clear field of vision and a rapid takeoff to avoid would-be predators. These fast-flying beetles also need a clear place to land and forage for food.

The gophers dig primarily with their strong foreclaws, but their large front teeth are used to loosen soil and rocks, as well as to cut roots. They hold the loose earth between their chest and forelegs and push it to the surface, plugging the exits of their burrows with soil, thus creating an effective air-conditioning system and some protection against unwanted visitors.

Although the gophers are active aboveground primarily from the evening throughout the night into the early morning, they are active at any time on warm, overcast days. Underground activity seems to be almost continuous and is often heralded by muffled gnawing or scratching. The sound ceases, and the stem of a lupine or other favored food plant begins to wiggle as a small, brown nose appears. The hole is quickly enlarged to allow the gopher's head to emerge in the midst of the plant. A stem is cut off and drawn belowground. A good meal

Mazama pocket gopher digging its burrow.

is gathered within a minute, and the hole is securely plugged with soil.

While gathering food in the evening, a gopher is alert and stays close to its burrow. It cuts vegetation quickly, crams as much as possible into its external, fur-lined cheek pouches, and disappears belowground. It reappears in a few minutes and gathers more food, which it takes into its burrow for storage in its food chamber. Although a gopher can withdraw food at will from its belowground pantry, much of the stored food is not eaten and decomposes, fertilizing the soil from below.

As mid-July approaches, the seed heads of the grasses form into a soft "dough" stage, and the gophers remain outside next to their burrows for long periods. They sit on their haunches in twilight and deftly and systematically bend down one grass stalk after another with their forefeet. The soft, green heads of grass are cut off, stuffed into cheek pouches, and transported below. The cheek pouches, which extend from the lower portion of the face back to the shoulders, are emptied, turned inside out, and cleaned. They are then pulled back in place by a special muscle.

More gophers leave the meadow and travel through the forest under cover of snow. On reaching the burn, they spread out and claim any unoccupied areas. Gophers are solitary except for the breeding season and the rearing of young. In fact, they are not only solitary most of their lives but also pugnacious. Their loose, flexible skin, thickest in the region of the head and throat, is advantageous both when they fight over home territories and when they try to fend off their main enemy, the long-tailed weasel, who hunts them in their burrows.

Between immigration and a growing number of youngsters being born each year, the burn supports an expanding population of gophers. And they in turn begin to alter the soil and so the burn. Their mounds cover 5 to 10 percent of the surface in some areas, and their burrows—six inches to a foot belowground—are so numerous that deer and elk keep breaking into them. The tunnels are constantly extended and gradually fill up as they are abandoned and the old nests, pantries, and toilets are buried well below the surface, while the mounds are constantly burying surface vegetation deeper and deeper. The soil thus becomes mellow, porous, and penetrated with the burrows of gophers; so a great part of the snowmelt and rainfall is held in the ground instead

Pacific treefrog (*Hyla regillia*).

of running over the surface, where it is likely to cause soil erosion. Thus, in their own unknowing way, the gophers help to prepare the burn for the coming of the new forest.

998

Vegetation is starting to change in parts of the burn. The grasses, herbs, and gophers have been working in concert and have gradually altered the characteristics of the soil. Consequently, the soil in some areas is no longer optimum for the survival and growth of grasses and herbs. Their offspring may germinate but do not survive, so these areas begin to be inhabited only by the remaining parent plants. As the parent plants age and die and are not replaced either by their off-spring or by seeds from outside the burn, openings appear in the veg-etative cover. Here and there, shrubs, such as snowbush and vine ma-ple, become visible in the openings amidst the blackened standing dead trees (snags) of the previous ancient forest. In this way, the grass-herb stage changes to a shrub stage, but that is still some years off. (This

Pacific treefrog being eaten by a common garter snake.

type of change is called autogenic succession, which means "self-generating" or "self-imposing" change; *stage* refers to one of the sequences that a plant community goes through in succession or change.)

The winter of 997–998 is mild, and the snowpack only moderate. Spring comes early with warm days and cool nights. The snow is largely gone by late April, and everywhere around the snowmelt ponds are the choruses of Pacific treefrogs. Groups of two or three males call in sequence during their calling bouts at night; the sequence is consistently started by one male, the bout leader. Females, attracted by these calls, usually select the bout leader to mate with. Eggs are deposited in packets that range from nine to seventy and average twenty-five eggs. The eggs, attached to vegetation underwater, begin to hatch during the first week of May. Tadpoles grow rapidly and begin changing (metamorphosing) into tiny frogs and leaving the drying ponds by the second week in July. The newly formed frogs will double their size by mid-September, prior to their first winter, and those not eaten by the common garter snake will add their voices to next spring's chorus of life and renewal.

Most of the Douglas-fir seedlings that germinated along the edge of the forest in 988 are now a decade old and are either intermingled

Black-tailed deer fawn (*Odocoileus hemionus*).

with the grasses, herbs, and newly establishing shrubs or are growing in clumps dense enough to exclude other plants.

Black-tailed deer have been increasing along the edge of the burn during the decade since the fire. The deer are well-muscled animals, the females of which may weigh around 100 pounds and the males around 150 to 200 pounds. They have relatively large ears, long, slender legs, and narrow, pointed hoofs. Both sexes have metatarsal glands, which are longitudinal glands located on the insides of the hind legs in the area of the hock or heel and are visible as tufts of long, stiff hairs. Their coats, which are composed of hollow hairs, vary from dull yellowish brown to reddish brown in summer and dark grayish to rich brownish gray in winter. The upper throat, insides of the ears, and insides of the legs are whitish; the belly ranges from white to tannish. The nose, forehead, and chest are dark brown to blackish. The rump patch is white, and the rather bushy tail is brown on top with a black tip. Youngsters are thickly spotted with white over tannish to reddish brown upper parts. The females are antlerless, whereas the males grow branching antlers each summer, only to shed them in winter.

The deer are primarily animals of the edge or ecotone between the grassy meadow and the forest, but they are also at home in small islands of trees or shrubs, such as those scattered throughout the burn. Deer occur wherever there is enough cover to protect them from the heat of summer and from predators. Because they are not herd animals, they require only scattered cover of sufficient size to protect at most a small family group. A family group includes at least a doe and a fawn; at most a doe, two fawns, and two yearlings.

One such family started with a doe that conceived on the 25th of November 997. She nurtured her developing young throughout the winter. Now, early in the afternoon on the 28th of May 998, she walks into a thicket and lies down in the bed she used yesterday. She lies quietly for fifteen minutes, then commences labor. A male fawn is born within ten minutes and is immediately licked clean by his mother. Fifteen minutes later a female is born and is also licked clean. The mother is alert and stays with her youngsters for some time. When she finally leaves in late afternoon, the fawns lie flat against the ground with their necks outstretched and their ears laid back against their heads. This flat, immobile posture, their white spots that disrupt the outlines of their body contours, and the fact that newly born fawns have little odor all serve as protection from predators.

Mother and young learn to recognize each other by sniffing one another's metatarsal glands. The fawns bleat for their mother during the day, but at night they rub-urinate to communicate as well as to give a distress signal. Rub urinating is ritualized in that the hocks are rhythmically rubbed together while urine is slowly released over them. As the youngsters mature, they will use rub urinating to threaten other deer. Smelling of the metatarsal glands is normally the first stage of aggressive behavior. As the young male matures, he will erect and rhythmically move the long hairs around his metatarsal glands, exposing the scent, and he will often combine this with rub urination.

Last year's fawns, two yearling females, try periodically to rejoin their mother, only to be rejected because of her new offspring. They are finally accepted, however, during the last week of June, and the family group is now complete.

Mutual grooming, licking one another, begins between the mother and her newest young and forms the initial ties within the family group. Grooming helps to establish strong bonds between members of a family and reestablishes them if they are weakened by frequent con-

tact with a relatively large number of deer during the gregarious win-
tering period. In addition to grooming, members of a family group
sniff the metatarsal glands of one another's legs once or twice an hour
during the day and as often as six times an hour during the night.

Adult females are mutually antagonistic toward one another much
of the year, and conflicts may arise when they come together. Such
antagonism results in a fairly regular spacing of the females' centers of
activity. A female occasionally remembers a conflict and avoids the
area of another female even if she is dead. Although family ties weaken
during late winter and spring when fawns have been weaned and when
females congregate in a choice feeding area, birth of new fawns renews
the mutual antagonism and thereby spaces the females throughout the
burn.

Most males are solitary, but some have a strong tendency to congregate throughout much of the year. They usually disperse with the
onset of the breeding season but may gather into groups again during
winter and spring. Several families and groups of males may come together in spring and form large feeding bands. Although these bands
resemble a social herd, each small group retains its integrity. Conflict
often arises when these small groups approach one another too closely.
No permanent social herd forms, however, because each group goes
its own way as the feeding period ends.

The males' centers of activity are often clustered, and other than
maintenance of social rank and sexual aggressiveness, no antagonistic
behavior occurs. Neither maintenance of social rank nor sexual aggressiveness seems to have any effect on the spacing among individual
males, and groups of males remain aloof.

The deer sniff and rub their foreheads against signposts (trunks of
trees, branches, twigs, and occasionally other objects) throughout the
year, forming an intricate system of communication. The material
from the scent glands on their foreheads is apparently washed off the
signposts by rain and melting snow because rubbing activity increases
following precipitation.

Males share rubbing sites as well as having some that are strictly
their own. Rubbing sites are established at strategic places, such as
resting areas and along commonly used trails. Males apply scent on
signposts, and both males and females sniff these sites. A correlation

Black-tailed deer antler eaten by deer mice (*Peromyscus maniculatus*) to obtain the calcium.

appears to exist between male rank and behavior at shared signposts. The dominant male frequently marks rubbing sites but seldom sniffs, whereas lower-ranking males sniff more and mark less, depending on their social status.

From spring to autumn, the frequency and intensity with which males mark shared rubbing sites increases, and the number of exclusive signposts that an individual maintains decreases. Rubbing, which reaches its peak during the breeding season, seems to advertise the presence and physiological state of a particular male because both females and males sniff signposts more frequently during the breeding season than at other times. In addition to absentee communication, forehead rubbing, including thrashing vegetation with the antlers, may be one method by which breeding males establish dominance while expressing a threat and at the same time avoiding unnecessary conflict.

Yearling and mature males begin to grow antlers in early summer (when day length reaches an exact number of hours and minutes); this timing ensures the maturation of antlers in time for the breeding season and therefore that the young will be born within a certain period in the spring.

Growing antlers are encased in a thin layer of skin covered with short, fine hairs called velvet. The antlers are soft, tender, and well supplied with blood. Antlers attain maximum size by late summer, when the supply of blood gradually decreases, then terminates. The velvet dries, loosens, and drops off; by this time the antlers are hard and dead. Once the velvet is off, the antlers serve as sexual character- istics as well as weapons. Antlers are shed on the winter range, only to grow again the next summer.

Antlers, containing much calcium, fall to the ground during a hard time of the year for most active rodents. So it is a fortunate deer mouse, chickaree, or flying squirrel that finds a discarded antler on which it can not only sharpen its ever-growing front teeth but from which it can also obtain a welcome supply of calcium and other minerals.

1000

Except for a few remnants on the north-facing slopes, winter's snow is about gone, and the high meadows just above the burn are resplendent with mid-June flowers that nod and sway in gentle breezes. Fluffy clouds drift slowly across a deep blue sky, followed always by their shadows. The shadows glide silently up one hill and down another, grow large only to shrink, combine and dissipate only to reform in some new shape. The shadows can only reflect the clouds, which in turn can only reflect the constantly changing universe.

This year, when the Norse navigator Leif Ericson discovers Vin- land on the coast of eastern North America and when the Early Middle Ages of European history are drawing to a close, a youth lies in the new grasses amidst the flowers of the meadow above the burn. The youth, whose ancient ancestors crossed the Bering-Chukchi platform between Siberia and Alaska in the dimly lit past, lies idly drifting with the clouds until his vision is riveted on a small, dark speck in the vast sweep of blue.

The midday sun warms the youth as he watches the speck sailing effortlessly in and out of cloud canyons and around cloud peaks. In his mind he journeys to the dark speck, the great golden eagle riding the currents of warm air reflected from the earth into the sky, into the immensity and freedom of space where there is no beginning and no end.

He soars wingtip to wingtip with the great bird. One with the eagle, one with the air, the warmth, the earth, the clouds, the sun, one with the Spirit that is the unity of all things, he is the Spirit and the Spirit is he.

Looking down, the youth sees that the meadow on which he was lying has become a riot of color surrounded above by the whiteness of snow, and along its sides and below by the dark green of forest that encloses the brighter green of the burn with its splashes of yellows, reds, and blues. And within the burn, connecting it within itself, connecting it with the forest, connecting it with the river of the lowland, and ultimately with the oceans of the world, is the pattern of the streams that from above appears like the naked branches of a maple tree in winter.

The smallest stream, the headwater, is called a first-order stream and is unique unto itself. Where two first-order streams come together they form a second-order stream that is unique among second-order streams but unifies the first-order streams that create it. Where two second-order streams come together they form a third-order stream that is unique among third-order streams but unifies the second-order streams that create it, and so on. The streams and rivers form the arterial system of the land.

A first-order stream flows out of a spring in the existing ancient forest where rain and melting snow, soaking into the soil from the high ridge at the head of the small basin, form an underground rivulet that comes suddenly to the surface. (The existing ancient forest south of the burn of 987, including the spring and high ridge, preceded and survived the fire.) The water issues through a crevice in a subterranean jumble of rocks hidden behind a huge, partly buried Douglas-fir tree that fell diagonally across the mouth of the spring in the winter of 900.

Hidden from the outside world in a partially water-filled cavity created by the buried portion of the Douglas-fir tree and by three large rocks that form the mouth of the spring lie two Pacific giant salamanders, the largest living land salamanders in the world. They are easily recognized by the marbled pattern on their backs, which is a dark

Pacific giant salamander (*Dicamptodon ensatus*).

brown to almost black background color with lighter tan or reddish tan marbling that is brightest on the head.

The salamanders have been together in and around the cavity since the 20th of May. Today, the 31st of May in the year 1000, the male walks over the tops of several smooth, flat rocks and deposits ten capsules of sperm, called spermatophores, from his cloaca. (A cloaca is the single chamber through which the contents of the digestive, excretory, and reproductive systems pass; it opens to the outside of the body at the vent, or cloacal opening.) The female follows behind and picks up four of the sperm caps with her cloaca, and then deposits her clutch of eggs in what is now her nest cavity.

She lays her eggs individually, side by side, and attaches them by a short, gelatinous pedicel to a smooth portion of the buried tree that forms part of the roof of the nest cavity. The female labors until she has safely laid 150 eggs where the water flows slowly over them. She guards her eggs until they hatch on the 2nd of March 1001, the longest incubation period known for any species of salamander.

The mother continues to guard her young from the time they hatch until they leave the nest, sometime before the end of March. She fends off males, including her mate, several times during the incubation period to prevent them from eating her offspring. Males that approach too closely are attacked with lightning quickness and severely bitten.

The newly hatched young, called first-year larvae, abandon the nest cavity and seek cover amidst the rocks and pieces of wood near the water's edge. Their dark brownish-back and light tannish stripes behind the eyes help them to blend into their habitat. Their short, bushy gills and stout, mottled tail fins adapt them to swift water.

If the first-year larvae move away from cover out into the stream, they risk being eaten by last year's young, called second-year larvae, which inhabit deeper water. Both first- and second-year larvae eat primarily aquatic, bottom-dwelling organisms, such as worms, larval mayflies, stone flies, alderflies, beetles, and tadpoles of the tailed frog. The larvae eat whatever is available, such as terrestrial beetles, leafhoppers, and crickets that fall off streamside vegetation into the water. And the larvae in turn are eaten by common garter snakes, northern water shrews, mink, river otters, and raccoons.

Although both first- and second-year larvae occupy the first-order stream from April through late July, the second-year larvae begin transforming into terrestrial adults in August and leave the stream because it is subject to low water during late summer. By mid-September, only first-year larvae remain.

Common garter snake (*Thamnophis sirtalis*).

The small stream flows from the forest into the burn, where it is almost immediately joined by another stream. The larger stream flows through a channel littered with partly buried trees that form waterfalls, at the bases of which are deep pools scoured out by the force of the falling water. Other pools are formed where large, fallen trees dam water behind them.

The fire of 987 missed some of the vegetation along the side of the stream, and since then, other vegetation has grown back and partly shades the water.

Some second-year larvae do not transform into terrestrial adults because their thyroid glands do not produce the necessary hormone (thyroxine). These individuals retain their larval form and grow large enough to eat any second-year larvae that venture within range of their lightning strike and powerful jaws armed with many sharp teeth. These larvae also become sexually mature in the larval form and are called paedogenic larvae, which simply means the early development of sexual maturity in larval individuals. Although a few such larvae inhabit some of the deeper, shaded pools in the burn, especially pools created by waterfalls, paedogenic larvae are far more abundant in the larger streams of lower elevations.

Paedogenic individuals eat whatever they can get and in turn are eaten by large fish, such as steelhead trout, and birds, such as great blue herons; they are also eaten by such aquatic mammals as mink and river otters. These larvae occasionally leave the streams during periods of prolonged, heavy rains; at such times they also fall prey to terrestrial animals, such as raccoons and long-tailed weasels.

Once transformed into adults, salamanders leave the water and find cover under large rocks and pieces of wood along the streams. They wander over the forest floor during prolonged wet periods, where they feed on invertebrates, such as snails, beetles, crickets, termites, and millipedes, and small vertebrates, such as frogs, salamanders, lizards, snakes, shrews, mice, and voles. Adult giant salamanders, which may grow to slightly more than twelve inches in length, are even able to climb up to six feet high in trees.

Pacific giant salamanders have a variety of defensive mechanisms, which include noxious and poisonous skin secretions, warning postures, and biting. Their defensive posture is to arch the body and to hold it high off the ground by standing on the tips of their toes. From this position, they can lash the tail, coated with repulsive skin secretions, at the would-be predator. Struggling prey is overcome by biting as the salamander simultaneously twists and spins. Transformed, adult salamanders also emit a rattling or growling sound while snapping the jaws sideways and lashing the tail.

Another amphibian, the tailed frog, shares the first-order stream in the ancient forest with the Pacific giant salamander and also is eaten by it. The tailed frog is the most primitive living frog in North America because it has internal fertilization that is adapted to breeding in cold, swift streams. The tailed frog does not have an external ear membrane. Its skin varies from almost smooth to warty, and when warty, the warts are small and sometimes have sharp, black tips. The back and sides are usually some shade of gray or brown to almost black, variously marked with dark lines and blotches. A dark eye-line is frequently present, and the top of the head from the snout backward to the middle of the eyelids is usually lighter than the rest of the back.

Breeding begins in late August and September for the tailed frog. During a successful mating, the "tail," which is really an outside extension of the male's cloaca, becomes engorged with blood and is directed forward. The male locks his arms around the pelvic region (waist) of the female and interlocks his fingers. Inserting his erected cloacal extension into the cloaca of the female, he copulates for twenty-four to thirty hours; the entire courtship and mating process, however, may last up to seventy hours.

Internal fertilization of the female prevents the swift currents from washing away sperm before the eggs can be fertilized. Sperm remain viable inside the female for at least ten months, and fertilized eggs are laid during July of the year following mating. Thus, females lay eggs every other year.

Up to ninety-eight eggs are laid in a string like a pearl necklace, which tends to become more of a globular mass as it is attached by means of a thick, tough outer membrane to the underside of large rocks that the stream's current is unlikely to move. Eggs, laid in July, hatch during August and September.

The tadpoles are either black or brown with or without lighter flecks. Most larvae have a whitish spot at the tip of their tails. They are unique among the tadpoles of northwestern frogs because their mouths are modified into an adhesive or suckerlike device that enables them to adhere to rocks in the swift current. In fact, tadpoles almost invariably occur in stretches of swift water, where they inch their way along the surfaces of smooth rocks as water cascades over them, often barely covering their backs.

Tailed frog tadpoles feed mainly on diatoms, which are small forms of algae. The tadpoles scrape the diatoms off the surface of rocks and therefore avoid moss-covered and silt-covered rocks. These tadpoles also consume large amounts of wind-blown pollen from the conifers of the ancient forest when the pollen falls into the water during pollination time in June.

Tadpoles transform into adult frogs during their third year, at which time they begin to spend days hidden under rocks and pieces of wood along the stream's edge and move about at night to feed. As frogs, they generally feed by sitting in one spot and devouring whatever comes their way, such as snails, spiders, flies, moths, ants, crickets, and lacewings. Although some aquatic insect larvae are eaten, adult frogs are inefficient at underwater feeding so spend most of their time along the stream's edge. On rainy nights, however, they may feed in the forest, as much as eighty feet away from the stream's edge.

Tailed frogs occurred throughout the burn for centuries prior to the fire of 987, but now stream temperatures are too high for them to survive. For the time being, they survive in the ancient forest above the spring, from which they will again enter the burn in centuries to come, when the new forest is old enough to keep the water cold by protecting the streams from too much sun.

IOIO

The burn, now twenty-three years old, is a vast mosaic of habitats arranged over the landscape according to Nature's combined patterns of soil types, slope, aspect, elevation, moisture gradients, and severity and duration of the fire, including areas the fire missed. Many of the south-facing slopes are shrubfields dominated by snowbush; other areas, where fire scorched the soil, are only now in grasses and herbs.

Streamsides are growing up with alder, willow, and vine maple, among other species. Where Douglas-fir seeds fell and germinated along the edge of the forested areas in 988 and 989, single trees, small clumps, and dense thickets are scattered around the burn.

The plant community is changing in some areas of the shrubfields. Snowbush, with nitrogen-fixing bacteria associated with its roots, has been adding nitrogen to the soil. In addition, its roots harbor some of the same mycorrhizal fungi that are symbiotic with Douglas-fir and thus have kept the inoculum alive in the soil. As soil conditions change, and the offspring of snowbush cease to survive, spaces become available between parent shrubs, and where space and Douglas-fir seeds come together, seedlings are becoming visible. And so the burn progresses from bare ground, to grasses and herbs, to shrubs, to young forest.

Although the fire of 987 killed many trees, it destroyed very little wood. Many snags of fire-killed trees stand like black and silver spires and columns of various sizes and shapes, regal sentinels against time, a measure of the burn's renewal. A few snags are already surrounded by thickets of Douglas-fir, as though they are trying to hide but can't quite cover all of themselves.

Many of the snags already have cavities that were excavated over the years by various woodpeckers before and after the fire. Some cavities, high up in tall snags, are used for nesting by tree swallows; lower cavities are used by western bluebirds. And amongst the solid snags are a few hollow ones that are open to the top. Because of their scarcity, these hollow snags are a premium habitat in the burn as they are in the ancient forest.

The small, migratory Vaux's swift comes each summer to the ancient forest to nest. The swift is a small bird that seems to fly continuously, feeding almost exclusively on small, flying insects, such as leafhoppers, that it catches on the wing in the open sky above the forest canopy. Built for speed, the swift's wings are long, slender, stiff, and slightly decurved, and its streamlined body tapers to a narrow, slightly rounded tail. It nests in the large, hollow snags. Although most snags used by the swift for nesting are tall, some are only 20 feet high. Nest snags are often hollow nearly to the ground, and many are charred by past fires.

A swift's nest consists of twigs that the bird breaks off from dead limbs as it flies past. Having secured a twig, the swift flies down inside the hollow snag and glues the twig to the inside wall with its gluey saliva. Although the swift normally fastens its nest well below the top of its snag, it occasionally nests almost at ground level in unusually large snags. Once constructed, the saucer-shaped nest is lined with the needles of Douglas-fir to receive the three to six dull white eggs that are usually laid in June.

The ground is covered with varying numbers of large, fallen trees. Some are left over from the previous ancient forest and are rotten and soft; others that had sound wood at the time of the fire were charred and case-hardened by the flames. Some of these fallen trees lie on open ground, some amidst shrubs, and some hidden in the scattered thickets of Douglas-fir. Scattered amidst the remnants of the existing ancient forest are the blackened trees that have fallen since the fire.

Trees in the oldest thickets average 8 inches in diameter 5 feet above the ground and are about 20 feet tall. Inside, the thickets are dark and closed in with many dead limbs and a few dead trees. The trees in this stage of forest development are competing intensely with each other for soil nutrients, water, sunlight, and space in which to grow; this competition results in the more vigorous trees suppressing the growth of the weaker. Barring catastrophic disturbance, such as trees blowing over in windstorms or fire, 93 to 99 percent of all mortality of trees in these relatively even-aged thickets will be from suppression until they reach 120 years of age in 1108. After their death, most of these trees will remain standing for a few years. Suppression prunes, thins, and supplies the maturing thicket with dead wood.

One thicket near the first-order stream that flows out of the small basin below the high ridge covers many acres. It extends along the edge of the forest and from the forest out to some scattered islands of ancient trees. The area in between the forest and the islands is also interspersed with a few individual live trees and others that lived for a year or two after the fire and shed thousands of seeds, some of which are now the growing forest.

It is the 15th of May, and a female snowshoe hare emerges from the thicket. Her back and sides are covered with a long, thick, soft, relatively light reddish brown coat with a few intermixed black-tipped

hairs. Her throat is also reddish brown, as are her ears, with their blackish tips and white margins. The reddish brown gives way to clear white on her chin, belly, the insides of her long legs, and the tops of her large hind feet. She has an inconspicuous tail that is blackish on top and light whitish gray underneath.

Before she became pregnant, she weighed about two and a half pounds, but now, heavy with young, she moves cautiously along the edge of the thicket. She pauses and tests the breeze with her keen, blackish nose and long, delicate ears. All is still except for the croak of a raven and the high whining of a hovering yellow-and-black syrphid fly. She hops farther, following a faint trail through the growing grasses between the shrubs and the thicket until she comes to a jumble of five fallen trees that form a protected alcove open to the warmth of the May sun shining through a snowbush. She enters the alcove and becomes quiet. She is a different hare than she was thirty-five days ago on the 10th of April when she was bred.

The 10th of April was clear and balmy, and the snow lay melting and dirty as winter retreated northward. As the sun slid silently below the western rim of the world, two hares, a male and a female, met in a small clearing between the shrubs and the thicket. They sat quietly for a time. Then the male began to chase the female, running beneath her as she leapt into the air and, in midair, urinated on him. She then ran beneath him as he leapt into the air and, in midair, urinated on her. They played for a while, and the time came when she was ready to receive her mate.

Now the sun graces the western tops of the trees and shrubs as the last of three babies is born. Each baby snowshoe, two males and a female, is fully clothed in soft fur; its eyes and ears are open. Each can hop around within a few minutes after birth. They begin to nurse after their mother has completely cleaned them and they are soft and fluffy.

The snowshoes grow rapidly throughout the summer and are fully grown by mid-October. Each hare now has its own area or home range where it knows all the safe places, all the trails, and has a number of hidden, shallow nests or "forms" where it spends most of the days sitting quietly, watching and listening without being seen or heard.

Hunger induces the mother snowshoe to leave the alcove where her youngsters were born five months earlier. She hops into the light mist

on a cold afternoon in late October and sits, listening intently. The wind shifts. She freezes, sitting absolutely motionless for several minutes. The wind shifts again, and she begins to relax. Suddenly she panics and screams the peculiar distress cry of the snowshoe hare. A blurred shape springs from behind; sharp claws grip her right hind leg; fangs pierce her skull. Her life's blood trickles down her fur to mix with the mist and wet soil at the edge of the snowbush—ten feet from the hidden alcove. Alive or dead, the mother snowshoe is an eternal link in the unbroken chain of ancestry from the hares of the past to the hares of the future.

The mother snowshoe's death means life to the young bobcat who, driven by extreme hunger, almost muffed his chance for a meal. He caught the snowshoe by two outstretched claws and then almost lost her because of youthful ignorance and impatience. He wastes little time nosing her but picks her up and carries her into the gathering darkness.

Mist turns to rain. The wind grows stronger and moans through the thicket. Night claims the land. The mother snowshoe's youngsters wait out the night, each alone in its own shelter and unaware that its mother has joined her ancestors in time beyond the world.

In another part of the burn, the young bobcat eats the snowshoe, cleans himself, and lies down. The mother snowshoe lives on as part of the bobcat, now sleeping soundly while the wind howls around his hollow, fallen tree. Her life has helped ensure that his seed will pass to yet another generation of bobcats, and another, and another as the cosmic dance of life and death and change continues to unfold in the evolving forest.

By midmorning the sun is shining; the sky is blue; and wispy fog is rising in long fingers from the warming land. Leaving the shelter of a fallen tree, the daughter snowshoe hops along the faint trail toward the alcove. She passes the place where, less than eighteen hours ago, her mother's life suddenly ended. She knows nothing of the event, and rain has erased all signs of it. It is as though neither the mother snowshoe nor the event had ever existed. The only proof that the mother snowshoe once lived is her three offspring; the only proof that the event took place is the absence of the mother snowshoe.

October sees days becoming shorter and a sun that rides lower and lower in the southern sky. The lessening daylight triggers a change in the snowshoes, and they begin to shed their summer coats of soft brown fur. The brown is replaced by their first winter coats of white. They will become all white except for blackish tips on their ears, but for now they are mottled in transition and relatively conspicuous because snow is late this year. The transition is a genetic response to millennia of climate—not an environmental response to local weather conditions.

The burn is covered with two feet of snow by December and appears as a white world with black spires of snags extending skyward. One of the male snowshoes, now in his winter coat of white, hops along a large, blackened fallen tree. Snow is falling quietly, softly, flake upon flake, each dazzling in its microscopic beauty.

A line of diagonally paired tracks dot the snow's surface a hundred yards north of the snowshoe. The tracks come from the thicket's edge and disappear under a snow-covered fallen tree. All seems still—motionless. A dark nose and a pair of bright, dark eyes appear from under the fallen tree. They remain an instant and disappear. Minutes pass. The nose and eyes reappear at another spot. Then the long, white body of a large male long-tailed weasel bounds into sight, followed by his black-tipped tail. And the diagonally paired tracks continue to dimple the snow, wending here and there as the weasel searches likely nooks and crannies for prey.

The snowshoe, meanwhile, sitting within a hop or two from the safety of a large fallen tree, idly licks falling snow off its nose. Because the snowshoe is a prey item for several predators inhabiting the burn, or the forest, or both, Nature has endowed the hare with eyes set in the sides of its head. This adaptation allows it to see with binocular vision to the front and to the back as well as with monocular vision to the sides. It is this ability that allows the snowshoe to detect the flicker of movement behind it as the weasel bursts suddenly over a fallen tree and bounds toward it. The snowshoe leaps under the fallen tree and dashes out the other side, the weasel in close pursuit. Now the hare's large hind feet, covered with stiff hairs, act as nonskid snowshoes holding the hare on the surface of the snow as it propels itself forward with mighty thrusts of its powerful hind legs.

Racing along remembered paths of summer, the snowshoe evades the weasel for a time, but the weasel closes in. The snowshoe screams and kicks viciously with its large hind feet armed with surprisingly long, sharp claws. The blow sends the weasel flying into the snow. The snowshoe races on, the weasel in pursuit. As the weasel again closes the distance, the snowshoe turns abruptly down a dimly familiar path under a snowbush and a hidden, fallen tree.

Intent on the path, the snowshoe is suddenly boxed in. The weasel leaps. The snowshoe kicks, raking an extended claw along the weasel's side, knocking the weasel hard against the underside of the tree. The weasel leaps again, this time sinking sharp fangs into the muscles of the back of the snowshoe's neck. Clinging with locked jaws, the weasel throws its sinuous, snakelike body against the struggling snowshoe, knocking it over. The weasel bites frantically at the base of the snowshoe's skull. The struggle ceases.

The weasel has its meal, but not without a price. The white-and-black world of snow and charred wood is now also red with the blood of both snowshoe and weasel.

The weasel eats its fill, pulls and pushes the remains deeper under the tree, and crawls into an old pileated woodpecker cavity in another fallen tree just behind the one under which the snowshoe ran. Tired, full, cleaned, and growing stiff from its deep wound, the weasel curls into a ball and sleeps, unaware that the tree in which it sleeps stood as a charred snag until a week ago when it fell and blocked the faintly remembered path of the snowshoe hare.

Awakening stiff, sore, and hungry, the weasel ventures from its warm cavity into a gray, overcast day. It goes to retrieve the carcass to eat but is suddenly gripped by sharp talons that pierce its chest and neck. A strong beak smashes against the top of its head, and its world fades as the great horned owl covers the weasel with outstretched wings to protect it from any would-be thief. No threat in sight, the owl takes wing, with the body of a white, red, and black weasel hanging limply in its tight grasp.

The owl had simply been on its way to its roost in an ancient Douglas-fir near the edge of the forest on the far side of the thicket after an unsuccessful night of hunting when the weasel came suddenly into view. Detecting stiffness in the weasel's movements, the owl knew it would be easy prey.

Yesterday the snowshoe's blood reddened this spot. Today it is the weasel's life that ebbs so that the owl might live. But would the weasel have been more alert and have reached safety if it had not been wounded by the snowshoe hare? After all, the weasel could have dived under the snow and escaped because weasels are excellent undersnow travelers. This is but one of many unanswered questions in the burn. And under the fallen tree, a tiny, pointed-nosed, grayish black Trowbridge shrew has found chance's bounty in the carcass of the snowshoe hare.

Mid-December brings a blizzard. Wind whips the trees, screams over the shrubs, and stings the world with blinding snow. The remaining daughter snowshoe sits hunched in her most sheltered winter nest, a protected hollow created by the lower limbs of a young grand fir. The fir's limber, downward sweeping boughs with their flat needles are weighted down and frozen into the snow that is continually piling up around the base of the tree. Here the snowshoe is safe and warm, out of the bitter, cold wind.

The storm lasts two days and covers the burn with three more feet of snow, but the forest floor inside the thicket is protected. Some areas are almost free of snow. The wind has broken many small, living limbs and twigs from the tops of the Douglas-firs and has cast them onto the forest floor. The female snowshoe enters the thicket and begins to eat the needles. Not being able to manipulate with her front feet, she can eat only those needles that are readily available.

Winter passes and the days grow longer. Change again takes place in the snowshoe hares as they shed their winter coats. Mottled hares hop over familiar trails in the burn, but now they blend in with patches of bare earth, green vegetation, and melting snow. The daughter is bred by the end of April, and elsewhere in the burn her sibling sires his first young. The generations of snowshoes continue.

Young Forest

❖

1020

It is September. A man and two boys pause at the edge of the meadow above the burn. The man leads the boys to a small clump of subalpine fir in the upper part of the meadow and instructs them to make camp. The boys gather wood, build a small lean-to shelter of dead sapling poles and fir boughs, and then explore the small stream rushing its way through the meadow.

The man leaves and walks quietly along the edge of the meadow toward the burn looking for signs of elk, which they have come to hunt. He pauses, climbs a small, rocky promontory, and surveys the existing ancient forest and the burn. He remembers how it looked when he had first seen it in his sixteenth summer, when he had lain in the meadow and had soared with the great eagle. This is his thirty-sixth summer, and the burn looks very different, its changes dramatic. Most of the shrubfields are gone, replaced by young forest, dense in many places, scattered in others, but still with a few persisting openings. He thinks how both he and the burn have grown and changed since that day in his youth, and how the ancient forest seems not to have changed at all. He is glad that he brought his sons to this place.

A few reddish orange paintbrushes still grace moist places along the stream, and asters in their blue autumn glory dot the meadow. Dry,

49

Clump of subalpine fir (*Abies lasiocarpa*) as it might have appeared in 1020.

golden seed stalks of summer grasses resist the breeze that tries to bend them, and butterflies search for waning flowers. A bull elk bugles and is answered. A varied thrush calls, its trill floating on the September breeze. Flies buzz. A thin wisp of smoke rises into the clear, warm air of late afternoon.

The man sends his sons, in their fifteenth and sixteenth summers, to catch trout at the lower edge of the meadow where the stream is larger and deeper. They obey gleefully for they often compete to see who can catch the most fish.

They move very slowly and quietly as they approach the stream, each going to his chosen place—deep water with an undercut bank where the meadow, in effect, grows over the stream. Approaching the water's edge, they crawl slowly, gently, close to the ground. They lie down at the stream's edge, and each slowly puts a hand into the water under the overhanging bank of meadow. Then, ever so slowly, they move their hands upstream, feeling for the tail and belly of a fish. The fish are still, simply maintaining their positions in the current, as the hands slowly, gently rub their way up the bellies to the gills. When the fish open their gill covers, fingers shoot into the gills and the fish are flung into the meadow. As each trout is retrieved, the youth who caught it pauses and apologizes to the fish's spirit, explaining that the fish's life is needed so The People Of The Land can live.

The boys meet within three hours and decide they have caught enough fish. The fifteen-year-old caught the biggest fish, and his brother caught the most. This time they both win. They return happily to camp.

The fish are cleaned, spitted on thin sticks, and roasted over the embers of the small cooking fire. The skin holds in the juices as the fish cook, so each is hot, juicy, and delicious.

It is dark by the time they finish eating, and the clear sky is filled with stars so bright they appear close enough to touch. The night breezes explore the faces of the man and his sons as they lie watching the stars, each alone with his thoughts, each listening to the distant howling of wolves.

Morning dawns cold and clear. After completing their duties, the man and his sons take their short, heavy elk bows and quivers of stout arrows and leave camp. They move along the edge of the meadow toward the burn. The boys are going to learn how to hunt elk, and they are excited. Hunting elk is a special event in the life of a boy because it takes a special, stronger bow than it does to kill a deer. To hunt elk is therefore an important step toward manhood, a rite of passage, and a lesson in humility because elk, the second-largest deer in the New World, can be elusive and dangerous, especially the bulls during the breeding season.

Elk are slender-legged animals with necks that are thick in proportion to their heads. The hair along the sides of the neck is long and dark, forming a dark brown mane on the throat. The hair on the back and sides is shorter and varies from light grayish, to yellowish gray, to yellowish brown, to brown. The head, neck, mane, and legs are dark brown to almost blackish; the underparts are darker than the back. The rump patch and tail vary from light yellowish to dark yellowish or tannish yellow. Cows and calves are darker than the bulls. Young calves are brownish with large yellowish white blotches. There are whitish metatarsal glands below the hocks on the outsides of the hind legs. Females are antlerless, but males develop large, widely branched antlers. The main backward-sweeping beam may reach three and a half feet in

High ridge as it might have appeared in 1020.

length. Adults have a well-developed brow tine, or "dog killer," and normally five other tines.

The father leads his sons to the burn, where they begin to follow a well-used elk trail through the thickets of young Douglas-fir toward the ancient forest. They walk in silence for three and a half hours and come to the spring where twenty years ago a giant salamander laid 150 eggs in a hidden nest behind a large fallen Douglas-fir tree. The three hunters drink from the spring's water and rest against the tree, knowing nothing of the generations of salamanders that began life in this spring.

The hunters follow the elk trail further into the ancient forest. It goes steeply up to the base of a cliff at the bottom of the high ridge. Here they find the disarticulated, partly eaten skeleton of a cow elk. They stop to examine it. The father points to what is left of the ribs and tells his sons that wolves have eaten on them. "You can tell by the way the softer parts of the bones have been chewed off." "What killed the elk?" asks the younger son. "I don't know," answers the father. "The bones are too scattered to tell even though they have only been here since last winter. You can see that by these small pieces of tough sinew that still cling to the spine." The older son brings the skull to his father. He looks at it and says, "She was very old; look how her special teeth are worn down." (Elk, as all deer, do not have upper front teeth, but they do have a pair of upper canine teeth that wear down with age.)

The group moves on without unraveling the history of last winter's incident in which, during the first snows before migration, a pack of seven wolves chased the cow along the ridge until she panicked and ran toward the cliff, where she slipped in the snow and fell over the edge, breaking her neck. The wolves and ravens did the rest.

Father and sons climb a steep trail at the end of the cliff and come to a small pass that leads down into the next basin and headwater stream. Here they find a fir sapling completely shredded from the ground up to seven feet where a large bull elk has thrashed his antlers. Next to it is a larger sapling with its bark scraped off on one side. The father points to it and tells his sons how the cows mark the area with their lower front teeth by scraping them upward against the trunk of the tree, letting the shavings drop to the ground.

Again the hunters follow the elk trail and periodically come to bull rubs and cow scrapes. The boys learn that a mature breeding bull usually holds a small basin as his breeding territory and marks its boundaries with signposts alongside of which the cows scrape. They learn that each territory has at least one pass into another drainage that serves as an escape route and that each territory has at least one well-concealed, well-protected high spot where the bull can rest in safety and know what goes on around him without exposing himself.

They learn that elk are noisy when undisturbed, the cows and calves calling back and forth, rustling branches, breaking twigs, snorting and wheezing as they breathe, and that these huge animals can suddenly become like spirits, moving silently and swiftly with nothing but their tracks and a warm, musky odor to attest their passage.

There is much to learn. So the father and his sons spend several days among the elk because the elk, when they move to lower elevations for winter, will be hunted by the tribe. And a successful hunt depends on a hunter's knowledge, for this is in the days before horses, when The People Of The Land must stalk their quarry very closely and must carry everything on their backs. The more skillful the hunter, the closer to camp the kill can be made.

The father allows his sons to kill a calf so they might learn how to hunt and feed their families and eventually their parents in the seasons to come. He allows them to kill only a calf because that is all they can use until the tribal hunt. The father is pleased with his sons, and it is wiser boys who leave the meadow and the burn and the elk, who travel through a land of yellows, reds, browns, and oranges of vine maple in the waning days of September.

Like their father before them, they leave something of themselves, of their youth, in this high country, and they leave an arrow with its obsidian head deeply buried in a young Douglas-fir tree, lost when the oldest boy, aiming downhill, overshot his target. Thus deep in the sapwood of the fir is Nature's glass spewed from a volcano even before the ancient people reached the New World. And in turn, the boys take a measure of adulthood, a measure of dignity and of humility, back to their village at the base of the great mountains.

The land again belongs to the elk and to the wolves and puma that hunt the elk year round for food. For now, the elk continue to live as elk live without human intrusion.

Elk have a matriarchal society in which the adult bulls live separately from the adult cows during the nonbreeding season. A matriarchal herd (cow-herd) is composed of cows, which weigh an average of about 400 pounds, their calves, and subadults (adolescents) of both sexes. The degree to which a member of any particular sex and age class associates with the central cow-calf unit is determined by the behavioral interrelationships of that individual with the other members of the herd. Yearling bulls, for example, show a strong cow-herd attachment at times of the year when they are not driven out by an adult bull during the breeding season or when the cows are not giving birth to their calves. The composition of a cow-herd dominated by an old "lead" cow seems most stable from November to May, and the association of subadult bulls with the cow-herd reaches a peak during the winter. But the duration of these visits decreases annually as the bulls approach maturity. Adult bulls, weighing an average of about 500 pounds and as much as 1,000 pounds, join a cow-herd only temporarily during the breeding season. When not accompanying the cow-herd, bulls gather into groups.

A cohesive herd has a central area that it uses to the exclusion of other individuals or herds even though the area is not actively defended. As the distance from the central area increases, use by the resident herd decreases and competition with other groups intensifies. A herd's strong orientation toward its central area is probably based on the area's availability of preferred food, water, cover, and a knowledge of the escape routes. Although precise boundaries do not exist, closely adjoining herds seldom overlap or trespass, perhaps because the resident herd signposts trees more frequently within its central area than it does outside it, which communicates its monopoly of the area.

The herd in the burn near the spring uses the lower portion of the meadow as its primary feeding area. It also uses the existing ancient forest, which has cool temperatures on hot days and a good ground cover of herbs and some grasses. In addition, the stream within the ancient forest has several places to drink.

Thus the herd's central area has water, food, and cover—both hiding cover and thermal cover. Hiding cover is used for escape, to see without being seen, and is capable of concealing 90 percent of a standing elk at a distance of two hundred feet or less. Thermal cover, on the other hand, can act as hiding cover but also is large enough in size and dense enough to produce its own internal climate—cool in summer and warm in winter—thus allowing an elk to maintain a nearly constant body temperature, which conserves its energy. The boys had learned about thermal cover one very hot afternoon when they had crawled into the coolness of a dense thicket and saw nothing but the legs of elk moving among the young trees.

The boys had also watched a cow signposting along the edge of the big thicket. She had started by carefully drawing her nose several times up and down a small tree as though sniffing it. She then scraped the tree with her lower front teeth, drawing them in deliberate vertical strokes from the bottom to the top of the area she had marked with her nose. The shavings simply fell and accumulated on the ground. She then deliberately rubbed the sides of her muzzle and chin against her flanks.

When the boys told their father what they had seen, he said, "Bulls of five summers and older do the same thing, but they use the base of their antlers to scrape the trees."

The boys had heard from other boys in their village that bulls rub the velvet off their antlers because it itches. They asked their father if what the other boys had said was true, because all the bulls they had thus far seen already had shiny antlers without velvet. Their father told them he had seen bulls go for many days with bothersome masses of stripped velvet hanging over their eyes without making any attempt to remove it, even though it was obvious that it was causing them a great deal of annoyance. He said, "The velvet does not itch because the antlers are dead and hard when the velvet begins to come off. It comes off by accident or when the bulls start to signpost early enough to rub it off before it simply falls by itself. Such early rubbing," he said, "is always rather gentle and hesitant as though the antlers are not yet completely hardened and capable of withstanding the heavy pressure and rough use we have seen in the last few days. The antlers are a dingy brown when the velvet has just dropped off, but as breeding intensifies and bulls begin to thrash vegetation, as we saw yesterday, their antlers become even more polished and gleaming than they are now. Not all bulls have antlers of the same color because they become stained by whatever vegetation the bulls most frequently attack."

The boys remembered the bull they had watched the day before. It had been a big, light tan bull with a dark brown head and long, dark brown mane; in fact he had been so big that he had thrust his head against a young tree, just over two inches in diameter, and had shaken his head so vigorously that the tree had broken. The bull had then attacked a shrub, and while attacking the shrub had unsheathed his penis and eliminated copious amounts of urine in spurts that had carried over three feet. He had directed the urine along his belly, thoroughly soaking the dark brown hair, and had then lowered his head and saturated the long, dark mane on his throat and the sides of his face. He backed out of the shrub after a few minutes and dug his antlers into the urine-soaked grass and herbs, flinging them over his back. Finally, he lay down in the urine-soaked area and rolled several times before leaving.

The boys had watched another bull wade into the stagnant water and foul-smelling mud of a wallow and submerge his head and neck in the water. He had then knelt and rubbed his chest, neck, and face in the slimy mud on the bottom. After having watched the bulls, the boys decided they were glad men didn't have to go through all this just to interest girls. If they did, the boys would have remained bachelors.

"Do bulls get killed very often when they fight?" the younger boy had asked his father. "No. They do get hurt and even killed, but not so many as die in the winter of hunger," his father answered. "I remember watching one fight many seasons ago. A young bull approached a herd of cows that belonged to a large bull. Each of the bulls bugled several times and circled the other about fifty feet apart. Suddenly they stopped and charged, their antlers coming together with a terrific crash. They pushed and twisted. Finally, with a sudden twist of his head, the big bull threw the young bull to one side and taking advantage of the opening, charged into the young bull's right side with his antlers, knocking him off his feet. When the young bull got up, he left in a hurry."

The last day of September becomes the first day of October, and by the end of October most of the cows are bred and on their way to the winter range. Some of the bulls will follow the cows to lower elevations, but the biggest ones will stay in the high country until the snow is so deep they are forced to leave or die.

The cows will carry their calves for 255 to 275 days and will give birth during the last week in May and the first week in June. Just before giving birth, a cow leaves the herd and selects a place where she will give birth to a single young, seldom two. The mother and her new offspring will rejoin the herd in a week or so, at which time the calf is well coordinated and able to keep up with its mother.

When alarmed or frightened, cows emit a call similar to the bark of a dog; this call warns the calves, especially before a mother and her new offspring return to the safety of the herd. A newborn calf reacts immediately to the bark of a cow. It conceals itself in any available vegetation by dropping to its belly, stretching its head out flat on the ground, and remaining motionless. The light blotches on its overall dark coat help to disrupt its outline, making it difficult to see. Once a mother and her calf return to the herd, however, a bark does not cause the youngster to hide, but it does direct its attention to whatever made the cow give the alarm.

Calves depend mainly on their mothers' milk for the first four to six weeks and may nurse five or six times a day. They are tended by a "babysitter" cow who keeps them together while their mothers feed. When it is time for a youngster to nurse, its mother calls her baby with a high-pitched neigh. When the nursing period is over, the calf's mother simply walks away and starts to eat. Further attempts by the calf to nurse may bring a resounding whack across its back from a front hoof or a butt from the side of the mother's head, but her youngster normally returns to the babysitter without hesitation. As the calves become less dependent on milk, the babysitter becomes more lax in her efforts to keep them together. By autumn the calves are feeding with the herd and have outgrown the need for a babysitter, but they still tend to remain together.

December is very cold, and the snows are deep, forcing the elk into the ancient forest at the lower end of the burn along the big river. Here, protected from the snow by the huge trees, the elk have good thermal cover and food. Although not all will survive until spring, the cows will add new life to the herd when the sun is again warm and the breezes gentle.

1037

Most of the thickets in the vicinity of the spring are 30 to 50 years old and have grown together, forming a dense forest with an almost bare floor. It is dark inside the forest even on bright, sunny days in mid-summer, and all living limbs between the ground and 50 feet in the air have died over the years from lack of sunlight. The last pocket gopher died four years ago, his small opening surrounded by dense trees. The elk herd has shifted its center of activity and uses the area less frequently because available forage is now insufficient for its needs. And the remaining black bear are forced to eat the inner bark of the young trees if they are to survive in the face of a rapidly dwindling supply of food.

When the burn was younger and covered with a wide variety of grasses, herbs, and berries, especially huckleberries, food was plentiful, and the bear population increased. As time advanced, however, and trees replaced the grasses, herbs, and shrubs, the bear's food supply began to decline and now has all but disappeared. Bear living along the margin of the burn have been able to make some adjustments in their home ranges (those areas that an individual uses during its normal

Left: Bark stripped off a young Douglas-fir by a black bear (*Ursus americanus*). The bear hooked the claws of its front foot under the bark and pulled it off. The arrows point to some of the bear's claw marks on the inside of the bark. *Right:* Once the outer bark is removed, the bear scrapes the inner bark (cambium) off the stem with upward vertical strokes of its lower incisor (front) teeth. Bear characteristically do not remove the small branches but work around them.

daily routine), but not without conflict with neighboring bear. Some, mostly the old and weak, have died, and reproduction has declined because of poor nutrition. The rest struggle to survive in the fifty-year-old burn at the expense of the trees.

Bear, along the gentle slope at the edge of the big thicket, make their initial attack on the trees on the open side that faces away from the inner portion of the thicket, the side with living branches. They begin by ripping at the bark with their foreclaws at a slight angle from the vertical, and then work their claws under the loosened bark and pull it off in strips and pieces two to six inches wide and six to thirty inches long. The bear eat the living tissue that they scrape off the trunk with their lower front teeth, which leaves a large number of overlapping grooves running almost vertically along the trunk of the tree.

Bear in other parts of the burn that live on the steeper slopes often climb two-thirds of the way up the Douglas-firs in the thickets and eat the tender bark off the open, downhill side of the tree.

Some trees are killed because the bear girdle them by removing the living tissue all the way around their trunks, which causes the trees to starve. These girdled trees can be seen easily in the spring of the following year because of their faded shades of green. Such severe damage often triggers seed production, and when this happens in an off-seed year, the heavily cone-laden limbs make the trees even more conspicuous. As spring gives way to summer, the dying trees' foliage turns varying shades of reddish brown and can be seen from great distances.

Other trees so injured are not killed outright but die later from diseases that enter the wound. Still others, wounded by bear more than once, may be healthy and heal or begin to heal only to be damaged a second or third time, become diseased, and die. Thus, as bear injure the trees, bear also add to the diversity of the evolving forest because each injured tree is altered and will live or die differently than it would have had the bear not eaten from it. In turn, dying and dead trees become homes of cavity-excavating birds, such as woodpeckers, whose abandoned cavities are then used by secondary cavity-nesting birds, such as western bluebirds and house wrens.

On the 19th of June, lightning starts a fire in the existing ancient forest at the northwestern edge of the burn, near the big river. The fire creeps around the forest floor, consuming twigs, branches, and now and then large fallen trees that are dry enough to burn. One large, almost buried, fallen tree near the edge of the existing ancient forest smolders belowground for days before it finally reaches mineral soil and burns out. This low-severity fire also removes fire-sensitive species, such as seedlings and small saplings of western hemlock and western redcedar, as well as some of the smaller Pacific yew trees. The fire not only adds to the overall diversity of the forest but also fireproofs this portion of it to some extent by removing the easily combustible fuels on the ground.

The giant Douglas-firs are not injured by the fire because the outer bark at their bases is ten to twenty inches thick, which protects their living tissue from the heat, and their crowns are far too high above the flames to sustain damage.

When the fire reaches the burn, however, it climbs quickly into the trees at the edge of the young forest because their living limbs form a ladder from the ground up. Once in their crowns, the fire races up the mountain, burning unchecked until heavy rains from a thunderstorm on the 22nd of June, followed by an overcast day, and more rain on the 24th puts it out. The fire has blackened a strip that is a mile wide when it reaches the scattered clumps of trees in the subalpine forest.

The fire affects nutrient cycling throughout the forest. Nutrients, such as nitrogen, are converted to gas as the vegetation burns and are lost into the atmosphere; some are lost in the ashes that become wind-borne and leave the site on the huge blasts of heat from the fire; still others combine with oxygen and so become different compounds.

Once the fire is out, more nutrients are lost from or redistributed within the burned area by wind that blows the ashes around, and later by rain and melting snow, which leaches some of the nutrients out of the soil and carries them into the streams and into the big river and ultimately into the sea.

Not all of the nutrients are lost, however; rain replaces a little of the nitrogen and in a small way balances the account. In addition, some of the nutrients that remain will be more readily available to the plants soon to inhabit the burn.

The new burn's loss of nutrients becomes some other area's gain because the nutrients are all eventually redistributed within the water catchment, the landscape, the geographical area, the continent, and the world. Nothing is truly lost, only removed for a time. And some-day, some other area's loss will be the new burn's gain.

Streamflows increase strikingly after the fire has killed most of the vegetation. Runoff from the melting snow begins earlier in the spring of 1038, and the runoff peaks are higher. The fire not only has black-ened the surface of the soil, causing it to increase dramatically in temperature on sunny days, but also has altered its behavior. Blackened soil absorbs heat, and water therefore evaporates more readily. Where the soil is severely burned, it becomes more repellent to water than before the fire; so rather than infiltrating deeply into the soil, the water runs off at or near the soil's surface.

Water temperature increases immediately after the fire because stream channels, now devoid of protective vegetation, are exposed to direct sunlight. But not all vegetation along the streams is killed. Some of the shrubs live below the surface of the soil and will resprout by early summer of 1038 and, within a year or two, will again shade the water of the first-order streams.

1042

Three men and three boys arrive in the meadow in late September as evening shadows begin creeping eastward, away from the setting sun. They arrive later than anticipated because the father, now fifty-eight summers old, is not as spry as he used to be. With him are his two sons, now thirty-eight and thirty-seven, and his three grandsons, fourteen, sixteen, and seventeen summers old. The two younger boys belong to the oldest son.

They make camp in the same clump of subalpine fir in which the father and his sons had camped in 1020. Supper finished, stars twinkling, and the soft, quiet light of the rising moon casting gentle shadows prompt the father to tell his grandsons the story of the Great Fire that killed his uncle fifty-five summers ago. "When I was but three summers old, the Great Fire that swallowed my uncle burned westward from this meadow down to the Big River and northward six days' walk from the Hidden Spring. When I was sixteen summers old—forty-two summers ago—my father brought me here to learn of the elk." He tells them also of the great eagle. His sons then tell their sons about the meadow when they first saw it, twenty-two summers ago. Finally, as the moon begins to descend, the camp becomes quiet.

Dawn brings a red sun into the eastern sky. The men and boys stand in the meadow and watch the huge plumes of thick smoke in the south and east as fires rage through distant forests. Some of the fires have been burning since the dry lightning storms of mid-August. One fire, however, was started only days ago when hunters left a smoldering fire in their camp, and before the day was over, they not only had lost their camp but also had to flee the pursuing flames. The fires will continue burning until either rain or snow extinguishes them.

The largest fire is in the east and has been years in the making. It started with several extensive areas of dense lodgepole pine forest that had become stagnant because of lack of fire, which normally thins the forest and keeps it healthy. A portion of the forest becomes stagnant when it is so dense that the trees are weakened through intense competition with their neighbors for nutrients, water, and space. This situation begins as the trees reach 30 to 40 years of age, when their tops form a closed canopy and the growth of the trees begins to slow down. The time is now right for an outbreak of the mountain pine beetle.

A bark beetle outbreak builds gradually. One generation of beetles flies each year and attacks trees during late July and early August. They eat the inner bark of green trees, mainly lodgepole pine. The beetles, with the aid of a symbiotic fungus, normally kill the trees in which they feed, and because the host tree dies, the beetles must find new trees each year. To successfully attack a tree, the beetles must overcome its defenses and therefore select weak trees. Weak trees are widely scattered and rare in a young, vigorous forest, and the beetles must be able to aggregate to ensure enough individuals for successful mating and to help overcome the defenses of the tree.

The outbreak therefore builds gradually over a period of progressive killing of trees and growth in the numbers of beetles. Trees are killed in small groups—first two to three trees, then four to five, then six to seven, and so on. Trees are killed in groups because an aggregating pheromone—a specific chemical compound—produced by attacking, unmated females lures a large number of beetles to the first tree selected for colonization. As the beetle population grows, more beetles, both male and female, are attracted to the tree than can be accommodated. Those individuals not needed for mating and colonization switch their attack to the next-closest tree they can handle, which establishes another pheromone source and brings in more beetles. The groups of attacked trees thus expand in a chainlike process throughout the flight period. The number of trees killed depends on the size of the beetle population within "calling" distance of the pheromone cloud and the number of large trees in close proximity. Finally, in the spectacular phase of the outbreak, the beetle population grows so large that even small trees and very vigorous trees cannot withstand the mass attacks of the large, concentrated beetle population.

Near the end of the outbreak, group killing of trees is no longer a meaningful term because hundreds of trees may be killed in one locality in a single flight of beetles. As the reservoir of suitable lodgepole pine becomes depleted, pressure from the beetles on the remaining species of trees in the forest becomes more intense, and near the end, trees are killed that are normally resistant to attack. Although the outbreak of mountain pine beetles has been collapsing over the last three years, mile upon mile of standing dead trees have been made vulnerable to the lightning that has finally come.

The two oldest sons leave camp by midmorning to scout for elk. They are amazed, as they stand on the rocky point, to see how the burn has changed. And they discuss what they remember from twenty-two summers ago.

After much walking, they have found little sign of elk, and what they have found is not very fresh. So they return to camp and discuss the matter with their father. A day and a half ago they had seen a more recent burn to the north, and after some deliberation, they decide to explore it.

Men and boys are a mile north of the abandoned camp by sunup the next day. Theirs will be a short hunt this year because cold arctic air, pushing southward from northern Canada, reaches the mountain on the 2nd of October, bringing with it a warning of imminent snow and an early winter.

Five feet of snow lie over the ice on the mountain lakes by the 21st of November, and still it snows. Before winter is over, the lakes will be buried under twenty feet of snow, and snow will accumulate in drifts over thirty feet high.

While snow falls in the Cascade Mountains of Oregon and Washington, the mountain range between France and Spain is also receiving its winter's ration of white. The Pyrenees, Pirineos in Spanish, extend 260 miles between the Bay of Biscay (an inlet of the Atlantic Ocean bordered on the south by Spain and on the east and northeast by France) and the Mediterranean Sea. Their highest point, Pico de Aneto, is 11,168 feet. On the Spanish side in this year of 1042, a small boy, Rodrigo Días de Bivar, is experiencing a childhood winter, and as is often the case, people like Rodrigo disappear for a time into the background of history only to reappear as prominent actors.

1075

The oldest trees of the young forest in the vicinity of the spring are 88 years of age, and their tops are at the lower levels of the crowns of the old trees along the edge of the existing ancient forest. Some of the young Douglas-firs have their branches interlaced with those of the shade-tolerant western hemlock. As in other parts of the existing ancient forest, hemlock forms a ladder of seedlings, saplings, young trees, mature trees, and a few that are 500 years old. The ladder extends from the forest floor into the canopy. It is this intermingling of tree species and the interlacing of their branches that gives the Oregon red tree vole easy access to the young forest.

The Oregon red tree vole occurs only in western Oregon from the crest of the Western Cascade Mountains westward to the shores of the Pacific Ocean, and from the Columbia River southward to the vicinity of the Winchuck River at the border between Oregon and California. Adult tree voles are from six to eight inches long, including their tails. The fur on their backs varies from dull brownish red along the northern coast, to brighter brownish red along the middle coast, to more

Oregon red tree vole (*Arborimus longicaudus*).

orangish red along the southern coast and along the western flank of
the Western Cascades. The undersides of the voles are light gray, and
their long, hairy tails vary from rich medium brown to black.

Adapted to a life in the tops of a few select species of coniferous
trees, primarily Douglas-fir, the red tree vole is one of the most specialized arboreal (tree-dwelling) mammals in the world. It is not surprising, therefore, that most of the voles have used the hemlock to
travel above ground from the existing ancient forest into the young forest, although a few have reached the young forest by way of the
ground.

On the 5th of May, a female tree vole gives birth to a litter of three
young in a "nursery nest" 50 feet up in a Douglas-fir tree in the young
forest, and the mother is bred again within twenty-four hours. But the
sexual encounter is brief in the life of the red tree vole because male
and female lead separate lives, each with its own nest, getting together
only when the female is receptive.

Although a mother may produce one to four youngsters, the usual
litter is two to three naked, blind, helpless babies. A nursery nest normally contains a single litter, but occasionally two litters of two different ages occupy the nest simultaneously. The youngsters stay in the
nest until they are a month or more old, at which time they construct
their own nests. Slow development seems to offer a survival advantage;
by leaving the nursery nest at a more advanced age than their ground-
dwelling cousins, the meadow voles, who can reproduce when twenty-
five days old, tree voles have relatively good balance in addition to
being more self-sufficient. Extensive wandering outside a nest before
they are adequately developed would increase accidental mortalities—
such as fatal falls—and predation.

Red tree voles disperse slowly through the young forest, partly because of the small size of their litters and slow development, and partly
because they tend to move only short, horizontal distances in young
forests, which results in a colonial, or clustered, distribution throughout the forest. In the ancient forest, on the other hand, many hundreds
of generations of tree voles can live in one ancient Douglas-fir over the
years because they disperse vertically up and down within the crown
of the tree and horizontally from the trunk to the outermost living
boughs of the tree's branches. In addition, the voles will only inhabit

trees that are 25 to 30 years of age and older because younger trees are not structurally able to fulfill the tree voles' nesting requirements or give them adequate protection from inclement weather.

Although the tree voles have been dispersing into the young forest for a little over four decades, they have not penetrated very far. The existing ancient forest in the vicinity of the spring is therefore an important reservoir for voles, as well as for flying squirrels and a pair of spotted owls because, except for the small basin of the spring at the base of the high ridge, the surrounding previous ancient forest was destroyed by fire in 1069, as was part of the young forest to the east and to the west of the spring.

On their own by the end of June, the young tree voles begin construction of their nests. The height above ground that a nest is built is limited by the height of the living branches. In the existing ancient forest, nests are among the living boughs usually at the outer limits of the branches and often over 150 feet above the ground. Nests in the young forest are normally built on a whorl of branches next to the trunk of the tree as high as 60 to 70 feet above the ground. Occupied nests may be found, however, anywhere along the trunk of the young trees as long as they are within the living branches. Old, abandoned nests are also visible in the young forest as dilapidated clumps of debris on the dead branches below the living crowns of the trees. Such nests were once occupied by the tree voles, but as the trees continued growing toward the sunlight, the living branches grew away from the nest and the lower branches became shaded and died from lack of sunlight. This left the voles' nests exposed, without a close supply of fresh food—the living green needles of the tree; so the nests were abandoned as the voles followed their food supply ever upward toward the sun.

For the most part, a nest is constructed from twigs that a vole cuts from the tree in which the nest is situated, but voles are also inclined to renovate the abandoned nests of birds, squirrels, and woodrats. The outer nest is made of twigs, whereas the inner nest chambers are lined with the discarded resin ducts from the needles of the Douglas-fir, which constitute the voles' diet in the young forest. (Each needle has a resin duct along each outer edge; these are bitten off and discarded as refuse; the middle portion of the needle is eaten.)

A nest constructed entirely by a tree vole is a more-or-less haphazard affair. The nest begins as a platform of food twigs on which the vole feeds; as additional twigs are carried to the foundation, food refuse accumulates. The vole's movements, along with deposition of feces and urine, continuously pack the material down. As larger twigs collect, the vole crawls under them to feed. The discarded resin ducts are pushed and pulled around as the vole moves, making a small cavity for itself. It pushes and scratches the resin ducts up and over the sides and top until a completely enclosed chamber is formed. Food twigs are brought to the nest nightly, and although some are stripped of their needles, others are not. As the vole alternately feeds in the nest and on top of it, the nest gradually increases in size and settles until it becomes firmly packed and well anchored. From then on, the growth of the nest is incidental, but the stages of growth are fairly standard. The nest changes from the original small structure to a large, roundish structure situated on one side of the tree. As growth progresses, the nest spreads out, continuing around the trunk until it connects with its beginning. Thereafter, growth of the nest is up and out. Rain, snow, and the constant movement of voles inevitably pack the structure. As generation after generation of voles inhabit the nest, a thick layer of fecal material accumulates, further anchoring the nest firmly to the tree.

The various portions of the interior of a nest are connected by a series of tunnels that lead to the outside. Although the system of tunnels has no predictable pattern, one particular tunnel exists in every nest; this is an escape tunnel leading from the interior to an exit at the bottom of the nest next to the trunk of the tree, through which the vole can escape undetected.

One or two tunnels usually lead to the top of the nest and the daily supply of food. These tunnels are normally situated in such a way that a vole can reach food without exposing itself for any length of time.

The system of tunnels within a nest changes constantly as the nest is altered. If a nest is large enough to surround the trunk of the tree, however, a circular runway going around the trunk is normally present; at times such a runway is found both inside the nest and on top of it.

In old, long-established nests with a thick layer of decomposing, earthlike manure, tunnels and chambers lined with resin ducts penetrate the fecal mass. These tunnels and chambers are dry and relatively permanent. Possibly such a nest can be inhabited constantly, despite changes in the weather.

All inner chambers are lined with resin ducts. The chambers are of two types, nest chambers and fecal chambers or toilets. Old nest chambers become toilets as new living quarters are established. The toilets become filled with feces and urine that gradually decompose, along with the resin ducts, forming a soil-like layer typifying nests of long use. Tree voles are clean and do not defecate or urinate in their sleeping quarters or tunnels that are being used; they do defecate on top of the outer nest, however, while feeding during the night.

On being evicted from their nests by predators, such as raccoons, the voles often move headfirst down the trunk of the tree, and if they reach the ground, either go into a handy burrow or under any available debris. Or they may go out onto a branch, cross to an adjoining tree, and suddenly stop, crouch, and remain motionless. In deep twilight, when they begin to be active, a motionless red tree vole is almost impossible to see among the branches because red is one of the first colors to fade or become neutral as darkness approaches, and without the red of their pelage or their motion to attract attention, a crouching tree vole is easily mistaken for a fir cone that has become lodged on a branch.

Some tree voles, usually adults, launch themselves into space when confronted by a predator instead of going onto a branch or down the trunk of the tree. Although many have their falls broken by lower branches, to which they are adroit at clinging, others merely free-fall to the ground. In so doing, they almost invariably land on their feet—uninjured. During free fall, they spread their legs out and use their tails for balance as they descend straight to the ground. Some voles free-fall from as high as sixty feet up in the trees, land, and head for the nearest cover. Age, and perhaps a degree of learning, seems necessary before such a feat can be accomplished successfully because young voles seldom land on their feet. They appear to lack the ability to spread their legs and do not seem to have control of their tails; thus, they land on their backs.

Although Douglas-fir needles are the chief food of the red tree vole, at times they also eat the needles of grand fir and western hemlock in the ancient forest. In addition to needles, they eat the tender bark off the twigs, and some individuals split the twigs open, apparently to obtain their pithy center.

Twigs are cut by a vole during its nightly twig-gathering forays. Some feeding is done away from the nest, but the nest seems to be the main dining area, both in it and on top of it. Twigs, one inch to nine inches long, are cut and carried to the nest; the bulk of them are stored on top of the dwelling. Other, shorter twigs are often partially or completely pulled into the nest and stored in the tunnels.

A tree vole bites the needles off near their bases, one at a time. Holding a needle with one or both forefeet, the vole rapidly and mechanically bites along the edge of the outer resin duct with its front teeth, flips the needle over, bites off the other resin duct, and then eats the rest of the needle. Young, tender needles are often eaten entirely. Although a vole spends much of the day sleeping in its nest, it periodically arouses and goes to its pantry for a snack.

Tree voles obtain most of their moisture requirements from their food, but they also lick dew and rain off the needles of the trees in which they live. Along the big river, the fog that condenses on the needles of the ancient trees is also an important source of water for the voles.

Even before the red tree voles began their explorations, northern flying squirrels had begun nightly visits to the edge of the young forest. The northern flying squirrel has long, very fine, soft hairs. Because all the hairs are about the same length, the fur is not separated into guard hairs and underfur; hence the coat appears sleek. One of the distinctive features of this squirrel is the loose fold of skin that stretches from the wrist of the foreleg to the ankle of the hind leg.

The hairs on the back are bicolored; the shafts are dark gray, and the tips are dark reddish brown, giving the back a predominantly dark reddish brown appearance. The hairs on the underside of the body are gray, tipped with light to dark tan, and give a tan appearance. The cheeks are light grayish brown, and dark gray hairs encircle the large eyes. The top edge of the gliding membrane is dark gray, and the hairs along the margin of the membrane are tipped with light tan, giving the appearance of an almost-white stripe. The underside of the membrane is tannish. The tail is relatively wide and horizontally flat; the hair of the tail is dense and of the same texture as that of the body. The top of the tail is dull; it is brownish gray along the basal one-third, becoming dark gray toward the tip. The underside is dark tan with a dark gray margin.

The flying squirrels first began to explore the forest in earnest in 1008, when the oldest trees had lived 20 years, and those that found abandoned cavities of pileated woodpeckers and common flickers in the snags left from the time of the fire in 987 took up housekeeping. Over the years, as flying squirrels moved into those areas in which the trees were large enough to allow them easy access through the forest, they gradually became established. All their nests at first were in abandoned woodpecker cavities and any other suitable cavity that could be found in the large snags. Woodpecker cavities are favored by the females, who have family responsibilities, so males take the less adequate cavities and live a bachelor life, either singly or in twos, threes, or fours.

The snags have been falling gradually over the decades and now, in 1075, they are far fewer than before. As the snags were falling, the forest was growing, and the flying squirrels began more and more to build thick, outside nests of twigs and moss, and when they could find a dead tree with loose outer bark that could easily be removed, they removed it, stripped off the dead, dry inner bark, and used that for their nests. Outside nests in the ancient forest were often made with the lichens (*Usnea* spp. and *Bryoria* spp.) that grew on the trees. (A lichen is actually two plants in one. A fungus forms the outside body, and an alga that can make its own food grows inside the body. Thus while the fungus protects the alga, the alga feeds the fungus.)

Flying squirrels are slowly becoming more abundant in the young forest as it grows and trees die, which create new snags large enough to house some of the larger woodpeckers and therefore the squirrels. Dying trees thin the forest and open space between living trees, which is important to the squirrels because, while they can't "fly," they glide downward through the air from one tree to another and need space to maneuver. They climb to an elevated point and launch themselves. As they leap into space, they extend their legs outward from the body. Such action erects the cartilaginous projections on the outside of each wrist. These projections help spread the large, loose folds of skin along the sides of the body so that a monoplane is formed, allowing the

A northern flying squirrel (*Glaucomys sabrinus*) eating a belowground fruiting body of the fungus *Hysterangium* spp.

squirrel to glide gently and quietly with good control. Steering is accomplished by raising and lowering the forelegs. The tail, flattened
horizontally, is used as a stabilizer to keep the squirrel on course.

Before a squirrel starts its glide, it carefully examines the chosen
landing site by leaning to one side and then to the other, possibly as a
method of triangulation to measure the distance. As a squirrel reaches
a landing point, normally the trunk of a tree, it changes course to an
upward direction by raising the tail. At the same time, the forelegs and
hind legs are extended forward, allowing the gliding membrane to act
as a parachute to slow the glide and to absorb the shock of landing.
The instant the squirrel lands, it races around the trunk of the tree,
thereby eluding any predator that may be following it, such as the
northern spotted owl, who inhabits the existing ancient forest and
whose favorite meal is flying squirrel. To make another glide, the
squirrel dashes to a higher position with incredible swiftness and agil-
ity and again launches itself into space. From a height of about 60 feet,
a squirrel can glide about 163 feet at a rate of 6 feet per second.

These bright-eyed squirrels of the night feed mainly on truffles during spring, summer, and autumn. They thus descend each night to the forest floor and dig out the belowground fruiting body of the fungus—the truffle—which they detect by odor. Truffles are abundant in and around the large, fallen trees from the ancient forest that still lie decomposing on the floor of the young forest. In addition, these decomposing trees, protected from drying by the dense tops of the young trees, act as reservoirs that hold water all year and thus prolong the fruiting season of the truffles well into the summer. Flying squirrels are therefore most abundant in those areas that have large numbers of slowly decomposing ancient trees. In winter, the squirrels also eat the two lichens used to build their nests in the ancient forest and glean truffles later into the year in the young forest because the dense canopy protects the floor from snow, keeping truffles available. They can also eat what few lichens they find in the young forest.

Because these squirrels get most of their food from below the surface of the forest floor, they are vulnerable to predation while on the ground, which explains how pumas, bobcats, coyotes, and marten are able to catch them to eat. Their vulnerability to predation makes it imperative that flying squirrels be familiar with their home areas. One way the squirrels mark their home areas is by cheek rubbing. They have a scent gland in the corner of each side of their mouths, and as they move about their home areas at night, they find an appropriate place and, twisting their heads, drag one side of their faces across the object. They generally mark only with one side, but on some occasions they mark with both. Such scent marking is done primarily at sites of grooming, feeding, and resting and probably acts to keep a particular squirrel oriented to and reassured that it is in its home area.

Breeding begins in March and April, and most youngsters are born in May and June, after a gestation period of thirty-seven days. Some mothers have from one to six young, but most have from three to five. Born in snug, soft, warm nests, babies weigh about two-tenths of an ounce at birth. Their eyes open when they are about thirty-two days old. By this time they are fully clothed in exquisitely soft fur, and their locomotion and coordination are well developed. They begin leaving their nest for short periods when they are about forty days old.

As tree voles and flying squirrels occupy the treetops of the young forest, the western red-backed vole takes over domination of the forest

Baby northern flying squirrels in their tree nest.

floor from the creeping vole. Populations of both the creeping vole and the pocket gopher have begun to decline as the grasses and herbs gradually disappear and young Douglas-fir trees begin in earnest to occupy the burn. Although the gophers disappear altogether as the forest grows, the creeping vole remains, but subordinate in numbers to the western red-backed vole.

The red-backed vole spends much of its time underground and flourishes among the decomposing ancient trees because its specialized food—the truffle—is again available in abundance. The creeping vole, on the other hand, will survive the years and decades in relatively low numbers until the advent of another fire.

Fire, that ever-unpredictable agent of change, releases the creeping voles from within the forest and makes the heretofore-uninhabitable forest floor available to the pocket gophers from without. It also immediately kills the red tree voles and flying squirrels, only to renew the Douglas-fir forest and thus ensure their survival over time.

1080

Rodrigo Días de Bivar, now a man of forty, is known as El Cid, "the Lord." He is uniting the Christians and the Moors throughout Spain against a common enemy from North Africa, the Moorish emir Ben Yousef, who threatens to overrun Spain. (History named these Muslim conquerors of Spain Moors, perhaps because they arrived by way of Morocco. Moors are a people of mixed Berber and Arab descent.) And while Rodrigo is building bridges between two cultures in an effort to unite Spain before the onset of an inevitable war, the young forest near the spring, now 93 years old, is in the middle of a long summer drought.

1099

The forest is entering its 112th April. Warm Chinook winds have already started the snowpack melting, and a few areas of bare soil are visible. The sun shines uninterruptedly for three weeks, causing the rivers to swell as snow and ice become trickles, rivulets, streams, rivers, and the ocean, only to return again to the forest as fog, rain, and snow.

It is the 15th of May, and the old female black bear is ready to emerge from the winter's den that she had dug under a pile of large fallen trees killed in the fire of 987. She comes out gingerly because the hairless pads on the soles of her feet have recently been shed and the newly formed pads are still tender. In fact, the local Native Americans hold the belief that bears eat the skin off their feet during their winter sleep. And if the Indians were to look at bear droppings near their winter dens, they would indeed find portions of the bears' foot pads in them.

The black bear is one of the largest mammals and is the largest carnivore in Oregon. It is exceeded in size only by some of the hoofed animals. Black bears are massive, with strong, heavy bodies and moderate-size heads; their facial profile is rather straight. They have small eyes and small, round, erect ears. The tapering nose has a broad pad and large nostrils. The wide feet terminate in five digits, each with a strong claw. Compared with other species of bear, the claws are relatively short and those on the forefeet are sharply curved. The short tails are hairy and inconspicuous. The black bear has a number of color phases, but only the black, brown, and reddish brown phases occur in Oregon.

The female, who was bred on the 1st of July last year, produces twin cubs while she sleeps on the 6th of February, 220 days after she conceived. The newborn cubs are between six and ten inches long and weigh between seven and twelve ounces. Their eyes are closed, and they are sparsely covered with fine, stiff hairs. They develop slowly for the first few days but then grow rapidly, nourished by their mother's milk. On the 3rd of March, at the ripe old age of twenty-five days, the cubs receive their first glimpse of the world as their eyes open. They are now covered with short, fuzzy brownish hair, even though they will be black as adults. The cubs are already playful by the time they are three months old on the 6th of May, and it is a bright, warm, sunny world that greets them on the 15th of May as their mother leads them out of the den for the first time.

The cubs grow rapidly, and the 15th of July finds them romping amidst the flowers of the meadow above the old burn as fluffy, white clouds drift slowly overhead. On this day, while the cubs are playing, Jerusalem is falling to the Christian crusaders, who finally conquer the Seljuk Turks and occupy the Holy City for the first time since the seventh century.

By mid-August, the cubs are six months old and can fend for themselves, but they will remain with their mother for a year or more and will even sleep with her or near her during their first winter. The bear family will separate during the breeding season of the year following the cubs' birth. The cubs will weigh between forty and sixty pounds by the time they are a year old, and between one hundred and two hundred pounds by the time they are fully adult.

August becomes September, then October. And before this year of 1099 comes to a close, Rodrigo Días de Bivar, after a long campaign and an arduous battle for the strategic city of Valencia on the Mediterranean coast, will finally bring peace to Spain after almost four hundred years of Moorish conquest. Rodrigo will not live, however, to see the peace his vast army of Christians and Moors will have won against the Moorish emir from North Africa, Ben Yousef. Wounded in battle, Rodrigo dies. And it is a dead Rodrigo that the next day, mounted and strapped to his horse as though alive, leads his army to victory and to peace. Thus, Rodrigo Días de Bivar becomes the epic hero of Spain.

The victory is short-lived, however, because the Moors recapture Valencia in but a short time, and Spain remains in the throes of battle over Moorish versus Christian domination for almost another four hundred years. Finally, in 1469, Ferdinand II of Aragon weds Isabel of Castile, and using their combined military might, they finally enter the Alhambra in Granada in 1492 and end Moorish rule. But for now, 1099, snow is falling in the Pyrenees; Spain is at peace, and the young black bears of the forest by the spring are sleeping through their first winter.

Mature Forest

1112

The forest is now 125 years old. The Douglas-firs are from 120 to 150 feet tall and 20 to 25 inches in diameter 5 feet off the ground. Suppression is no longer the main cause of tree death. Now and throughout the rest of the forest's life, the Douglas-firs will die for other reasons, but not old age. The trees of the forest, unlike people and animals, do not have essential organs, such as hearts, livers, and brains, that wear out and are irreplaceable. The trees produce new functional tissues every year and replace their defenses against threats such as harmful fungi and insects. Although trees can live for thousands of years, most are weakened and finally die from injury, disease, or both. Those species with thick bark or resinous wood tend to live longer than others, but all trees accumulate wounds and infections throughout their life or suffer from detrimental changes in their environment.

How and when a tree finally dies determines what type of diversity it will add to the forest. Diversity in this sense includes a tree's structure (how the tree appears), how it falls (whole or broken, across the contours or up and down the contours of the land), and its function (how it decomposes and recycles into the soil and how plants and animals can use it as habitat or food during the decomposition process). For example, the Douglas-fir sapling that died standing from suppres-

An ancient Douglas-fir blown over by wind and caught in a neighboring tree.

sion in 1010 and the 700-year-old Douglas-fir that has been weakened by root rot and is suddenly blown down today present very different opportunities as food, shelter, and support for the plants and animals growing and living on, in, and around them.

Trees in the forest are injured and weakened by physical forces, such as wind, lightning, fire, snow and ice, and drought. Wind rocks trees back and forth and rubs one against another (which can often be heard as a squeaking sound on a windy day) and abrades their roots against rocks in the soil. Wind also breaks the trees' branches, and their tops often suffer from decay.

Exceptional loads of snow and ice may break branches or entire tops off the trees. Although such damage is often concentrated around the top of the high ridge, not all the trees are affected. Those with asymmetrical crowns are most likely to be damaged because ice builds more heavily on one side than the other. These are most likely to be trees below the tallest trees in the forest, whose crowns are influenced by the growth of the tallest trees. The tallest trees, on the other hand, are most likely to be struck by lightning, which shatters or kills their tops or kills the entire tree.

Left: The snag of an ancient Douglas-fir (*Pseudotsuga menziesii*) with the spiral wound of the lightning strike that killed it. *Right:* An ancient Douglas-fir wounded when the tree in the foreground struck it while falling four years earlier.

Over the years, ground fires kill some trees outright, stress others, and leave still others unscathed; what happens depends on many factors, including the thickness of the bark and the height above ground to the live crown. Or a fire may kill a small area of the trunk of a tree, usually near the ground where dead woody material lies against it. On the conifers, the fire scar that results is often covered with pitch and becomes even more flammable in subsequent fires.

Wind, ice, and fire generally damage trees by destroying their protective bark. Other environmental effects are more subtle but ultimately more debilitating. Prolonged or unseasonable drought, for instance, reduces a tree's growth, creates physiological stress, and weakens its chemical defenses against pathogenic fungi and insects. Suppression of small trees by larger neighbors has a similar effect.

The live trees provide food and shelter for many living things, often to the long-term detriment of the trees. Bear, beaver, and por-cupines feed on the inner bark (which is the living tissue just under-neath a tree's outer, protective bark). Although bear and porcupines often attack the young trees with thin outer bark, they will climb into older trees to reach the thinner outer bark near the treetops. Beaver inhabiting the big river simply select a tree along the water's edge and chew it through near the base, thus bringing the thinner outer bark to their level on the ground. Deer and elk strip bark off trees during sign-posting, and sapsuckers, relatives of woodpeckers, remove bits of bark from favored trees with almost surgical precision.

Fungi, some higher plants, and insects parasitize the trees. Many such organisms are secondarily taking advantage of wounded or weak-ened trees, but some organisms are primary agents of damage. Defoli-ating insects, such as tent caterpillars, western spruce budworms, and Douglas-fir tussock moths, occasionally eat so much of the green fo-liage that they reduce the tree's ability to produce its own food from photosynthesis. Fungi that cause a tree to lose its needles (called needle-cast fungi) have a similar effect. Primary decay fungi, such as laminated root rot, structurally weaken specific tissues. And dwarf mistletoes and rust fungi actually increase growth of tissue, but only in the area of infection. Such tissue growth produces an altered growth form, and with the mistletoes, eventually may starve the uninfected portions of some trees.

Although tree injury in the forest results from many causes, the immediate effects fall into a few broad categories—wounded, weak-ened physiologically, or altered structurally. Any agent damaging a tree in the forest can kill it outright if the agent's action is extreme, prolonged, or concentrated, but in many cases, the tree survives the initial injury only to be attacked secondarily by fungi or insects. The ultimate fate of a tree, however, depends on its health, the potency of the pathogens attacking it, and its ability to limit or recover from the damage.

The outer bark of a tree provides primary protection against the desiccation and death of its living tissue and against decay of its struc-tural tissue. A break in the outer bark, whatever the cause, exposes the living tissues to the air, which causes them to dry out and die. The damaged area is walled off by the formation of a reaction zone within the living tissues around the wound. If a wound is sufficiently severe, the nutrient-rich, moist sapwood, originally protected by the bark, is exposed to wound-decay fungi and wood-boring insects that open channels for still deeper penetration by decay fungi. The decay spreads slowly (one to two inches per year) and is generally limited to the wood already formed before the wound occurred. Decay usually becomes inactive when wounds heal and seal off the supply of oxygen to the pathogens.

The probability of decay following injury is influenced by the size of the wound, whether the wound is in contact with the soil, and the species of tree that is wounded. Large wounds provide a bigger target for airborne spores of fungi and release more volatile terpenes (also called essential oils), which attract wood-boring insects. Large wounds heal more slowly than smaller ones, and wounds in contact with the soil may be kept moist, but the soil also contains many decay fungi. Some species of trees in the forest, such as the western redcedars across the big river and the Douglas-firs, store materials in their heartwood that are toxic to fungi, so decay around a wound is confined to the sap-wood for many years. But other species of trees in the forest, such as the red alders and bigleaf maples along the streams and the big river, the grand firs and the western hemlocks near the spring, lack this chemical protection and decay soon after being injured. Small, some-times superficial wounds of sapsuckers heal quickly unless they are invaded by fungi that kill additional tissue and ultimately girdle the tree and kill it also.

Death and decay of the sapwood and later of the heartwood structurally weaken a tree, making it more likely to break at the point of infection, and create opportunities for animals, such as cavity-nesting birds, to take up residence. Carpenter ants extensively colonize decayed wood, especially at the base of trees; they accelerate the decay as their galleries extend into sound wood and increase aeration and moisture. The pair of pileated woodpeckers that live in the forest by the spring then feed on the ants, chopping through the outer, protective wood to excavate the ants, and thus expose the soft, decayed interior wood.

Trees physiologically weakened by fungi or defoliating insects or by suppression may die outright or may survive for some time in a precarious state. Often, only the extremities die or a secondary agent kills part or all of the tree. Repeated defoliation ultimately results in decay of the tree's top like that caused by any other wound or break. Some of the trees are chronically weakened and lack the defense chemicals to resist attack of normally benign canker fungi and some wood-boring insects. Canker fungi girdle branches or even whole tops. A tree suffering chronic stress is especially vulnerable to the mass attack of bark beetles. Woodpeckers, pursuing the beetle larvae, then strip the bark off dead trees or portions of trees and either hasten or retard the rate of subsequent decay, which depends on prevailing conditions of temperature and moisture.

The initial effect of tree damage is to alter the tree's form and structure, but additional, secondary effects often occur as well. Rust galls, with their distorted wood grain, are likely points of breakage in wind. Branches with witches'-brooms (masses of rather small, bushy branches caused by some fungi and dwarf mistletoes) tend to break under stress of heavy snow. The dense clusters of fine branches also increase fire hazard to the tree and the forest. Primary decay fungi that destroy cellulose (the main constituent of all plant tissues and fibers) in the otherwise healthy trees also increase the chance of breakage. Root rots, for example, so weaken a tree's roots that the likelihood of the tree's being blown over in a windstorm is increased—if the disease-stressed tree does not first succumb to bark beetles. The condition of a tree at death is determined by its species, where in the forest it grows, and how it was damaged while alive.

From now on, chronic, single-tree mortality is a built-in component of the forest that adds greatly to its diversity and is a continuous supply of snags and fallen trees.

1137

The large snags left from the fire of 987 are all but gone; piece by piece they have ended up on the floor of the forest, where they are recycling into the soil and hence into the next forest. Now 150 years old, the forest near the spring is beginning to show signs of maturity in the form of new, large snags. Although the snags of today are not as large as those that will characterize the developing ancient forest, they still go through the following five generalized stages of decay when they die.

Stage 1 (0–6 years): A flush of activity from wood-boring beetles (bark beetles, pin-hole borers, round-headed wood-borers, and flat-headed wood-borers) erupts when a tree dies. The beetles riddle the bark, cambium (the living tissue that is renewed annually), and sap-wood with holes and galleries (tunnels chewed through the wood). Such activity introduces symbiotic wood-staining and wood-decaying fungi and bacteria into the snag and loosens the bark. The flurry of insect activity triggers feeding by woodpeckers. Needles, twigs, and fine branches fall to the ground.

Stage 2 (7–18 years): The bark and sapwood that have been extensively mined by wood-boring beetles begin to slough. Round-headed and flat-headed wood-boring beetles penetrate into the heartwood and open avenues for decay. The wood is physically softened, and cavity-nesting birds begin to excavate their residences. The height of a snag decreases rapidly and erratically as large pieces of the trunk break and fall to the ground. The top breaks where wood-boring beetles have penetrated most deeply, and branch stubs are formed as large branches break and fall.

Stage 3 (19–50 years): The sapwood becomes considerably decayed and partly sloughs. Wood-borers extensively mine the heartwood. The snag's height continues to decrease, but the rate of decrease slows to about 1 percent per year when the diameter of the broken top approximately equals 50 percent of the snag's diameter at 5 feet above the ground. (Decay processes are similar in small and large snags except that snags less than 12 inches in diameter at 5 feet above the ground decay and break near or below the ground.) Only small pieces of bark and wood slough from the top and sides, and only the largest branches remain.

Stage 4 (51–125 years): All the sapwood sloughs, and all the heartwood becomes soft. The snag's height continues to decrease slowly as chunks of wood and bark fall and accumulate as a mound around the base of the snag. Although the external changes are subtle, green plants begin to colonize the snag and the mound of woody debris on the ground.

Stage 5 (126 years and older): The snag approaches dynamic equilibrium in that the wood continues to deteriorate, but roots of colonizing shrubs and trees stabilize the sloughing of decayed wood and bark and hold it in place. Only snags greater than 21 inches in diameter at 5 feet above the ground reach this stage; these snags are yet to come in the ancient forest.

Snags are a vital component of the forest and provide habitat for many species of animals. Each stage differs in characteristics and is therefore used by a variety of different species. For example, wood-boring beetles are active in stage 1, and woodpeckers take advantage of this source of food. Large branches persist in stages 1 and 2 and provide perches for birds. Many species of vertebrates find nesting sites in snags of stages 2 through 5. Red-breasted nuthatches, for instance, frequently nest near the top of a stage-2 snag, whereas northern flickers prefer snags that are more decayed. And brown creepers and bats roost and rear young under loose bark on snags in stages 3 and 4.

To be suitable for nesting, a snag must be large enough to accommodate the cavity nester. Most cavity-nesting birds prefer snags with a diameter greater than 15 inches at 5 feet above the ground, and they select specific stages in decomposition of a snag to fulfill their requirements for feeding and nesting. The ability of woodpeckers to excavate in snags that differ in soundness of wood is related to a species' adaptations for drilling. Strong excavators, such as the pileated woodpecker, can excavate in harder snags than a weak excavator, such as the Lewis' woodpecker. A snag's hardness is therefore an important characteristic in determining its value for nesting and foraging.

Broken tops, one characteristic that separates snags of stage 1 from the remaining four, are important to the decay process of both live and dead trees. Broken tops provide an avenue through which heart-rotting fungi can invade the heartwood, primarily of live trees, and expose heartwood to weather and insects. The presence of decayed heartwood is important in the selection of nest sites by primary cavity-nesting birds, such as woodpeckers, which make their own cavities.

Natural cavities and those constructed in snags by primary excavators provide thermally regulated refuges for animals, such as the northern flying squirrel, in which to nest and overwinter. Cavities in snags are cooler for nesting animals during hot weather than are nests in the open, and the thick walls of cavities also ameliorate temperature fluctuations. This temperature stability may increase the survival of cavity-nesting animals and result in higher production when compared with species or individuals that nest in the open.

Cavity-nesting species usually roost in cavities overnight, during stormy weather, and during winter. Such behavior enables many cavity nesters to be permanent residents in a generally harsh winter climate; in fact, a high percentage of permanent resident birds and bats use cavities.

Twelve species of vertebrates, mostly bats, use the spaces under the loose bark on the snags near the spring. Because these spaces are used for roosting and rearing young, the rate at which bark sloughs off snags over time determines how long the habitat is usable. The average rate through which bark is lost from a snag through fragmentation is about 11 percent per year on small Douglas-fir trunks, about 6 percent per year on medium Douglas-fir trunks, about 4 percent per year on large Douglas-fir trunks, about 14 percent per year on small western hemlock trunks, and about 10 percent per year on large western hemlock trunks. Bark is lost three to six times faster from Douglas-fir snags through fragmentation and disintegration of the snag than from sloughing of the bark, and three to twelve times faster on western hemlock.

Snags are a rich source of food for the vertebrates that forage on them, especially birds. Snags provide four areas for foraging: external surface of the bark, cambium, sapwood, and heartwood. The use of snags as areas on which to forage varies among species of animals; how and when a snag is used depends on its age because decomposition continually changes the texture and moisture content of the wood fibers, which in turn alters the snag's suitability as insect habitat—the birds' food supply. In addition, different species of woodpeckers forage on snags of different diameters. Northern flickers and pileated woodpeckers forage on snags that have larger diameters than the snags in which they nest. Hairy woodpeckers, on the other hand, do the reverse. As a whole, however, woodpeckers forage on the larger snags in the forest, and as the forest ages, its trees, and therefore its dead snags, become larger and larger.

1187

Now 200 years old, the forest near the spring is taking on the characteristics of an ancient forest. The dominant Douglas-firs are beginning to suppress the western hemlocks growing beneath them, which creates a continual supply of small snags. From now on, suppression will again be a dominant cause of mortality, but only in the understory (those trees growing beneath the canopy of Douglas-fir) and only until the forest is again started over through some future catastrophic event.

Although snags have been forming, decomposing, and falling piece by piece to the floor of the forest over the years, only the wind uproots and blows over whole trees that fall intact to the ground, some healthy and some weakened by root-rot fungi. In the broad biological sense, however, both a snag and an intact fallen tree are only altered states of the live tree. And when a tree falls—be it a windblown, healthy tree or a decomposing snag—it exerts a series of effects within the forest.

One ancient Douglas-fir amidst the 200-year-old forest has survived the fire of 987 and stands in the old burn by the spring on a pleasant, sunny, and warm September day, but in another part of the world, a battle for the city of Jerusalem is underway. A gentle September gives way to a stormy October in this year of 1187, and while high winds periodically buffet the ancient tree, Saladin, sultan of Egypt and Syria, is finally reconquering Jerusalem after its having been in Christian hands for eighty-eight years. While that battle rages over Jerusalem, and while a small lad named Giovanni Francesco Bernadone, destined to become the beloved Saint Francis of Assisi, is in his third year of life, in Assisi, Italy, a violent windstorm topples the ancient tree.

With the victory of Sultan Saladin, Jerusalem is again in Islamic hands and there, except for a brief interlude in the thirteenth century, it remains until modern times. But while the status of Jerusalem becomes stable, the falling of the ancient tree forever alters the forest and starts an irreversible chain of events that will last for more than four centuries.

The initial response of the forest denizens to the falling of the ancient tree varies. By night a deer mouse, who felt the vibrations sent through the earth by the impact of the old tree, comes to investigate. A passing black-tailed deer stops to eat lichens off the branches that are suddenly and unexpectedly accessible. By day, a chickaree (the small tree squirrel) climbs onto the old tree and establishes a lookout from which to defend its territory. Birds land on the branches and search for insects or simply warm themselves in the sun coming through the new opening in the forest canopy. Flies land on the tree to sun themselves, and ants include the newly fallen tree in their foraging territories. Within a week, a snowshoe hare finds protection beneath the branches of the old tree's crown.

Spring comes. The fallen tree is warmed in the sun and attracts thousands of bark beetles that chew through the bark and thus connect the outside world with the inside of the tree. As they enter and begin to use the tree, they introduce fungal spores and also initiate the nutrient cycle with the first deposit of their bodily wastes.

The character of the available wood varies greatly in different parts of the tree. Proteins are concentrated in the living tissues (phloem—the inner bark and cambium). Carbohydrates are concentrated in the dead woody tissue (xylem). The living inner bark and cambium are more easily digested than is sapwood, but moist sapwood is more digestible than is the drier heartwood. Each portion of a fallen tree therefore supports a characteristic group of insects adapted to a specific microhabitat. The numbers of any one species are also regulated by the quantity and quality of their food supply. Inner bark and cambium furnish the most nutritious food, so this microhabitat is promptly occupied. The area of next-greatest importance is the sapwood, then the heartwood, and finally the bark.

Douglas-fir beetles (a member of the bark beetle family) arrive at the old tree. They breed in both live trees and in newly fallen trees that have been blown over by the wind. Because they depend on fresh, green tissues of the inner bark and cambium, their larvae must develop rapidly before their perishable habitat and food supply dry out and become chemically and physically altered by other organisms.

A female Douglas-fir beetle attacks the wood early in spring by chewing through the outer bark. In the inner bark and cambium, she chews an egg gallery that is usually two feet long and has small grooves on alternate sides; she then lays ten to thirty-six eggs in the grooves.

When the eggs hatch, the larvae chew lateral feeding galleries through their food supply—the phloem. As the larvae grow, the feeding galleries increase in size. Larvae pack their feeding galleries with borings (refuse) and frass (feces) as they feed throughout the spring, summer, and autumn. In autumn, each larva creates a pupal cell at the end of its feeding gallery, where it overwinters as a mature larva. Adults overwinter also and begin to emerge in April. The cycle, from egg to sexually mature adult, is about one year long, and one generation is produced annually.

For all its complexities, the life cycle of the bark beetle can be generalized into three stages: production (mating, construction of galleries, laying of eggs, and development of brood); dispersal (flight and host-tree selection); and colonization (aggregation and overcoming host-tree resistance). The beetle leaves the tree only in the dispersal stage.

Ambrosia beetles also enter the fallen tree and live primarily in the sapwood. They differ from true bark beetles by constructing galleries that go deep into the wood. They are unique among the wood-boring insects in that they do not eat the wood, so the borings are cast out of the tunnels, where they collect on the surface of the bark or wood as light-colored powder. Adult beetles, depending on the species, construct a variety of tunnels: an open cavity; a long, winding, branched or unbranched cylindrical gallery in which larvae move about freely; and a compound tunnel in which "larval cradles" or small pockets are chewed at right angles along the main channel. Ambrosia beetles, especially the females, store certain fungi in specialized structures called mycangia. The fungi, called ambrosia fungi, are introduced into the beetles' galleries during burrowing. Particular species of fungi are host specific to certain species of beetles. As the fungi grow, they are eaten by both the adults and the larvae. The beetles' requirements, however, are very exacting; if moisture in the galleries is unsuitable, the crop of fungi either fails and the beetles starve or the crop explodes and the beetles smother in their own food. Hence, the stage of decomposition of a fallen tree is critical.

Flat-headed wood-boring beetles, such as the golden buprestid, also arrive at the tree. Some develop in the inner bark and cambium; others feed there only for a short time and then enter the sapwood. Still

Golden buprestid (*Buprestis aurulenta*).

others go directly into the sapwood and the heartwood. Many flat-headed wood-boring beetles are host-plant specific or at least confine their activities to closely related species of trees.

The golden buprestid, for example, feeds briefly in the cambium but prefers the sapwood and heartwood of freshly fallen trees. It will, however, inhabit partially to completely seasoned wood. A female deposits her eggs in flat masses wedged in crevices in the bark, or in cracks in exposed wood, or in holes that she creates, or she may be attracted to the pitchy wood of a fire scar. The young hatch and immediately start chewing into the wood. Their oval tunnels increase in size as they grow. The tunnels range in length from three to fifteen feet from where the eggs hatch to where the larvae mature. As they feed and grow, the larvae pack their tunnels with borings and frass. The larvae mature in two or more years, construct pupal cells near the surface of the fallen tree, overwinter, and emerge in spring as adults. Before laying eggs, the newly emerged adults feed on needles of Douglas-fir, then find a recently fallen tree and start the cycle again.

Although the normal life cycle of the golden buprestid from egg to mature adult is usually two to four years, the length of the cycle is influenced by the quality of a larva's habitat. In poor-quality habitat, the life cycle may take a decade or two.

As the fallen tree is penetrated by wood-boring beetles and they begin to thrive within it, Nature's system of checks and balances is also activated. At first this system is composed primarily of predaceous beetles in the families Cleridae (checkered beetles) and Trogositidae (no common name). The redbellied checkered beetle, for example, is an important predator of bark beetles in Douglas-fir trees and helps to keep their populations in check. Adult redbellied checkered beetles prey on the adult bark beetles, and larvae of the checkered beetles prey on the larvae of the bark beetles. One generation of redbellied checkered beetles is produced annually in the forest of the old burn.

A year passes. Needles and bits of lichen from neighboring trees join the snow and rain as they come through the forest canopy to collect in the fissures in the bark of the fallen tree. Another year passes. Seeds of western hemlock land on the fallen tree and germinate. Those that land in a crevice filled with organic debris from the canopy can grow for a time. But as summer arrives and the forest becomes hot and dry, the seedlings shrivel because their tiny roots cannot yet penetrate the thick outer bark of the fallen Douglas-fir. A Townsend chipmunk, collecting salal berries in its cheek pouches, scampers along the top of the fallen tree. Suddenly, out of the shadows bounds a long-tailed weasel and bites the chipmunk through the base of the skull. Some of the salal seeds spill onto the tree. Again, it is too soon, and they germinate only to perish.

During the tree's first two years on the ground, an ever-changing variety of animals use it for shelter, food, and foraging, and as perches. And throughout each year, the surrounding vegetation continues to grow and change, gradually adding another dimension of ever-increasing diversity to the fallen tree.

When the old tree fell, it created a notable hole in the forest canopy. Without further disturbance, the increased light striking the ground will release the shade-tolerant understory trees to grow and, with time, to fill in the hole. (Shade tolerant means that a plant can survive in the shade of another plant; when the shade is removed, however, the plant responds with increased growth.) The extent of an opening can be increased considerably if the falling tree starts a domino effect—the successive uprooting and breaking of neighboring trees. The probability of a falling tree initiating a domino effect increases as its size and vigor increase. A large, healthy tree is more likely to knock over the trees it strikes as it falls than is a decayed snag, even a large one. A snag will most likely break or shatter when hitting a large tree, but a snag may knock down a small tree if it strikes the tree directly.

Understory vegetation covered and crushed by a falling tree is either killed by injury or dies from lack of light. Vegetation may also be uprooted or buried by soil as a tree's roots are pulled from the ground. In addition, falling trees create opportunities for new plants to become established. For example, the bare mineral soil of the root pit and mound, and with time the fallen tree itself, present habitats that can be readily colonized by tree seedlings and other plants. (Pit refers to the hole left as a tree's roots are pulled from the soil, and mound refers to the soil-laden mass of roots, termed rootwad, suddenly projected into the air above the floor of the forest.)

The response of ground vegetation to the falling of a tree will vary according to how the tree falls, its size, species, and health, as well as characteristics of the surrounding forest. It is likely that understory vegetation, both existing and potential, will be released when a large Douglas-fir falls because of the large opening created in the canopy that admits light to the floor of the forest. Space and resources for plants to become established and grow are also created: first on the mineral soil of the newly exposed rootwad; second on the fallen tree itself as the thick, furrowed bark accumulates litter for a seed bed; and third as the trunk decays, which allows plants to become established in the wood under the bark.

A newly fallen tree interacts only passively with the surrounding forest because its interior is not accessible to plants and most animals. But once fungi and bacteria, which are smaller than the wood fibers, gain entrance, they slowly dissolve and enter the wood cells, and wood-boring beetles, carpenter ants, and termites chew their way through the wood fibers. Meanwhile, many other organisms, such as plant roots, mites, springtails (also called collembolans), amphibians, and small mammals, must await the creation of internal spaces before they can enter. The flow of plant and animal populations and communities, air, water, and nutrients between a fallen tree and its surroundings increases as the tree's decomposition process continues. For example, the water-holding capacity of a large fallen tree varies by day, season, year, decade, and century, adding yet another dimension of diversity to the forest.

Surface area develops within a fallen tree through physical and biological processes. A tree cracks and splits when it falls and then dries. Microbial decomposition breaks down the cell walls and further weakens the wood. Wood-boring beetle larvae and termites tunnel through the bark and wood, not only inoculating the wood with microbes but also opening the tree to colonization by other microbes and small invertebrates. Wood-rotting fungi produce zones of weakness, especially between the tree's annual growth rings, by causing the woody tissue laid down in spring to decay faster than that laid down in summer. Plant roots that penetrate the decayed wood split and compress it as the roots elongate and thicken in diameter. Because of all this internal activity, the longer a fallen tree rests on the forest floor, the greater the development of its internal surface area. Most internal surface area results from biological activity, the cumulative effects of which not only increase through time but also act synergistically—insect activity promotes decomposition through microbial activity that encourages the establishment of rooting plants.

Thus, fallen trees offer myriad organisms multitudes of external and internal habitats that change yet persist through the decades. Of the organisms, only a few of the fungi, such as mushrooms or bracket fungi, might be noticed by the casual observer. These structures, however, are merely the fruiting bodies produced by mold colonies that run for miles within the tree. Many fungi fruit within the fallen tree, so they are seen only when the tree is torn apart. Even then, only a fraction of the fungi present might be noticed because the fruiting bodies of most appear only for a short time. The smaller organisms, not visible to the unaided eye, are also very important components of the forest. We human beings do not begin to grasp the notion that microbes and fungi change a forest just as surely as a raging fire, only inconspicuously and more slowly. Theirs is an unseen function that is just as critical, and just as great, as any in the forest. We are awed by a towering fir but not by a lowly fungus, and yet it is the fungus that converts the tree to soil and eventually, by mycorrhizal associations, a seed to a new tree.

The interaction of a fallen tree with the slope and other fallen trees determines how much of a fallen tree is actually in contact with the ground. A tree that falls down a slope will likely have more of its volume suspended above the ground than in contact with it. The same is true with a tree that falls across other down trees. Such elevated relief adds complexity to the forest floor. Cover and shade are created in the space between the undersurface of a fallen tree and the forest floor. Trees suspended above the forest floor decay more slowly than those in contact with the ground, but the tree collapses to the ground as decay advances.

Fallen trees often seem to be randomly oriented to a slope, but trees blown over by wind usually fall in a relatively consistent direction. These become mixed with snags that break as they fall and trees that fall from causes other than windstorms. Regardless of how jumbled the fallen trees are at first, eventually they all make complete contact with the floor of the forest.

Trees that fall across a slope seem to be used more by vertebrates than are trees that fall up or down a slope, especially on steep slopes. Large, stable trees lying across a slope help reduce erosion by forming a barrier to creeping and raveling soils that gradually work their way downslope and may eventually end up at the bottom. Soil deposited along the upslope side of fallen trees reduces loss of nutrients from the site. Such spots are excellent for the establishment and growth of vegetation, including tree seedlings.

As vegetation becomes established on and helps to stabilize this new soil, and as invertebrates and small vertebrates begin to burrow into the new soil, they not only enrich it nutritionally with their feces and urine but also constantly mix it by their burrowing activities.

The interactions of fallen trees with soil are affected by steepness of slope and ruggedness of terrain; a tree on flat ground is much more likely to be in contact with the soil along its entire length than is one on steep or rough ground. The proportion of a tree in contact with the soil affects the water-holding capacity of the wood. In a dense forest, moisture retention in the wood during summer drought is greatest on the side of the tree in contact with the soil. The moisture-holding capacity of the wood in turn affects its internal processes and therefore the plant and animal use of the tree. How a tree lies on the forest floor and the duration of sunlight it receives strongly affect its internal processes and biotic community.

When you look closely at the surface of the forest floor, it becomes apparent that there is no such thing as a smooth slope. The forest floor is roughened by the scattered pieces and stumps of collapsed snags and by whole fallen trees, their uprooted butts, and the pits and mounds left after their uprooting. Living trees roughen the surface of the forest floor by sending roots outward along slopes, often near the litter layer. Tree trunks also distort the surface by sloughing bark and by arresting creeping soil at their bases.

Decomposing woody roots of tree stumps also have distinct functions in the forest. Tree roots contribute to the shear strength of the soil. (Shear strength is a root's ability to hold soil in place.) Declining shear strength of decomposing woody roots increases mass soil movement after such disturbances as catastrophic fire. Another related function of decomposing tree stumps and roots is the frequent formation of interconnected, surface-to-bedrock channels that rapidly drain water from heavy rains and melting snow. The collapse and plugging of these channels as roots decay may force more water to drain through the soil matrix, which reduces soil cohesion and increases hydraulic pressure that in turn may cause mass soil movement. Finally, decaying woody roots that harbor root-rotting fungi, such as the laminate root rot fungus, contribute to the continuation of the disease in the forest as the roots of healthy trees come in contact with the already-infected dead roots.

Of all of the factors that affect the soil of the forest near the spring, surface microtopography, particularly the pit-and-mound topography, is the most striking. The effects of this topography have a major influence on creating and maintaining species richness of the herbaceous understory and on the success of tree regeneration. Pit-and-mound topography, for example, has been, is, and will be a major factor in mixing the soil of the forest floor as the forest evolves through time. Thus is the Earth's mantle of soil an integral part of a universe ever in creation and never created, always becoming and never finished, always expanding, always infinite.

1210

Francesco Bernadone, known as Francis of Assisi, reaches his twenty-eighth year, and the Franciscan order of monks is recognized by Pope Innocent III as the forest below the high ridge reaches 222 years of age.

1215

The sound English constitutional system, gradually building during the Middle Ages, is in acute danger of going awry under the rule of King John should he overstep the fine line between necessary strength and outright despotism. The English nobility therefore force King John's recognition, by signature, of the Magna Carta—the great charter, which reaffirms the traditional rights and personal liberties of free Englishmen—at Runnymede on the 15th of June. Although King John continues to resist the Magna Carta in every way he can, Henry III, his son, ratifies it, and it has ever since remained a cornerstone of English law.

1223–1228

Francis of Assisi is forty-one years old in 1223, and Pope Honorius III officially approves the Franciscan order.

Francis is said to have had miraculously received stigmata (bleeding wounds similar to those of Jesus when he was crucified) in a vision on Mount Alverno and to have borne them for almost two years before his death in 1226. Even as Francis of Assisi dies, a small boy, Thomas Aquinas, now one year old, awaits his destiny.

Pope Gregory IX canonizes Saint Francis of Assisi in 1228. It is both a fitting tribute to Francis and a stroke of political genius on the part of the pope. By bringing Francis, the age's most popular religious figure, firmly within the confines of the Roman Catholic Church, Gregory greatly enhances papal authority over lay piety. Thus, as Pope Gregory IX secures a place in history for Francis of Assisi, the forest halfway around the world is passing from maturity to the veneration of old age.

Ancient Forest

1237

The Douglas-firs in the burn near the spring are now 250 years old and between 200 and 220 feet tall and 40 to 45 inches in diameter 5 feet above the ground. They have changed considerably from their youth. When young, their crowns formed broad, sharp pyramids. Their branches formed in whorls around their trunks; the lower branches were straight or drooping, whereas the middle and upper branches trended upward and formed an open crown. All of the branches had numerous long, hanging side branchlets. In the dense thickets, one-half to two-thirds of the lower branches were shaded out and dead by the time the trees were 10 to 15 inches in diameter 5 feet above the ground.

By now, 1237, their crowns have lost much of the pyramidal form and have become rounded or somewhat flattened. And by the time they are 450 years old in 1437, their crowns will be cylindrical and resemble a bottle brush (albeit one missing many bristles). Their trunks will be clear of branches from 65 to 130 feet above the ground. Branches, scattered throughout the lower two-thirds of the canopy, will often have gaps between them of many feet on one side of a tree. Many of the lower branches will become horizontally flattened fan-shaped arrays that will arise from stubs of older branches that will have been repeatedly broken. Although such massive, irregular branch systems may be on one side of the trunk, their foliage will often spread out to surround over three-quarters of the circumference of the trunk. The upper surfaces of the large branches will become covered with perched, organic "soil" several inches thick that will support entire communities of epiphytic plants (plants growing on other plants, in this case primarily mosses and lichens) and animals. Large branches will become the home for myriad invertebrates, as well as some birds and a few mammals. Branches in the upper one-third of the canopy will remain numerous and regular in shape and will resemble those of younger trees.

Many of the trees will have broken tops by the time they are 450 years old, in which case one or several of the lateral branches will have grown upward and assumed the leadership role. These lateral branches of the secondary tops will resemble those in the upper portions of the intact tops.

Some trees have their crowns concentrated at the tops of their trunks in a spherical rather than a cylindrical shape. These trees will often grow above the adjacent canopy, and their crowns will be dominated by much larger branches than will be found in those with cylindrical crowns. Although their crowns may differ in shape, a single ancient tree can have over 60 million individual needles that have a cumulative weight of 440 pounds and a surface area of 30,000 square feet, or about 1 acre.

The bark of the young trees was whitish gray, thin, and smooth except for resin blisters (little blisters in the bark that contained resin or pitch). The bark remained smooth, except near the ground, until the trees were 12 to 14 inches in diameter. As the trees aged, the lower bark became 5 to 10 inches thick, rough and furrowed with intervening ridges, although it remained thinner near the top of the trees. Trees that live 800 to 1,000 years will have shinglelike bark that varies from 18 to 24 or more inches thick at their bases. The bark will be dark brown on the outside, often very rough with deep, wide furrows and great ridges that connect at intervals by narrow cross ridges. The character and marking of the bark will vary between the dry and moist and exposed and protected parts of the burn. Trees in dry, exposed situations will have rougher, harder bark than will those in sheltered, moist situations. Their massive trunks will remain clear of branches for 100 feet or more and will have only a slight taper below the crown.

By the time the trees are 450 years old, few of them will have vertical trunks. The lower trunk will lean away from the hillside yet become nearly vertical where it extends above the surrounding canopy. Trees growing on level ground will have trunks that appear to slope almost at random. Even a slight inclination of a tree's trunk will result in an important difference in the habitats of its two sides. The upper side will receive almost all the moisture from direct precipitation (rain and snow) and from water either dripping from the canopy or running down the trunk. The bark on the wet upper side of the trunk will be easily eroded and will appear to be held in place only by the colonization of epiphytic plants, mostly mosses, that require a moist habitat. The lower side of the trunk will become a desert occupied by scattered colonies of lichens that will form a crust over the surface of the bark. The bark on the lower side will be hard and deeply furrowed, an indication that it will remain in place for a long time.

1247

The summer is hot and dry. Because of a mild winter with little snow, the forest is like tinder as August approaches. Lightning cracks and thunder rolls on the 3rd of August as heavy clouds pile one on another over the forest south of the high ridge by the spring. Lightning strikes an ancient tree, shattering its top. It strikes another and another. Then an ancient tree, whose top is above the surrounding canopy, seems to disintegrate as lightning strikes, shattering limbs and spiraling down its trunk, igniting pitch oozing from old wounds. Bits of burning pitch-covered wood drop to the ground and start the fine twigs on fire. The fire spreads quickly, driven by hot east winds. The winds shift and swirl as the fire climbs into the crowns of the trees and races through the forest. Smoke blots out the sun. The fire, stopped in the north by the high ridge, races southward, spreading eastward toward the crest of the mountain range and westward toward the big river. By dawn on the 10th of August, the fire, still burning unchecked, is miles away from the high ridge. On the 13th of August, moist air from the

A high-elevation forest as it might have appeared after the fire of 1247.

ocean increases the humidity and brings rain. The fire is out by the 25th of August, and it is a blackened, smoldering world that ushers in September 1247.

Winter comes early this year, and, by December, five feet of snow blanket the new burn. It snows all winter as one storm after another adds its infinite variety of flakes to the white-and-black world. January, February, and March see no letup in the fury of winter. On the 12th of April, however, a sudden warming trend begins and continues. The snow, melting fast now, is saturated by warm rains that begin on the 15th of April and continue on and off until the 2nd of May, when the daily temperature ranges between 65 and 70 degrees Fahrenheit for three weeks.

The streams and rivers swell as the rain and early snowmelt saturate the soil beyond its capacity. Here and there, mass movements of soil carry live trees, dead wood, and rocks downslope toward the streams and rivers. Some of these mass movements actually flow into streams and form dams. As the streams fill and the dams collapse, the debris is washed downstream by the water, scouring the channel to bedrock. Some woody debris then collects at other obstructions in stream channels and accumulates in large jams ten to fifteen or more feet in height and, in some cases, approaching a quarter mile in length.

A few become so well anchored they survive the flood intact. Most, however, break and are washed into the rivers. The floodwaters also pick up many large pieces of wood and whole trees that have gradually accumulated along the banks of streams and rivers. Whole, live trees are also added to the drifting wood as streambanks and riverbanks are washed away. Some of the trees will remain in the river systems for many years, but most are spewed out as driftwood from the mouths of the rivers into the sea to float until they land on shores of the Pacific Northwest or on the sandy beaches of the Hawaiian Islands where they, especially Douglas-fir, are highly valued and are made into canoes. But that is another story.

1252

It is September, and the forest near the spring north of the high ridge is 265 years old. South of the high ridge, however, the burn is 5 years old and is becoming good habitat for elk. It is not surprising, therefore, that once again smoke rises from an early morning campfire in the meadow above the spring. It has been 210 years since the native people hunted elk here in 1042. But now, for a few years, depending on fires and how the new forest develops in the burn, some men of the tribe will again come here to teach their sons and their grandsons how to hunt the largest deer in their world.

1274

The burn south of the high ridge is 27 years old and still has much bare soil along its upper margin just below the meadow. As early July arrives and the snow melts, small, absolutely round burrows appear in the game trails and in the patches of bare soil. They are visible in three sizes. The smallest is about the diameter of a pin's head, and the largest is about the diameter of an ordinary wooden pencil. These are the larval burrows of the Cascade tiger beetle (so named because of its fierce predaceous habits). Here and there a still-soft, greasy-looking adult, newly emerged from its belowground pupal chamber, runs swiftly over the bare soil, often of gopher mounds, in pursuit of an ant, its major diet. The newly emerged adults will harden in a day or two, and the greasy appearance will be replaced by metallic brilliance. But those individuals that emerged last autumn overwintered as adults and are an iridescent green that changes to blue as they move about over the soil and alter their bodies' angle to the sun. They have no pigment; the change in color is caused by the tiny, roughened pits sculptured into their wing covers that refract light and produce different colors of the spectrum as they move. Most have small white markings about mid-way down the outer margins of their wing covers that do not refract light and so remain white; a few do not.

They are exceedingly alert and are so well camouflaged that they are difficult to see until they fly, which they are quick to do when approached too closely. If disturbed, they take off and fly from three to five feet above the ground. When they land, they usually do so facing whatever disturbed them.

If you were to sit quietly and watch, you would see the smaller males race recklessly at the larger females and try to grasp them with their first pair of legs, which have hairy pads on the feet. Because size is a determinant of sexual recognition, an amorous male occasionally rushes a bit of dead wood if it is relatively the right shape and size. If the female is receptive, the male mounts, inserts his "penis," and grasps the female with his mandibles (jaws) and rides her around until mating is completed. The fertilized female will then feed for a time before she finds a patch of bare earth that suits her and lays her eggs singly in the soil.

When they hatch, the larvae excavate the round burrow in which they live and grow for a year or a little more. The larvae are whitish and elongated with a large disk-shaped head. Their eyes are on short stalks, and their upward-directed, sickle-shaped mandibles are exceedingly sharp. When the larvae are hungry, they move to the top of their burrows and fill the entrance with their head, which just fits the hole. Their eyes and mandibles ready, they seize any passing insect they can catch, although their main diet is ants. The larvae have a pair of upward-curved spines or hooks in a hump midway down their backs that they dig upward into the soil so that they cannot be pulled out of their burrows. If the prey they capture is too large and strong, the larvae simply release the grip of both their mandibles and the spines and drop safely to the bottoms of their burrows.

Some larvae mature to adults in spring and others in autumn. Those that mature in spring will lay their eggs in the autumn of the year they mature and then die. Those that emerge in autumn over-winter as adults, breed in the spring, and then die. The greatest number, however, seem to emerge in the spring.

Other tiger beetles inhabit the mountains, such as the Oregon tiger beetle, which occurs mainly along sandy shores of the lakes and rivers, and the *depressula* tiger beetle, which occupies the open areas of the burn and bare areas above timberline. And in the forest is the black, flightless Dejean tiger beetle, peculiar to the Pacific Northwest from northwestern California through western Oregon, western Washington, and into extreme southwestern British Columbia. This beetle lays its eggs in the compacted soil of elk trails, and its larvae differ from others in that they have two pairs of spines in the hump on the back.

And in this year of 1274, Thomas Aquinas, a monk of the Dominican order, dies at the age of forty-nine, but not before having written his magnificent *Summa Theologica*, a summary or reference book of the entire theological knowledge of his time from the Creation to the Last Day. In it, Aquinas seeks to reconcile the reasoning of Aristotle with traditional Christian religious teaching. Although the premises and data for the *Summa* come from divine revelation instead of empirical observation, in the Middle Ages theology was considered a science in its own right. Aquinas was canonized Saint Thomas in 1322 by Pope John XXII, and the *Summa Theologica*, considered by many to be the greatest theological work ever written, remains the basis of Catholic doctrine.

Meanwhile, amongst the heather in the meadow above the forest, the small, grayish, docile heather vole is released from its winter quarters under the snow, but its winter activities are visible in the scattered, elongated piles of slightly curved fecal pellets that have been deposited in special toilet chambers in the snow. These pile of feces are important to the dynamics of timberline because heather voles include the fruiting bodies of belowground, mycorrhizal truffles in their diet, and thus their toilets inoculate the meadow soils with viable fungal spores that eventually allow the establishment of trees. The forest's timberline is therefore in constant change as trees germinate and die and soils are built and eroded, inoculated, and sterilized, and it is all somehow interdependent on those dynamic actors, the animals amongst the heather.

1287

It has been a century since the ancient tree fell in the forest near the spring, and it has undergone many changes. The succession of plants on a fallen tree is mediated by changes in physical properties and the availability of nutrients over time. Early invaders prepare the tree as habitat by altering its physical and chemical properties while the bark is still intact and the heartwood is sound. The altered tree provides the best habitat for a wide array of organisms as long as the sapwood is still present. Ultimately, the depletion of nutrients, sloughing of the sapwood, and physical deterioration of the remaining heartwood diminish its value for many organisms, thus fewer species will inhabit the old tree during its final phase of existence as a fallen tree.

The earliest use of a newly fallen tree is likely to be by heart rot or butt rot fungi and associated microorganisms that inhabited the tree before it fell. Other organisms quickly enter where the tree's interior is exposed at breaks or splits in the bark. When beetles chew through the bark, they create additional ports of entry. The beetles also carry spores of decomposition fungi that thrive in the beetle galleries, which are excellent incubators filled with nourishment for the fungi and protected by the bark from drying and extremes in temperature. These earliest invaders are opportunistic scavengers—fungi and bacteria that join the insects in exploiting the readily available carbohydrates of the cambium, phloem, and sapwood. As the most easily extracted nutrients are depleted, these early invaders sporulate (bear spores). The spores are then carried off by the emerging new generation of insects reared from eggs laid after the tree fell. And even in death inside the tree, mites and other invertebrates interact with plants; their empty exoskeletons serve as incubators for the spores formed by certain mycorrhizal fungi.

Meanwhile, free-living, nitrogen-fixing bacteria are active in the wood and add to the nitrogen pool available for growth of the wood-decaying fungi. In the ancient forest, other nitrogen is added by rain falling through the canopy rich in lichens that fix nitrogen, and much of the nitrogen extracted by the initial decomposers is still present in their dead cells or in the frass of wood-boring insects, ready to be recycled.

The early scavengers are succeeded by fungi more competent in decomposing cellulose and lignin in the sapwood. This process moves relatively fast, as long as the bark holds together on the fallen tree to maintain the incubator environment within. Furrows in the bark on the upper side fill with leaf litter and for several years provide sites for seeds to germinate. Where the bark is intact, seedlings generally die during summer drought. If, however, a seedling's roots find a crack or hole in the bark and grow into the decomposed layer between bark and wood, it may find enough moisture to survive the summer. Western hemlock, spruces, huckleberry, and salal commonly become established on fallen trees in this way. Seedling top growth is generally poor at this stage because nutrients are limiting and the roots may not have contacted the mycorrhizal fungi needed for nutrient acquisition. Root growth may be extensive but it is trapped in the zone of decomposition between bark and heartwood.

When the bark sloughs off, it may take with it some of the plants that have grown through it to form roots in the decaying sapwood. Plants that remain will have much of their root systems exposed to air and sun. As the sapwood deteriorates and sloughs off, additional plants are removed with it.

As most of the bark and sapwood slough off the old Douglas-fir, there are striking changes in the fungal populations. In addition, the heartwood is much decayed, usually by brown cubical rot. Wood thus rotted becomes spongy and tends to separate into angular chunks, and the intervening cracks provide interior surfaces for the fruiting of fungi and for the growth of roots. Insect tunnels provide additional passages for root growth.

Mineral content of the fallen tree at this stage may exceed the original content of the wood because minerals have been added by organic materials from the canopy and by rain falling through the canopy; other minerals have been brought in by animals and have been trans-

inches in cross section) and are filled with frass and refuse. When they are mature, the larvae construct pupal chambers at the ends of their feeding tunnels and pupate. They emerge as adult beetles in summer, lay their eggs, and die.

As the tree continues to change, but still has sound sapwood, the carpenter ants begin to colonize it. The ancient forest or a young forest with many snags and fallen trunks of ancient trees provides numerous sites for queen carpenter ants to establish new colonies. As these sites deteriorate, however, the queens die and the weaker colonies subsequently become decadent and die also. Although fallen trees, stumps, and the bases of snags serve as initial nesting sites, they are not permanent. Permanent nesting sites are provided by living trees that contain dead wood, often from old injuries. The reproductive success of carpenter ant colonies is related both to their age and to the number of ancient trees that provide such permanent nesting sites. When a nesting site finally deteriorates, a strong ant colony can move to another location and withstand catastrophes that would eliminate a weak colony.

Young, winged males and females leave the nest in early spring and fly in all directions. The males die shortly after mating, but the young, mated females may go into old, established colonies to replace decrepit queens, or each may form a new colony. In the latter case, a young queen seeks a small cavity (for example, in the old, fallen tree) and constructs her brood cell by completely enclosing the cavity, leaving neither exit nor entrance. In this sense, carpenter ants (of the genus *Camponotus*) differ from other ants in that a queen works alone in founding a colony.

Once the brood cell is complete, the young queen breaks off her wings as they are no longer of use. And after sealing herself in, she does not feed again until her first brood of young is mature. She lays a few eggs that hatch in about ten days. The newly hatched larvae are fed a secretion from the queen's salivary glands. The larvae complete their development, spin their cocoons, pupate, and emerge as adults in about thirty days after hatching. The only food the first brood has during their development is the material from the queen's salivary glands. Although this first brood of workers is small, they take over the work of the nest as soon as they mature.

located from underlying soil into the wood by fungi or roots. Nitr
may be added by similar means and by biological fixation. These
cumstances provide an excellent rooting medium for plants. A g
variety of fungi, both decomposers and symbionts, thrive in the c(
plex of microhabitats within the fallen tree. Lichens, mosses, and
erworts become established on the surface and stabilize it after the s.
wood sloughs off. Hemlocks and other plants become established
the upper surface of the tree, but their roots grow through it into t
underlying soil as well as throughout its length. Nutrients may th(
be acquired from the tree itself and from the soil. Although this sta
may last for many decades, in time the fallen tree enters the final, mo
depauperate stage.

In the final stage, the tree loses structure and shape and become
increasingly low and covered with material from the forest floor tha
buries the lichens, mosses, and liverworts. Roots of overstory trees and
of trees that became established in the earlier stages of the old tree's
decomposition now permeate it and bind it together. Establishment of
new plants in the remains of the old tree is rare because of the humus
cover and because of the intense competition of roots already there.
Relatively few decomposers remain because only the lignins, the most
resistant to decay, are left. Mycorrhizal fungi seem to predominate and
are the primary fruiters. The moisture content of such material remains high during summer drought compared with that of soil, and
roots and fungi can grow actively in it long after most roots in nearby
dry soil have become dormant or desiccated.

While the bacteria and fungi are altering the structure and composition of the wood, insect activity increases. The ponderous borer is
the largest western round-headed wood-borer (one and a half to two
and a half inches long). It is a brown beetle with long antennae and
papery wing covers that directly penetrates the sapwood and heartwood while the wood in the tree is still sound. Adults emerge during
summer. After they mate, the female deposits her eggs in crevices in
the bark or in cracks in exposed wood of fallen trees. The eggs hatch
and the larvae chew their way into the sapwood and then deep into the
heartwood of the tree. They grow to nearly three inches in length by
the time they are mature; one generation requires three to seven years.
The oval, meandering galleries of mature larvae are large (one to two

Formation of a colony may initially follow the burrows of wood-boring insect larvae, such as the golden buprestid. First-year colonies contain a single queen, an average of 9 or 10 workers, and an average of 17 to 19 larvae. A new colony produces winged females in three to six years, at which time there would be about 2,000 workers. Some colonies become large and contain about 12,000 workers, 1,000 females, 10,000 larvae, and between 50 and 100 males. As colonies become old and decadent, large numbers of males are produced but no females. About 500 workers seems to be characteristic of decadent colonies.

The workers feed the queen, care for the eggs she lays and for the larvae that hatch from the eggs, and feed the larvae secretions from their mouths. The "nurses" continually move both larvae and pupae to the most favorable places in the colony. When young adults are fully developed, the nurses assist them in emerging from their cocoons and treat them with great consideration.

The workers cut approximately parallel, concentric galleries that run longitudinally through the wood, primarily where it is soft from decay. These galleries are continually increased to accommodate the enlarging colony. The wood is not eaten, as it is by beetles, but is cast out through openings to the outside, sometimes called windows. Excavation of the galleries causes piles of wood fibers or sawdust to accumulate below the access holes. Food secured by the workers is also brought into the colony through these openings.

Most species of carpenter ants feed on honeydew produced by aphids. Honeydew is emitted from an aphid's anus and consists mainly of excess plant sap ingested by the aphid, to which are added excess sugars and waste materials. Carpenter ants even shelter the eggs of aphids in the nests during winter and carry them out in the spring and place them on plants to develop, so they can be "milked" of their honeydew. With this exchange of materials, the ants establish a purposeful physical link between the inside and the outside of a fallen tree.

Other species of carpenter ants not only connect the fallen tree to the ground through predation and scavenging but also connect the fallen tree to the forest canopy through predation. Foraging by carpenter ants in the canopy is important for the health of the forest in that the ants prey on eggs, larvae, and pupae of defoliating insects, such as the Douglas-fir tussock moth and the western spruce budworm.

Ants replace birds in preying on western spruce budworms where alterations in habitat more or less exclude those birds that feed on the same insects. Birds are equally effective as predators in high branches of ancient trees and in short, young trees, but ants become ineffective in the tops of the ancient trees. The ground-layer, shrub, and tree components of a forest influence the species richness of those forest birds, such as the dark-eyed junco, that feed on the western spruce budworm. Forests with diverse and abundant bird communities are resistant to outbreaks of this insect. Potential bird predators are less abundant, however, in the dense thickets of young trees that lack an understory, such as those that had developed by the year 1020 in the burn following the fire of 987. Thus, the characteristics of a forest can influence the population dynamics of defoliating insects, such as the western spruce budworm, indirectly through the structure of the plant community, which in turn determines the species richness and abundance of the bird community.

When the old tree has rested on the floor of the forest long enough to have a high moisture content but still sound wood, it will be suitable for habitation by the Pacific dampwood termite, which sooner or later colonizes most large fallen trees in the Pacific Northwest.

Colonies of Pacific dampwood termites contain reproductively active individuals (called primary reproductives), sterile soldiers, and nymphs, but no workers. Warm evenings in August, September, and October become alive with the rattling of wings as the reproductively active termites sally forth by the thousands to mate and form new colonies.

Typically, colonies are formed by swarms of primary reproductives. Such individuals appear in established colonies and accumulate for a short period before departing on their nuptial, colonizing flights. During the predeparture period, the primary reproductives become sexually mature. Their sexual maturity culminates as they take wing in about equal numbers of males and females.

Termites are weak fliers and seldom travel far without the assistance of a breeze. They are also vulnerable to predators, such as bats.

The survivors cast their wings on completing their flights. When a survivor encounters an individual of the opposite sex that has also cast its wings, the pair walks in tandem—the male following the female—as they seek a fallen tree in which to excavate a small nuptial chamber and copulate.

Individuals produced during the early stages of colony development are sterile; winged, reproductive individuals develop when a colony is about four years old and contains 400 to 500 individuals. Individual termites are long lived (several years), an important factor in permitting a close relationship between successive generations and an important element in the termite's social organization.

Pacific dampwood termites feed on the rotting wood in which they live. They even appear to be attracted to a specific fallen tree when it is ready for their habitation; its readiness depends on the presence of certain acids and aldehydes produced by particular tree-inhabiting fungi. These substances initially attract termites to the fallen tree and then attract them inside the tree to the wood that is appropriate for consumption.

A termite can digest the wood it eats because of a mutually beneficial, three-way relationship between the individual termite, cellulose-digesting Protozoa (one-celled animals), and nitrogen-fixing bacteria that live in the termite's gut. The Protozoa digest the cellulose in the wood and convert it to a form that the termite can use as food. In turn, the termite's body provides an anaerobic chamber (a chamber without oxygen) that is replete with food for the Protozoa. Wood particles eaten by the termite pass into the chamber and are engulfed by the Protozoa, which ferment the cellulose. Major products of fermentation are carbon dioxide, hydrogen, and acetic acid. The acetic acid is absorbed through the wall of the termite's hindgut and is oxidized as energy.

Nitrogen is important in the termite's diet, especially because it is required by the cellulose-digesting Protozoa. Wood, the primary ingredient of the diet, is low in nitrogen, although termites consume mostly wood colonized by fungi, which probably supply vitamins and some nitrogen. Whenever the nitrogen intake by a termite is deficient, the nitrogen-fixing bacteria in a termite's gut make up the difference. The bacteria respond rapidly to changes in dietary nitrogen. The nitrogen-fixing system is efficient and is potentially capable of quickly supplying a termite with usable nitrogen should its dietary level suddenly drop.

The Pacific dampwood termite lives in a series of galleries eaten in the wood and without any external sign of a colony. Even so, by the time a colony has run its course, it has greatly altered the interior microhabitats of the fallen tree. The abandoned galleries form a major network of passages used by other animals and through which plant roots find easy access and ready nutrition.

Two species of lungless salamanders are also associated with fallen ancient trees in the forest near the spring—the Oregon slender salamander and the Oregon salamander. Although these amphibians may only require the large, wet, decomposing, fallen trees for two or three weeks per year, particularly during summer drought, that time can be critical to the salamanders' survival.

The Oregon slender salamander is endemic to the northern half of the Western Cascade Range in western Oregon. (Endemic means that an organism has a specific, narrowly limited geographical distribution.) As the name implies, the salamander is long and slender with short legs and a wormlike body. Individuals generally reach between three and four inches in length. They have a reddish brown stripe down the back, from the head to the tip of the tail. The stripe is often interrupted with black pigment along the midline and fades to a duller color in old, large individuals. The background color along the upper sides is black to dark brown. The lower sides are dark grayish black covered with large white spots; the belly is the same but with fewer white spots.

These small salamanders normally inhabit the spaces under loose bark and in termite channels deep within the tree. Large, moist, cool, fallen trees are important to these amphibians in the heat of summer because they are prone to fatality from heat stress. Courtship occurs from February to April. Females lay about eight to eleven eggs in June. This salamander eats springtails (also called collembolans), mites, pseudoscorpions, fly larvae and adults, spiders, tiny snails, small beetle larvae and adults, centipedes, and earthworms. These amphibians are well suited to the role of a predator within the narrow confines of wood-boring beetle and termite galleries.

The Oregon salamander, although thought primarily to inhabit rodent burrows in forested areas, frequents spaces under pieces of bark that slough off large, fallen Douglas-firs. This salamander is easily recognized in that it is the only Northwestern salamander with a distinct constriction around the base of its tail. The tail is round and notably thicker in the middle than near the basal constriction or the tip. The body is short and is a nearly uniform light to dark orange-brown on the back and pale yellowish on the underside. A fine, black speckling covers the entire body, and the bases of the relatively long, slender legs are yellowish on top.

The Oregon salamander also inhabits well-decomposed trees during cold or dry weather. Individuals are usually solitary except when they are breeding or are associated with young. Courtship takes place from April through early June. Females lay their clutches of eggs in hidden nests under bark and in well-decomposed fallen trees. Clutches, averaging eleven or twelve eggs, are often deposited under the bark or within fallen, rotting Douglas-firs. The two most important foods of the Oregon salamander are springtails and spiders, followed by isopods (sowbugs), millipedes, and adult beetles. These salamanders also eat camel crickets, all of which can be found in and under a fallen tree.

The clouded salamander also inhabits large, decomposing Douglas-firs that have fallen to the ground, but these amphibians are primarily creatures of fire-created open areas. This is a slender salamander with long legs and square-tipped toes. Its head is dark brown with a brassy triangle between the eyes. The back is brownish clouded with pale gray and scattered brassy flecks, and the underside is grayish with light flecks.

These salamanders are often found in the spaces excavated by wood-eating insects under the loose bark. In fact, young clouded salamanders show a striking affinity for bark. Adults may also climb up to twenty feet above the ground in ancient trees. Eggs laid in late spring or early summer under bark and in cavities in rotten wood are guarded by the female. The eggs may be attached separately by their stalks but close together, or they may have their stalks twisted around one another and be attached to a common point on the ceiling or wall of the nesting chamber. The major foods of adult clouded salamanders are isopods, beetles, ants, and termites.

As the old tree decomposes, it creates a gradually changing myriad of internal and external habitats. Plant and animal communities within the fallen tree are very different from those outside, but both progress through a series of orderly changes. The old tree's internal structure becomes simpler as it decomposes, whereas the structure of the plant community surrounding it becomes more complex.

Internal succession (how the tree decomposes) is related to the following factors: (1) the species of tree and its inherent decay-resistant chemical properties; (2) its size—the larger it is, the longer it lasts; (3) what killed the tree; (4) whether it originated as a tree or snag; (5) the microclimate around it; (6) its placement on the ground; (7) the biotic community peculiar to it; (8) the daily, monthly, and annual temperature; (9) precipitation and the tree's internal moisture content; and (10) the stage of decay.

External succession is related to the changes that take place in the plant community surrounding the tree. A fallen tree is a connector between the successional stages of a community; it provides continuity of habitat from the previous forest through subsequent successional stages. A large, fallen tree therefore provides a physical link—a nutrient savings account—through time and across successional stages. Because of its persistence, a fallen tree provides a long-term, stable structure on which some animal (both invertebrate and vertebrate) populations appear to depend for survival.

External succession is influenced by the same factors as internal succession, with the additional influence of light. Consider, for instance, a well-decomposed fallen tree that supports a lush community of mosses, liverworts, hemlocks, and other flowering plants. As the canopy closes over the opening created by the original falling of the tree, light becomes limiting to the growth of green plants. If, at this point, a nearby tree falls, the environment can change immediately and strikingly. Greater solar radiation increases the amount of light but may also raise the daytime temperature of the fallen tree. In turn, nighttime temperature may be lower because of the increased heat that reradiates to the atmosphere. In addition, more rain and snow reach the ground.

The ancient, fallen Douglas-fir will disappear gradually through the decades and centuries, and its nutrient capital will be reinvested in the forest. Weathering processes, such as freezing and thawing, and animal activities contribute to the disintegration and disappearance of the old tree. Some residue will remain another 404 years until 1691– 71 years after the Pilgrims will have founded Plymouth Colony on the eastern coast of a New World—as the residue of the ancient Douglas-fir slowly becomes incorporated into the soil.

1337

It is estimated that the human population in Europe doubled between the years 1000 and 1300. By 1300 the balance between the food supply and the population was precarious at best. Crop failures between 1315 and 1317 produced the greatest famine of the Middle Ages. Then, in May 1337, the Hundred Years War begins, a futile and devastating war between the English and the French. And as the first battles of the Hundred Years War are being fought in France, the last ancient Douglas-fir in the basin between the spring and the high ridge dies. This portion of the forest has now reached climax and is dominated by western hemlock with some intermixed western redcedar. The red tree voles and flying squirrels have been decreasing in numbers over the last three centuries as the old firs died and were replaced by the shade-tolerant hemlock and cedar, neither of which are conducive to habitation by these forest rodents. With the demise of their prey bases, the spotted owls move to more favorable areas of the developing ancient forest a short distance north of the spring in the old burn.

It has taken thirteen centuries without fire or other major disturbance in the basin between the spring and the high ridge for the forest to reach climax. Douglas-fir is a fire-dependent, subclimax species in that it cannot grow under its own shade and therefore requires fire to start the forest over if the fir is to remain the dominant species. Without fire, the shade-tolerant hemlock and cedar, whose seedlings can grow under the shade of the Douglas-fir and of their own parents, will replace the non-shade-tolerant Douglas-firs as they die out of the forest stand. (A forest stand is a plant community, particularly trees, that is sufficiently uniform in composition, constitution, age, and spatial ar-

Spotted owl (*Strix occidentalis*).

rangement so as to be distinguishable from other adjacent forest stands.)

The 350-year-old forest north of the spring is inhabited by a nesting pair of spotted owls. The spotted owl is a medium-sized owl of sixteen to nineteen inches in length. Its back is dark brown, and the head and neck are covered with round, white spots. The feathers of the wings are covered with pale brown and white spots, and the feathers are slightly tipped with white. The underparts are whitish and are barred and spotted with brown, and the tail is banded whitish and brown.

The owls' nest is in a cavity formed by the broken top of an ancient Douglas-fir. The fir's top had been broken off 50 years earlier in a winter windstorm. The wound then became infected with spores of heart rot fungi that gradually decayed the heartwood down into the live tree and formed a hollowed-out cavity surrounded by the hardened, still-living shell of the outer tree. Over the years, the side branches grew upward and took over the role of the tree's top and now shelter the cavity from both rain and sun.

Having selected the same tree to nest in that they have used for the past three years, the pair of spotted owls begin copulating on the 18th of March. The female begins to roost in her nest cavity three days before she lays her first egg, which appears on the 1st of April, and her second late on the 4th of April. After the second egg is laid, the female incubates them continuously except for occasional ten- to twenty-minute periods during the night when she leaves the nest to regurgitate a pellet, defecate, preen, and receive food from her mate. Her mate feeds her during the entire incubation period, and both adults aggressively defend their nest. The eggs hatch thirty days after they are laid, the first one on the 1st of May and the second one on the 4th of May.

The owlets are covered with pure white down and have their eyes closed when they hatch. They are relatively inactive until their eyes open in five to nine days. When the youngsters are ten to twenty days old, the pale brown, barred juvenile plumage begins to replace the white down on their wings, back, and the tops of their heads. They begin to sit upright in the nest at this age, become more active, and beg for food. The owlets grow rapidly and leave the nest (fledge) when they are thirty-five days old on the 8th of June. One of the owlets begins sitting on branches next to the nest three days before leaving, while its sibling is content to only peer from the entrance of the nest without leaving it before the day of final departure. The owlets are able to fly and climb, albeit clumsily, onto elevated perches within three days after leaving their nest cavity. They stay near the nest as their mobility and foraging skill improve gradually during the summer. As they mature, their parents roost with them less and less frequently but continue to feed them until early September. By the 1st of October the owlets are on their own.

As soon as the owlets hatch, they keep both parents busy hunting to feed two hungry mouths. And the parents' incessant quest for food puts additional stress on the lives of those flying squirrels in the vicinity of the nest. Each night the squirrels leave their treetop nests and glide to the forest floor in search of truffles. Each night they risk the parent owls' silent wings and sharp talons, and those female squirrels that have already given birth to their young are in double jeopardy because if they are caught by one of the spotted owls, then their own youngsters will starve. If a flying squirrel is caught by one of the parent owls, then the owlets are fed and may survive, but if a flying squirrel escapes an owl's detection or talons, it is able to perform another useful function in the forest.

As a flying squirrel searches out the belowground truffles, it digs in the forest soil. If in searching, a squirrel digs out the uninoculated root tip of a Douglas-fir and happens to void fecal pellets that fall into the hole it has dug, the fecal pellets can come into contact with the root tip. The spores of the mycorrhizal fungus that the squirrel ate yesterday or the day before will inoculate the fir's root tip when they germinate and will form the mycorrhizae (the fungus-root relationship) necessary for the uptake of nutrients and water by the tree, just as did the spores in the feces of the deer mice and red-backed voles after the fire in 988. The tree in turn will feed the fungus sugars produced in its green needles. If, on the other hand, the root tip that the flying squirrel digs up is already inoculated with the same species of fungus that the squirrel ate yesterday or the day before, then on germination, the nonreproductive portions of the fungi fuse—one of several ways their genetic material is exchanged.

Flying squirrels are associated with large amounts of rotting wood on the floor of the forest, especially large, fallen trees, because that is where their food, the belowground truffles, fruits most abundantly. Most of the truffles in one way or another are dependent on the rotting wood in the soil, and flying squirrels, whose main food is truffles, are the staple prey for the spotted owls. These owls are therefore indirectly dependent on the rotting wood.

In addition to flying squirrels, red tree voles also comprise a generous portion of the spotted owls' diet in the forest by the spring, as do western red-backed voles, snowshoe hares, and the large ponderous wood-boring beetles. The beetles, however, are an important food only in summer and early autumn when they emerge from the large, decomposing trees on the ground.

What the flying squirrel does through its feeding at night, the chickaree (the small tree squirrel) does during the day. Not vulnerable to the spotted owls because of its daytime habits, it is, however, vulnerable to other predators, such as the northern goshawk and the bobcat.

Unlike flying squirrels that forage by starlight and moonlight, chickarees arise at dawn to begin their day and usually retire with the setting sun. Chickarees are one of the three main sentinels in the forest; Steller's jays and belted kingfishers (mainly along the streams and rivers) are the others. Little escapes their attention. And throughout much of the year, the chickarees' commentaries call attention to a spotted owl trying to sleep, a sleeping raccoon exposed to view in a tree, or a weasel or bobcat abroad during the day.

The chickaree (see page 23) is a relatively small squirrel that ranges from ten to fourteen inches in length and weighs between five and ten ounces. Its eyes are encircled with short, orange hairs, and the small ears have short tufts of black hair at the tips. In summer, the back varies from slightly reddish brown to slightly grayish brown with many orange- and black-tipped hairs. A short, black stripe extends from the forelegs to the hips on each side. The underside and the tops of the feet are light to dark orange; however, white patches occasionally are seen on the throat, chest, and near the forelegs. The bushy tail is wide and somewhat flat. In winter, the squirrel's coat is slightly grayer than in summer, and the black stripes on the sides are less apparent. The orange of the underside is obscured by many gray-, brown-, or black-tipped hairs. The tops of the feet are dark gray. The short, sharply curved claws vary from brown to dark gray.

Chickarees spend much time climbing up and down trees, searching the ground for truffles and other foods, minding the affairs of others, or just sitting quietly on a branch next to the trunk of a tree with their tails over their backs.

When building a summer nest of twigs, a chickaree cuts many live twigs (primarily Douglas-fir), carries them to the selected site, and in a short time constructs a loose nest. In the nest, a chickaree uses soft, dry mosses, lichens, or shredded inner bark from bigleaf maple, red alder, or western redcedar for its sleeping quarters. Summer nests may be merely large balls of mosses, lichens, or shredded bark into which the squirrel burrows a hole and makes its sleeping quarters. Chickarees often take over and remodel an abandoned nest, such as that of a bird, flying squirrel, or red tree vole. Winter nests are often located in hollows in trees, frequently abandoned woodpecker nest cavities. When nests are constructed on limbs, however, they are well within the crown of the tree and are bulkier and much thicker than summer nests.

Chickarees have several calls, ranging from a low *chirrr* or *burrr* to an explosive *bauf, bauf, bauf*. Except during spring and summer when the young are being reared, chickarees are relatively vociferous, and noisy territorial disputes and occasional temper tantrums occur, especially in the autumn. Every now and then a chickaree becomes so irritated by the trespass of an intruder that it bounces up and down with such vigor on the top of its nest that the whole nest is knocked out of the tree. After a cooling-off period, the chickaree usually retrieves its nest to the last twig, packs it all back to the original site, and rebuilds it.

The diet of chickarees is usually associated with the cones of coniferous trees, such as Douglas-fir, and they are indeed an important part of the chickarees' diet. When seed-bearing cones of the Douglas-fir near maturity in early autumn, the chickarees cut them off the branches, extract the ripening seeds, and eat them. A cone is held with the forefeet, and individual scales are cut off the central core (called a rachis) of the cone. Good seeds are eaten, and defective ones are discarded. A chickaree normally eats in one or two selected places near its nest or food storage area. The discarded scales of the cones accumulate on the ground under a low branch, or a stump, fallen tree, or other elevated feeding perch. Chickarees do not normally eat cones on the ground where they cannot see what is happening around them. As the majority of the cones ripen, the chickarees ascend to the tops of the trees in the early morning, cut the cones off, and let them fall to the ground. The cones are then collected one at a time and carried to a storage area, such as an underground burrow, hollow stump, or hollow fallen tree. Cones are also deposited in small streams or springs. Cones are normally cached in a moist place that prevents them from drying out and shedding their seeds. For example, cones stored underwater remain fresh for a year or more. Those stored on land, however, become moldy and spoil much faster. An examination of a chickaree's kitchen midden in the winter will usually show whether the cones were stored underwater. (A kitchen midden is the refuse pile of accumulated, uneaten scales and cores of the cones on which the squirrel has been dining.) Cones stored underwater often have the scales pulled off, whereas those stored on land are hard and the scales have to be chewed off. A chickaree usually stores more food than it consumes during a winter. There is, however, survival value in this excessive harvesting of cones; should there be a failure in the next year's crop, the chickaree can rummage through its unused stores of cones and often find enough good ones to augment an inadequate harvest.

In addition to cones, chickarees eat a variety of foods. During early spring they frequently cut the newly active terminal shoots of Douglas-fir. They eat the developing inner bark and needles but discard the old, mature needles. Some chickarees also eat the mature pollen cones in great quantities, with the result that the pollen turns their feces yellow. During summer, the chickarees eat some green vegetation and various ripening fruits and berries. They may also eat sap that oozes from the holes made by sapsuckers.

Chickarees' main food during spring, summer, and autumn is truffles, which are detected by odor and dug out of the forest floor in a manner similar to that of the flying squirrel and other forest rodents. When a chickaree, flying squirrel, or other forest rodent eats a truffle and defecates near the boundary of its home range, the spores germinate and form a fruiting body (a truffle) that is subsequently eaten by some other rodent, which in turn deposits feces still somewhere else. Thus the fungi's genetic material is continually moved throughout the forest to combine and recombine with other colonies of the same species of fungus.

The majority of the male chickarees are sexually active from March through May. Females usually have litters of four to six that are born from May through June. Chickarees are born naked and blind and stay in their treetop nursery nests until they are about one-half to two-thirds the size of their mothers. When first out of their nests, siblings stay close together and are tended by their mother. Families are still together by the end of August, although they are more independent of the mother, and sibling associations are less evident. Families tend to remain relatively close through December.

While a new generation of chickarees experiences its first winter and spring, in Europe the combined grip of growing pestilence and war plunges the people into the abyss of chaos and despair. Decades of overpopulation, economic depression, famine, and ill health so weaken the population of Europe that it is highly vulnerable to the virulent bubonic plague (caused by a bacterium) that strikes with full force in 1348. This Black Death, so called because of the way it discolors the body, first appears in Sicily in 1347 and, following the trade routes, enters Europe through the port cities of Venice, Genoa, and Pisa in 1348. Once established, it sweeps rapidly through Spain and southern France into northern Europe and reaches Scandinavia by 1350. Thought to have been introduced by ship-faring rats from areas of the Black Sea where the plague-infested rodents had long been known, the Black Death kills an estimated (one of the lower estimates) twenty-five million people.

1412

The winter snows are deep this year and are slow to melt. It is the 25th of June, and still snow clings to north slopes and in shaded areas. A tree at the stream's edge near the spring, one of the first Douglas-fir seedlings to germinate in 988 following the fire, dies. Its life, its last living cell, ceases to function and dies. The 424-year-old tree, which has been slowly dying of fungal infection, including heart rot fungus, that invaded a wound when another tree fell against it 73 years ago, is dead. And as the tree dies in this year of 1412, a peasant girl is born in Domrémy, France. The child, christened Joan, is destined to change the outcome of the Hundred Years War and to help bring it to a close, but that is still to come.

The newly formed snag is surrounded by forest canopy and is ideal for a maternity colony of twenty-five female long-eared bats secreted under a large slab of loose bark that is still attached by its upper end to the dead trunk forty feet above the ground. The bats average a little more than three and a half inches long and weigh about two-tenths of an ounce. They have dull yellowish brown to dull light brown backs and tan to light tan undersides. The large, black ears reach beyond the nose when laid forward, and the flight membranes of the wings are dark brown.

It is now mid-July, and the bats are about to give birth. They were

Deep snow as it might have appeared in the winter of 1412.

bred last autumn, and the sperm was stored in each female's reproductive tract through the winter; the eggs were fertilized when the bats
ovulated early in the spring. As the time of birth approaches, an ex-
pectant mother who has been hanging quietly from a vertical surface
suddenly becomes restless and changes position frequently. She is nervous, irritable, and reluctant to eat. She periodically grooms her underside, genitalia, and tail membrane; this behavior lasts from a few
minutes to an hour. Just before the onset of labor, the fetus changes
from a horizontal to a vertical position. The mother then also reverses
her position until, head up, she is suspended from a vertical surface by
her thumbs and feet. She spreads her hind legs and curls her tail forward over her vaginal opening, forming a cup with her tail membrane
into which her youngster is born. During labor she cries, closes her
eyes, bares her teeth, and makes chewing motions, indicating that labor is probably painful. A baby is usually born within thirty minutes.

In normal labor there may be as few as ten muscular contractions.
The young are born in a breech position. Unlike most mammalian offspring, a bat starts to grope with its feet and hind legs as soon as it is
freed from the birth canal. Its feet grasp whatever they encounter, usually the fur or its mother's leg. After securing a foothold, the youngster

Silver-haired bat (*Lasionycteris noctivagans*).

pulls vigorously with its legs and helps to draw its body from the vagina. In a few seconds, the body is free up to the head, which remains momentarily in the vagina. The baby may continue to pull with its legs or may bring them forward and brace its feet against its mother's body and push vigorously. Pushing or pulling by the baby, coupled with the muscular contractions of its mother, frees the head suddenly. Its mother then tears the birth membrane with her teeth.

After delivery, the naked, blind baby remains attached to the placenta (afterbirth) by a remarkably elastic umbilical cord. The expulsion of the placenta with its attached umbilical cord is delayed, and the cord functions as a safety line after the birth. Should the youngster fall off its mother, it remains suspended close enough to her to be able to secure a firm grip on her with its well-developed thumbs and feet. Free circulation of blood continues through the umbilical cord for three to ten minutes until it blanches and circulation ceases. The delicate cord dries rapidly. If the umbilical cord ruptures too early, the baby bat bleeds to death in minutes. After the expulsion of the placenta, it may be eaten by the mother.

During or shortly after birth, the mother resumes her normal head-down position. She then grooms her baby until it is clean and dry, after which she cleans herself, using her wings to shift her baby around. With the exception of the silver-haired bat, all of the bats that live in the forest give birth to a single young. The silver-haired bat has twins.

Long-eared bats are one of nine species of bats that live in the forest near the spring. Of these, only the silver-haired bat and the hoary bat migrate southward to Mexico to spend the winter. The Townsend big-eared bat lives in the cave at the base of the high ridge. The other bats live primarily in or on the ancient trees, in hollows created by injuries or disease, or in abandoned woodpecker cavities, or under loose bark on the trunks of the trees. The hoary bat hangs in the foliage of the trees, but only the males. Female hoary bats fly east of the Rocky Mountains on their return from winter quarters in the south, while the males fly west of the Rocky Mountains.

The only true flying mammal, each species of bat has different characteristics of flight and eats different foods, although there is some overlap in their diets. Bats therefore partition the forest as they feed: big brown bats come out early, before the swallows have gone to roost, and feed over the forest canopy and along its edges; long-legged bats feed amongst the trees; little brown bats, silver-haired bats, and California bats feed along the edges of the forest; Yuma bats feed over the

Long-eared bat (*Myotis evotis*).

streams and the big river; the swift, late-flying hoary bats feed over the tops of the trees; Townsend big-eared bats come out late and feed along the edge of the forest. And some bats, such as the silver-haired bat, in turn fall prey to the spotted owl, with whom they share the forest.

1429–1430

High, thin clouds filter the sunlight as a pair of pileated woodpeckers excavate their nesting cavity in the snag fifty feet above the ground. The pileated woodpecker is the largest woodpecker in the Pacific Northwest and is between seventeen and eighteen inches long. Males are dark brownish or grayish black with a conspicuous red crest on top of the head. The rest of the head is white except for a red cheek stripe on each side at the base of the bill that becomes a blackish stripe going down the neck. A blackish stripe extends through each eye. The wing patches are white, and the feathers of the belly are tipped with white. Females are similar except for a brown forehead and brown cheek stripes. The bill is longer than the head, straight with a wedgelike tip and beveled sides.

While the pileated woodpeckers are excavating their nest cavity in March 1429, the seventeen-year-old peasant girl Joan from Domrémy is presenting herself to the dauphin, Charles VII of France. When she declares to Charles that God has called on her to deliver the besieged Orléans from the English, Charles is, of course, skeptical. In desperation, however, he overcomes his skepticism and gives Joan his leave. Circumstances are perfectly in Joan's favor. The English, already exhausted from a six-month seige of Orléans, are ready to withdraw when Joan arrives with fresh French troops and wins a victory for France.

Meanwhile, the nest cavity finished, the female woodpecker lays four smooth, gleaming white eggs between the 1st and the 7th of May. The eggs hatch by the end of May, and the youngsters keep their parents busy collecting carpenter ants, which are the woodpeckers' main diet. The youngsters leave the nest by mid-June but continue to be fed for a time by their parents before they disperse as adults.

As the young adult birds find their way in the forest, pass their first winter, select their territories, find their mates, and produce their own young in May 1430, the French win victory after victory following the battle of Orléans, and the victories are attributed to Joan, who, although not a military genius, gives the French people something military experts cannot—a mystical confidence in themselves as a nation. But Charles, once he is crowned king in July 1429, forgets his liberator as quickly as he had embraced her, and Joan is captured in May 1430 by the Burgundians. Although King Charles is in a position to secure Joan's release, he does nothing, and she is given to the Inquisition in English-held Rouen. Both the Burgundians and the English want to publicly discredit Joan and thereby King Charles, which they reason will demoralize the French resistance. The inquisitors are skilled and break the courageous Maid of Orléans in ten weeks of merciless interrogation. Joan, now nineteen years old, is burned alive at the stake as a relapsed heretic on the 30th of May 1431. Charles VII and Philip the Good, the Duke of Burgundy, declare peace in 1435, and a now-unified France progressively forces the English back. By the end of the Hundred Years War in 1453, the English hold only the coastal enclave of Calais.

King Charles reopens Joan's trial at a later date, and on the 7th of July 1456, Joan is finally declared innocent of all charges. Joan of Arc, who turned the tide of the Hundred Years War in favor of the French, will be canonized Saint Joan by Pope Benedict XV in 1920. Throughout human history, our judgments of right and wrong determine our perceptions of the world. Our judgments of motive are inevitably in error, however, because we cannot see the whole picture, as illustrated by Joan of Arc's short life. If we could have observed the evolution of the 442-year-old forest by the spring, we could have learned something of patience and tolerance. Nature makes no value judgments, so in the forest time is perfectly in balance with events. Only we humans assign values to things, and our preconceived values impose time constraints that hide the true relationships because we bind an infinite Universe in finite time and space.

1451

It has been a dry winter, and what snow has fallen contains little moisture. April arrives, then May, and most of the snow is already gone. The avalanche lilies, following the retreat of winter, bloom along the edge of the melting snow. The meadow above the old burn is already resplendent in color because the flowers are blooming early this year.

The 18th of May dawns clear and warm, and the rising sun casts its light on a man and his fifteen-year-old son as they follow the game trail along the upper edge of the forest and into the meadow. The trail takes them past an isolated clump of subalpine fir in the upper northern quarter of the meadow. They turn aside into the clump of trees and sit down, thanking the Great Spirit for the warmth of the sun on this most perfect of days. Above them, deeper in the clump of trees, is a fire circle of stones in which are the remains of many campfires of those who went before. Signs of the old campfires are dim now because elk have been scarce in this part of the mountains for many summers, and the last hunting party camped here 199 summers years ago in the year of 1252.

The man and his son make their camp, ever mindful of those who went before. They treat the campsite with deep respect, and to themselves they wonder about the Ancient Ones, their ancestors, and how the hunting had been, for now there is little sign of elk anywhere in the vicinity.

Camp ready, they leave to search for elk. They spend ten days exploring the meadows, ridges, and upper areas of the forest. They kill a yearling deer and five blue grouse. And the youth catches trout in the stream flowing through the meadow; although the stream is different now, the youth catches the trout in the same way as did two boys on their first trip to this meadow 431 years ago.

Having found little sign of elk, the man and boy leave this meadow in the early morning on the 29th of May. They travel northward for three days and then head back toward the village.

June is hot, and by July the forest is dry as tinder. Dry lightning storms ignite fires in the grass- and shrublands east of the mountains, and hot, east winds blow the smoke toward the coast. By the 1st of

August, fires are sweeping through the forests on the southern horizon. As the smoke builds, the sun hangs red above the smoke, and the sky is empty of clouds.

Small, fluffy clouds begin to appear on the 17th of August, and the heat becomes oppressive, the air still. The meadow and the forest seem to hang limply in the heat that shimmers upward from the soil and the rocks. Even the grasshoppers are silent. By noon the clouds tower upward with great canyons dividing the cloud peaks, which have ever-darkening bases. The air begins to stir and the breeze to blow. In the distance, clouds are illuminated within as though neighboring gods are warring with swords of lightning. The breeze is replaced by wind as the sky darkens, lightning flashes inside the clouds, and thunder rumbles. It gets darker and darker, and the wind grows ever stronger. The storm, gathering its power, unleashes its fury in the late afternoon, and the crescendo of Nature's symphony engulfs the land as lightning slashes the gray-black sky and the thunder rolls. Lightning comes in tongues and sheets, here and there and here again. Small wisps of smoke begin to rise from the forest. The wisps become columns, and the columns begin to spread into broadening fronts of flame that are continually whipped by the wind.

A fire starts half a mile north of the spring and, fanned by southerly winds, spreads eastward to the high meadows and ridgetops and westward to the big river. Fires start to the south of the high ridge by the spring and seem to be spreading in all directions as the wind shifts.

The storm is over by late evening, leaving in its wake a red glow in the gathering night sky from fires seemingly burning everywhere at once. The flames reach the tops of the trees and race wildly through the darkness. The whole world seems aflame.

Dawn finds a pall hanging over the scorched, apparently lifeless land. Here and there the charred carcasses of deer that died in a running position attest to the speed of the shooting flames and intensity of the heat that kindled their panic and overtook them in their flight. Many of the old, fallen, rotting trees retain their moisture and living organisms in spite of the fire and act as refugia from which these organisms can reestablish themselves in the renewed forest. In the distance, fires still roar and smoke still billows before hot winds. But just below the meadow, in the old burn of 987, the fire is spent. And just north of the spring, three thousand acres of the now 463-year-old Douglas-fir forest survive, but not untouched by the flames. The fire skips some areas; in others, half the trees are killed, and still others lose only the fire-sensitive understory western hemlock and western redcedar. The climax western hemlock–western redcedar forest survives in the basin between the spring and the high ridge, as does the clump of subalpine fir in the meadow.

Meanwhile, in Italy, in this year of 1451, two boys are born, each of whom will leave his indelible mark on an unknown continent. One is Cristoforo Colombo (Cristóbal Colón as he will become known in Spain, Christopher Columbus as he will be known to the English-speaking peoples of the world), destined to become the navigator who will demonstrate that the world is round and will unite the Old World with the New. The other is Amerigo Vespucci, also destined to become a navigator. He will explore the coastline of the New World after its reported discovery by Columbus, and this new continent will be named America in his honor.

Again, in this year of 1451, Nature has altered Her forest canvas. Again human youth issues into life. And again the universe must wait in timeless patience for the unfolding of destiny that brings humanity from the Old World and the ancient forest in the New World ever closer together.

1492

The snag by the stream has now stood for 79 years, and a vast array of animals have used it. The abandoned nest cavity of the pileated woodpeckers has been used by tree swallows, flying squirrels, chickarees, bushy-tailed woodrats, a marten, bats, and finally by a western screech owl, who has occupied it for the last two years. In addition, red-breasted nuthatches have excavated their own nest cavities in the snag as the wood became soft enough, and one of their cavities was in turn used by a pair of chestnut-backed chickadees and then as winter quarters by a deer mouse. During this time wood-boring beetles have eaten their share of the wood; carpenter ants have been chewing ever-expanding galleries in the base of the snag; pileated woodpeckers have been chopping more and more, larger and larger holes into the mainstream of ant life; and fungi and bacteria have been decomposing the wood.

October arrives amidst heavy, wet snows. The forest is weighted under a blanket of white that is twenty feet deep on the burn, now 41 years old and still largely barren of trees. The snow continues to fall through November and the first part of December. A brief warming trend changes the snow to freezing rain in late December. The combination of wet snow and freezing rain on the 26th of December causes two 500-year-old Douglas-firs to topple, one of which strikes a glancing blow to the old snag. Whitened by years and weakened with age, it gives way at the base and falls along the side of the stream twenty feet from the high-water mark.

The terrific thud of the falling tree sends vibrations through the soil that faintly reach into the southernmost terminus of a large underground burrow, causing its occupant, a female mountain beaver, to start slightly and decide to go elsewhere in her extensive burrow system. The name *mountain beaver* was given to this unique rodent by the Sierra Nevada miners of California because it occasionally gnaws bark off and cuts branches off in a manner similar to the true stream beaver. *Mountain beaver* is really a misnomer, however, because this rodent, which belongs to the oldest known group of living rodents in the world, is more closely related to the squirrels than it is to the true beaver.

Mountain beaver are chunky with large, wide, flat heads; long, stiff whiskers; and small eyes and ears. A little patch of whitish hair marks the base of each ear. Their tails are small and inconspicuous, their legs short and stout. Their forefeet are relatively small and are armed with long, sharp, slightly curved claws adapted for digging. Their fur is dark reddish brown with numerous black-tipped hairs on their backs, and grayish brown to tan on their bellies, often with patches of white hair.

Mountain beaver have well-developed senses of smell, touch, and apparently taste. Their long, stiff whiskers are well adapted for detecting the sides of their extensive tunnels, through which they usually make their way in total darkness. Their small eyes may not be very efficient, but they can detect light and movement. A thick, sticky,

Mountain beaver (*Aplodontia rufa*).

whitish substance often covers the eyes and probably aids the animal in keeping its eyes clean of the earth through which it burrows.

Mountain beaver are burrowing rodents that are active primarily from late evening, throughout the night, and into the early morning, but they may be active during all daylight hours.

The burrow system of a mountain beaver is often conspicuous. It is characterized by large holes ranging from about thirty-eight to fifty inches in diameter and occasionally as large as sixty-three inches. The holes are surrounded by large piles of earth, rocks, and other debris. The burrows are frequently near the surface of the ground and are easily broken through. Caved-in burrow roofs are not repaired; the debris is merely removed from the tunnel, leaving an open trench. Burrow systems are normally located in or near cover. Most of the entrances and exits, as well as the short trails on the surface that connect entrances of burrows, are usually well hidden.

A mountain beaver's nest chamber is circular and is situated from fourteen inches to five feet below the surface of the ground. The nest of an adult may contain a bushel of vegetation and is composed of two layers—an outer layer constructed of coarse vegetation and an inner layer composed of soft, dry vegetation. Ferns and occasionally Douglas-fir and hemlock sprigs are used for the outer layer, but any readily available vegetation may be used. When available, the leaves of salal are used for the inner layer. Although nests may be moist on the outside, they are dry inside. For the inner nest, the animals gather from the ground the plentiful already-dry vegetation from a previous year.

Dead-end tunnels, located near the nests, are used as fecal and food refuse chambers. Fecal pellets are deposited at the rear of the tunnel, and when the tunnel is full, a new one is constructed. New nest sites, particularly those of young animals, have only one fecal chamber. But long-established nest sites, which may be used for as long as three and a half years, have several chambers that are completely filled with fecal pellets and other refuse. In addition to the "toilets," feeding and food storage chambers also are located near the nest.

Mountain beaver do not travel particularly far in their daily wanderings. Most adults stay within about twenty-five yards of their nest. The size and shape of a mountain beaver's home range is influenced by the arrangement and quality of the habitat, as well as by the territorial behavior of the animal. Nest sites, defended against trespass by these generally solitary rodents, are located in such a way that advantage is taken of both good drainage and available cover. The burrows that radiate from the nest site are also constructed to take advantage of available drainage and cover, although away from the nest site, much-used tunnels may have permanently flowing rivulets coursing through them.

Mountain beaver have various vocalizations, ranging from soft whining and sobbing to a kind of booming noise, hence another name for them—"boomer." The most frequent sound, however, is a harsh chattering-grating produced by gnashing the tips of the lower front teeth across the tips of the upper front teeth. Gnashing of teeth indicates irritation and is best heeded because mountain beavers are normally cantankerous and are swift, vicious biters.

Strictly vegetarian, a mountain beaver consumes a wide variety of plants, but swordfern is the most important food on a yearly basis. Thoughout the year, however, certain dietary changes occur related to the protein content of the various foods. Adult males, for example, eat principally ferns but shift to red alder for a short period in the early autumn when the leaves of the alders are amassing their greatest protein content. Because milk production in mammals depends on a high-protein diet, in spring the nursing females shift their diet from ferns to the new growth of coniferous trees, whose foliage is then high in protein. Later, when the protein content of grasses and herbs reaches its peak, the females again shift their diet.

Whereas plants gathered for inner nest material are always dry, plants gathered for food are never allowed to dry out. Food plants are cut while fresh and piled next to a burrow, under a fallen tree, or on top of one. There the plants are allowed to permanently wilt before a mountain beaver transports them by mouth into the feeding chamber. Since the relative humidity of the feeding chamber is 100 percent, the food does not dry out. Thus by wilting some vegetation and then later mixing it with fresh plants, a mountain beaver achieves a desired intake volume of water content.

Mountain beaver climb hardwood trees, such as red alder and vine maple, to get the leaves. The animals climb to heights of about fifteen feet in alder and about six feet in vine maple to lop off living branches that are sometimes nearly an inch in diameter. They cut the branches off as they climb, but the branches are not cut off flush with the trees, which leaves stubs for the mountain beaver's descent.

Mountain beaver produce two kinds of pellets—hard and soft. The hard pellets are fecal pellets of waste material and are discarded, whereas the soft pellets are produced in the cecum (the large, blind pouch that forms the beginning of the large intestine) and are reingested as soon as they are expelled. This secondary digestion allows maximum use of the nutrients contained in the food.

These chunky rodents also have chambers that provide for storage of their "mountain beaver baseballs." These "baseballs" are earth or stones that the animals find and keep while excavating burrows. The baseballs, composed of heavy clay or friable rock, may be spherical or lopsided, about three inches in diameter and about seven ounces in weight. Their function seems twofold: because the animals' diet furnishes little abrasive material, gnawing the balls keeps the animals' ever-growing front teeth in proper trim; the balls are also used as a wedge to close the nest–feeding chamber complex during an animal's absence, preventing trespass.

Mating occurs in January and February, and young are born after a gestation period of about thirty days. Litters usually are four or five young. Youngsters are born naked and blind with disproportionately large heads. Their front feet serve as hands for grasping, as they do in the adults. On the heel of the palms are two elongated processes, which, together with the thumb, oppose the four fingers and thus assist in grasping. Youngsters are evident outside their mother's burrow in early June. Although some young animals become sexually mature the year after their birth, most do not mature until the second year. One litter per year seems normal.

During dispersal, the young may follow existing burrow systems, or they may travel along the surface of the ground. When dispersing through existing burrow systems, they may attempt to establish several nest sites before finding one that suits them. Nest sites are established either by enlarging or extending burrows or by occupying vacant, already-established nest sites. After a nest site has been established, movements of the young are similar to those of the adults.

One such youngster leaves its mother's burrow system and, after several trial starts, ends up at the fallen snag on the 15th of August. By morning, it has dug a burrow beneath the prone snag and created a temporary nest chamber. It works diligently and has a well-established burrow system along the entire length of the snag by the time the first skiff of snow falls in mid-November.

Mountain beaver burrows are used by a variety of mammals: shrew-moles, coast moles, snowshoe hares, deer mice, western red-backed voles, long-tailed weasels, mink, and spotted skunks. Whereas most of these mammals are innocuous to the mountain beaver, the weasels and mink (primarily large males) prey on the young.

Meanwhile, in Spain, a new power is revealed through the promotion of overseas exploration by King Ferdinand and Queen Isobel. While the Portuguese concentrate on the Indian Ocean, Ferdinand and Isobel give their patronage to the Genoese navigator Christopher Columbus, who sets sail across the Atlantic Ocean in the hope of establishing a shorter route to the rich spice markets of the East Indies. While sailing west in search of the shorter route to the spice markets, Columbus discovers the islands of the Caribbean, and just before midnight on Christmas Eve, a sleepy helmsman of the flagship, *Santa María*, gives the tiller to a ship's boy, who runs the ship aground off the north coast of Haiti, near the present-day town of Bord de Mer de Limonade.

Columbus appeals to Guacanagari, the Indian *cacique*, or chief, for help in salvaging what he can from the wrecked ship. The Indians, whose village is about four miles from the wreck, help unload supplies and dismantle the ship for its boards and timbers. They carry the supplies, boards, and timbers by canoe to the village, where Guacanagari gives Columbus two of his best and biggest houses. Thus, a tiny settlement—named La Navidad for the infant child of Christmas—is established on the 26th of December 1492.

Before he leaves, Columbus instructs his men to build a fort and a moat to impress the Indians and to trade for as much gold as they can until his return. When Columbus returns in November of 1493, he finds the settlement burned and all his men dead, so he decides to move to a more hospitable location. The reason for the destruction of La Navidad is forever the secret of distance and time.

Amerigo Vespucci and Ferdinand Magellan (born Fernão de Magalhães in Portugal in 1480 and commander of the Spanish expedition that is the first to circumnavigate the world) will later demonstrate that the islands of the Caribbean are not the outermost territory of the Far East, as Columbus still believes when he dies in 1506, but an entirely new continent whose western shores embrace the still-greater Pacific Ocean.

The discovery of vast quantities of gold and silver more than compensate for Spain's disappointment in not finding a shorter route to the Indies. Still greater mines will be opened in the 1520s and 1530s when Hernando Cortés conquers the Aztecs of Mexico and Francisco Pizarro conquers the Incas of Peru. The native Indian populations will be enslaved and forced to work in the new mines, and as they die in large numbers from new European diseases, human dignity will fall prey to human greed and the lust for riches and power, and still another item of trade will be created—slaves from Africa. African slaves will replace the native Indians in great numbers as forced labor in the mines and on the sugarcane plantations of the New World. Spain will become Europe's dominant power in the sixteenth century—a power built not on humility and dignity but on humiliation and terror.

As the Spanish gather the forces of darkness in their bid to rule the

New World, a new generation of young mountain beavers is taking up residence in the ancient forest by the spring. The mountain beaver, in a sense, seems to be a timeless animal because the fossil record of its family, in what will be known as North America, extends back to the late Eocene, some 40 million years ago. And if the Spanish brutality and unconscious lust for the material wealth of the Earth is an omen of what is to come, is it possible that the humble mountain beaver will outlive humanity in this as yet unknown continent?

1513

Pope Julius II, born in 1443 and having been pope since 1503, dies. He is perhaps best remembered as the patron of Michelangelo Buonarroti, the Italian genius who excelled as a sculptor, painter, architect, and poet. Although Michelangelo was commissioned to produce works of art by four popes, it was during the pontificate of Pope Julius II that he painted the frescoes in the Sistine Chapel. The frescoes, a labor of love and reverence for God, originally covered 10,000 square feet and included 343 figures, over half of which were more than ten feet high and were painted on the ceiling while Michelangelo was standing with his head tilted back, or lying on his back, or stooping. It took Michelangelo and as many as thirteen assistants four years, from 1508 to 1512, to complete the frescoes.

In 1513, Michelangelo Buonarroti is thirty-eight and will live another fifty-one years. Christopher Columbus and Amerigo Vespucci are dead. Ferdinand Magellan is thirty-three and will live eight more years. Juan Ponce de Léon discovers the peninsula of La Florida; and the snag that fell on the 26th of December 1492, the day the *Santa María* ran aground in Haiti, has now rested on the ground for twenty-one years.

Much has happened in these past twenty-one years. The snag has settled to the ground and is gradually becoming part of the forest floor, and of late it has been discovered by a shrew-mole. The shrew-mole, the smallest mole in North America, is often mistaken for a shrew. It averages about four and a half inches long and weighs less than half an ounce. The nose is long, tapering, and sparsely covered with fine hairs, except at the tip, which is naked and reddish. The ears are merely holes near the shoulders and are seldom visible because of the dense fur. Minute eyes are nearly concealed by fur. The front feet are broad, and the stout claws are adapted for digging. The tail, constricted at the base, is relatively thick and encircled with rows of scales and sparse, long hairs. The fur is thick, relatively soft, and almost uniform in color, varying from dark brownish to blackish gray.

The shrew-mole living along the fallen snag makes two types of burrows, shallow and deep. The shallow, troughlike burrows are roofed by the decaying vegetation on the floor of the forest and by the fallen snag. They form a complex, intersecting network through which the shrew-mole regularly travels in search of food, invertebrates that have either crawled or fallen into the shallow burrows.

When digging, the shrew-mole pushes aside the earth with lateral motions of its forefeet. Using only one foot at a time, it rotates its body at a 45-degree angle and forms the burrow by pressing aside and packing the loose, damp earth. This tiny mole is an excellent digger because it is incredibly strong and can vertically lift almost seven ounces— twenty times its own weight. The mole makes its way through loose litter on the surface of the ground by pushing the litter sideways with its forefeet and pushing its body forward with its hind feet.

The shrew-mole constructs a tiny opening, too small to admit its body, in the roof of a shallow burrow just under the protective cover of the snag. Immediately beneath this tiny ventilation duct, it digs out a slightly larger chamber in which to sleep.

The shrew-mole does not construct deep burrows as often as it does shallow ones. The deep, narrow burrows branch, intersect, and cross one another at various levels but seldom go as deep as a foot below the surface of the soil. This burrow system contains a larger chamber built at the level of the water table between the snag and the stream along which it fell. The chamber is about five inches in diameter, with an arched ceiling about three inches high, and is close enough to the water table to have a soft, level, mud floor.

The shrew-mole moves in a slow walk with momentary pauses. When walking, it bends its elongated claws of the forefeet underneath the feet so that it actually walks on the backs of the foreclaws. It is not only graceful on the ground but is also a capable climber and spends time climbing about investigating the inside of the old flicker nest cavity that now lies with its entrance near the forest floor under the fallen snag.

When frightened, the shrew-mole makes an incredibly swift, scuttling dash for cover, where it remains crouched and, except for rapid breathing, absolutely still. If not too badly frightened, it faces the disturbance with one forefoot raised and its mouth open.

This tiny mole is a good swimmer and sometimes explores along the edge of the stream. One day, while burrowing under the litter on the forest floor above the streambank, it gets too close, and a falling branch from an ancient tree knocks a bit of bank and the mole into the stream. Astonished, the mole "flies" through the water with powerful movements of all four feet. Using the feet on each side of its body alternately, the mole creates an undulating motion with its body and tail. Its forward motion is so great that its head and fully two-thirds of its body are above the water.

The shrew-mole's periods of activity are interspersed with periods of rest and sleep. The periods of rest and sleep are longest and most frequent when the mole's appetite is satiated and shortest and least frequent when the mole is hungry. Periods of rest range from one to eight minutes at irregular intervals from two to eighteen minutes apart.

The mole's nest is a simple affair. The slight animal grasps small pieces of vegetation with its mouth and takes them to a selected place. When a sufficient pile of material is accumulated, the mole hollows out a cuplike depression in the material by moving about and tucking some of the material around itself with its mouth. To sleep, the mole places its feet under its body fairly close together and tucks its snout and head beneath its body and between its forelegs. Its weight is thus borne by the top of its head and by its hindquarters. The tail is placed around one side of the body. When the mole is resting, its nose is relaxed and flat against the ground. Periods of relaxation are occasionally interrupted when the mole raises its nose and half-heartedly sniffs the air or scratches itself vigorously with a forefoot or a hind foot.

Touch appears to be the most developed of the shrew-mole's senses. The mole's long, flexible nose guides it much like a blind person's cane.

The nose, in almost constant motion, quickly identifies any object it contacts. The gentlest contact of an object by one of the sensitive whiskers on the nose or face causes an immediate response. Debris adhering to a whisker makes the mole almost frantic in its effort to remove the material with its forefeet. The stiff hairs that encircle the openings of the ears are also very sensitive, and the long, stiff hairs on the tail may also be sensitive to touch. The shrew-mole's hearing apparently is adapted to the sounds made by the invertebrates on which it feeds.

Most of the shrew-mole's active time is spent in a ceaseless quest for food, and it may eat more than its own weight in a twelve-hour period. Its greatest enemy, therefore, is its own appetite. When hunting for food, the mole rummages through decaying litter, turns leaves and debris, investigates crevices, and patrols its burrows. It may climb into low vegetation and search the foliage for food, and it may search both the accessible inner and outer areas of the fallen snag. Its hunting is aided by an ever-active nose that is thrown high in the air, twisted to one side or the other, rapped on the ground, or hooked under the body. Although nose rapping appears to be a characteristic of the mole's hunting on the ground, the tapping sound made by a nose-rapping shrew-mole is not altogether beneficial. One shrew-mole, for example, helped a hunting screech owl to locate it by rapping its nose in dead alder leaves along the stream.

These tiny moles appear to be reproductively active throughout the year, but most reproduction seems to take place between early March and mid-May. Although litters range in size from one to five, three or four is probably the norm. Shrew-moles are naked and pink at birth and even lack whiskers. Their eyes are merely prominent black spots under a transparent covering of skin, and their external ear openings are not yet evident. Their broad forefeet are fleshy and paddlelike, and there is no indication of claws.

Much has happened in the collection of individual human events called history since the snag fell 21 years ago. The life of the shrew-mole is but an infinitesimal episode in the snag's journey through time. The decades, centuries, and millennia to come will weave the rest of the fallen snag's historical tapestry as its atoms and molecules recycle through the plants and animals into the soil, streams, rivers, ocean, and atmosphere.

1526

A wealthy lawyer from Santo Domingo, Lucas Vásquez de Ayllón, leads the first attempt to make a settlement (five hundred people) on the Carolina coast in what is known as La Florida, an area that is destined to cover the entire Southeast of the present-day United States. This settlement is possible because, following Juan Ponce de León's discovery of the peninsula of La Florida in 1513, two men—Pedro de Quexo Giovanni da Varrazano (for France) and Esteban Gómez (for Spain)—completed the exploration of the eastern North American seaboard in 1524 and 1525.

The events along the eastern coast of the New World are unknown in the forest, where the late-April sky is clear and blue and the day is sunny and warm with a light breeze that still has a nip of winter, where flies buzz and a Steller's jay mimics the cry of a red-tailed hawk. The stream, flowing from the spring near the high ridge, collects its tributaries as it bounces and leaps its way to the valley. Before reaching the valley, however, the stream slows. It flows quietly through a marshy area that was formed when the soil on the lower hillside began losing its grip in 1357 and settled gradually, gently to the bottom of

The big river as it might have appeared in 1526.

the slope, forming a flat bench just above the big river. Today the marshy area is dotted with the large, broad green leaves and the large, bright yellow flowers of skunk cabbage, a sure sign of the dying of winter and the birth of spring.

A month passes, and the air is warm and still. Here and there around the edge of the marshy area, bright yellow faces of wood violets, the bluish purple of spring queens, and the creamy yellowish of fawn lilies, colors hidden belowground all winter, lighten the somber greens, browns, and grays of last year's vegetation. Along the stream's edge, pinkish red blossoms of salmonberry attract a pair of rufous hummingbirds that diligently sip the nectar. The brilliant scarlet of the male rufous hummingbird's iridescent throat feathers (which look a little like a brilliant bib, termed a gorget) gleams like a gem, reflecting different colors—from scarlet to greenish to burnished gold—as the hummingbird flits about the salmonberry blossoms. His general body color is bright reddish brown glossed with bronzy green on the top of his head and back, which fades to white next to the gorget and on his belly.

The female, lacking an iridescent bib, ceases to feed and sits quietly on a twig near the top of a salmonberry bush. The male now ascends into the air with his back to his mate. He turns at the zenith and, facing her with fully expanded gorget ablaze with color, descends swiftly to within an inch of her, spreading both his wings and tail to check himself before soaring aloft again to repeat the performance. Each performance is accompanied by much twittering at its zenith and a whining note produced by the rush of air through his outspread feathers as he checks his flight near the female at the bottom of his dive. The female sits motionless on her twig, and as the male reaches the upward limit of his courtship flight, she turns her head slightly and glances aloft.

After the mating flight, the hummingbirds select a small branch on a young Douglas-fir that has germinated along the upper edge of the marsh after the fire of 1451. The outer part of their nest is made of fine, soft moss that is decorated with the scales from the buds of the newly opening Douglas-fir needles. The outside of the nest is then covered with lichens that blend in with the Douglas-fir's mottled bark and are held together with the webs of spiders. The inside of the nest is made of the soft, cottony material from spent willow blossoms gathered along the big river and is also held in place with spiders' webs. The inner cup of the nest is about one-half inch deep and about an inch in diameter, and the outside diameter is about one and a half inches.

The female lays two tiny white eggs on the 22nd of May. As soon as she settles into her nest with her eggs, the male disappears, and she is left with the family duties. She incubates her eggs, turning them periodically with her long, slender beak. One hatches on the 4th of June and the other on the 5th. The babies are almost naked, and their large, bulging eyes are closed. The female broods her babies, but with frequent intervals of absence. As the nestlings grow larger and the days become warmer, she eats mainly in the cool of the morning and spends the afternoons protecting her babies from the heat of the sun.

The young hummingbirds grow rapidly, feeding on nectar that is regurgitated into their mouths by their mother. By the time they are five days old, they struggle to get their rear ends level with the edge of the nest, and literally standing on their heads braced against the sides of the nest, they eject their excrement several inches beyond the nest. The youngsters' beaks appear above the rim of the nest by the 17th of June, and the nestlings are large enough to be compressing the pliable cup of the inner nest toward the less flexible edge of the outer nest. As the young continue to grow, the nest continues to be compressed outward, and by the 24th of June, they fill the nest, whose rim is now much thinner than when the nest was new. One youngster is squeezed out of the nest on the 25th of June and spends the night in a torpor on the ground. The 26th dawns clear and sunny, and by noon both fledglings are gone, and the nest, by comparison to its original architectural beauty, is a shambles.

Unlike that of the family of hummingbirds, Ayllón's attempt at settlement in 1526 fails, and the attention of the Spanish will turn toward the Gulf of Mexico, where Pánfilo de Narváez will land in 1528 at Tampa Bay with 400 men. Narváez's settlement will also fail, and eight years later four survivors, having walked thousands of miles, will arrive in Mexico. In 1539, Hernando de Soto will land at Tampa Bay with 600 men in ten ships. He will wander through the Southeast for three years and encounter the Mississippi River, in which he will be buried. Again, survivors will make it to Mexico. In 1559, Tristán de

Luna y Arellano will lead 1,500 soldiers and settlers to Pensacola Bay, where his fleet will be wrecked by a storm. The survivors will be rescued two years later by Angel de Villafañe.

From the first attempt at settlement in 1526, the Spanish will repeatedly try to control the vast continent to the north of Mexico. While Spain will grapple with the problems of La Florida, French Protestants in 1564 will establish Fort Caroline, which will intensify the conflict of control over the land and will bring Pedro Menéndez de Avilés to La Florida. He will annihilate the French in 1565 and will establish St. Augustine, which is today the oldest continuously inhabited European settlement on the North American continent, and where the oldest documents penned in the United States reside. Menéndez will also establish a town on modern Parris Island—Santa Elena, which will be the colonial capital of La Florida from 1566 to 1587. During these years, expeditions from Santa Elena will explore the Tennessee Valley and Chesapeake Bay. All this time, Menéndez, while serving King Philip II of Spain, will try to turn La Florida into his personal empire as Cortés did in Mexico, but Menéndez will die in 1574 with his dream unfulfilled.

On the day the young hummingbirds leave their nest, a female Pacific jumping mouse conceives her six young, which will be born pink and naked in a well-hidden nest of grasses and moss amongst the July grasses along the edge of the marshy area. Their eyes will be closed, and their ears will still be folded over and deaf. They will have short, stubby heads, relatively long tails, and will weigh less than one-twentieth of an ounce.

When the young jumping mice are grown, they will be as beautiful as their parents, which are about nine and a half inches long, most of which is a long, slender, sparsely haired, tapering tail that is distinctly bicolored—brown above and white below. Their fur will be composed of stiff, bristly hairs that lie close to the body and are strongly tri-colored. Their backs will be brown with an infusion of many yellowish-tipped hairs. Their sides will be yellowish orange with many scattered brownish- and blackish-tipped hairs, and their undersides will vary from clear white to white washed with light orange. Their feet will be long and narrow with long, slender toes, and their ears will be long and narrow.

Pacific jumping mouse (*Zapus trinotatus*).

Jumping mice occasionally walk on all four feet but normally progress in short hops in an upright position, solely on their hind feet. They steady themselves by using their long, strong tails as braces. Their tails also act as counterbalances that compensate for the vigorous thrust of their long hind limbs. When pursued, jumping mice propel themselves through the air in long leaps, covering from three to almost six feet in a bound. After a few rapid leaps, they stop suddenly, crouch slightly, and remain motionless. If pursued further, they take flight in earnest. At the height of a jump, a mouse turns its head down, arches its back, and dives headlong into vegetation. Even though it may strike thick vegetation, it lands on its feet. Landing on the forefeet, then bringing the long hind legs well forward beneath its body, it leaps again.

Jumping mice are noisy as they rummage in vegetation, and their rustlings can be heard for several feet. The mice are particularly noisy when foraging for salal berries up in the salal bushes, often six inches or more above the ground. The dense, shrubby nature of salal thickets, as well as the long hind feet and long tails of the mice, allows them to move freely in or on a thicket. When startled, the mice either dive head first into the thicket or escape by leaping across the surface of the springy top of the thicket. When resting on top of a salal thicket, the mice normally have their tails braced across the upper surface of the broad, stiff leaves.

The stream poses no barrier to the jumping mice, who are good swimmers, although they use branches and fallen trees for bridges when they are available. Many fallen trees, both ancient Douglas-firs and red alders, bridge the marshy area, so the jumping mice can go almost anywhere they choose without having to swim.

During summer, the jumping mice construct their well-hidden, fragile, spherical or dome-shaped nests on the ground; some are in slight depressions dug by the mice. Summer nests are composed of coarse or broad-leaved grasses that are loosely interwoven and about six inches in diameter and about four inches high. Nests in the marshy area are made of mosses and lined with grasses or sedges. Each nest has a single opening in the side and appears to belong to one individual.

Although jumping mice are usually silent, they do vibrate their tails rapidly against some resonant body, such as dry leaves, and produce a drumming sound. They also squeak when disagreeing with one another.

The jumping mice of the marsh eat the seeds of the skunk cabbage, the pinnae ("leaves") of some mosses, the seeds of grasses, and some of the belowground-fruiting mycorrhizal fungi. As summer progresses, however, and the fruits of salmonberry, thimbleberry, trailing blackberry, huckleberries, and stink currant fall to the ground, the mice eagerly concentrate on them.

As autumn approaches, the mice begin to accumulate layers of fat under the skin, over the muscles of the body, and throughout their body cavity. Although some individuals will begin to accumulate fat as early as the latter part of August, most will not begin until the latter part of September. With these accumulations of fat to sustain them, they will enter hibernation in their warm, dry, belowground nests in late October or early November. During hibernation, as the winter winds howl and the snow accumulates and the sun seems to be held hostage in the southerly latitudes, the jumping mice of summer are rolled up in little furry balls and appear to be quite dead. If, however, a mouse were to be given warmth, the latent spark of life in its body would soon respond, and in half an hour it would be fully awake. But remove the warmth and it would again doze off. Thus, the jumping mice will remain in hibernation until released by the warmth of the late May sun, when they will again grace the marshy area by the big river.

1555

January and February are months of softly falling snow that gently cloaks the ancient Douglas-firs (567 years old) and the surrounding young forest (which ranges from 50 to 105 years old) in a deep blanket of white. The snow comes and goes in early March but has ceased by late March, and the skies are clear and sunny. The second day of April brings a warm wind off the ocean, and the sparkling surface of the snow begins to melt. April is a month of contrasts with gentle, warm days and melting snow that is refrozen during the breathless, penetrating cold of night when the winking stars seem close enough to touch and the silence is so deep and profound that one can hear it.

Spring flowers begin to show their faces along the big river in late April as the bright yellow heads of skunk cabbage push upward out of the mud of the marshy area and reach toward the sun, and the white blossoms of Indian peach hang surrounded by new, green leaves. By early May, amidst molding leaves and dead stalks of last year's grasses are the dainty, pale pinkish flowers of the spring beauty, the white flowers of false Solomon's seal and lily-of-the-valley, which are complemented in the midcanopy by the large, white flowers of dogwood and the pink blossoms of Pacific rhododendron.

As the sun climbs higher above the horizon and the days of June grow warmer, spring moves up the mountain, accompanied by the yellow blossoms of the wood violet and shining Oregon grape, the white of bunchberry, salal, and the magnificent spikes of bear grass, along with the white blossoms of serviceberry bushes. Black-speckled orange tiger lilies grace openings along game trails, and pinkish, waxy-petaled prince's pine along with pink, bell-shaped twinflower dot brief sunny spots between the trees. And by July, the meadow above the burn, from its edge to the stream in its center, is like a painter's palette with the oranges and reds of Indian paintbrush, the scarlet and yellow of columbine, the yellows of avalanche lily, subalpine buttercup, Drummond's cinquefoil, monkeyflower, and goldenrod, the purple of alpine shooting star and subalpine lupine, the blues of camas, monkshood, gentian, and bluebells, the pink of mountain spirea, and the white of false bugbane, grass-of-parnassus, Gray's lovage, and white bog orchid. As July moves silently towards August, a hot afternoon is punctuated from somewhere along the edge of the ancient forest by the call of the olive-sided flycatcher: *Free Beer. Free Beer. Quick! Free Beer.*

August brings hot, cloudless days with occasional thunderstorms. A cold, sharp tang bites the night air by mid-August as summer passes toward autumn and the flowers of July mature. Although the eye may see their colors fading on the stalk, it cannot see the oranges, reds, purples, pinks, blues, yellows, and whites safely stored in the seeds, like artist's colors in their tubes, until once again Mother Earth paints Her mural of the flowers.

August becomes September, the Moon of Ripe Berries, as black huckleberries, dark blue salal berries, blueberries, and red elderberries ripen in the sun. Townsend chipmunks, yellowpine chipmunks, deer mice, and Pacific jumping mice all have telltale stains on their mouths from gorging on the fruits of autumn. And everywhere as high and as far as the eye can see are the drifting webs of spiders gleaming like silver threads in the afternoon sun amidst the silvery white fluffs of floating thistledown.

On one such mid-September afternoon, a man and his son of thirteen summers walk into the meadow and drink from the stream. They survey the meadow and the upper edge of the forest and then gaze on mountain after mountain after mountain until at last the silhouettes fade into the bluish haze of the horizon. A quiet contentment pervades the meadow, and the man decides to spend a day or two exploring the country, much to the delight of the boy.

It has been 104 years since the second great fire, in 1451, and it has been 74 years since the native people have hunted elk from the meadow. The man and boy do not find the old camp in the clump of subalpine fir with its ancient fire ring of stones originally built by a youth of sixteen summers in the year 1000. The camp, periodically maintained until 1483, was destroyed 72 years ago when lightning struck the clump of firs twice in one summer and the resulting fire destroyed most of the mature trees immediately. The three firs that survived the fire were so weakened that the severe windstorm of 1487 blew them over, and they now lie guarding the secret of the ancient fire ring of stones. Somewhere in time the clump of subalpine firs will disappear, and a simple circle of stones in a meadow of flowers will bear mute testimony to the daydreams of a youth over 555 years ago.

It is one of those rare, golden autumns that matures gently into winter as the sun rises lower and lower in the southern sky and each night grows a little colder and a little longer. Snow, when it comes in mid-November, falls quietly, covering the land, and the year closes as it began—a gentle year.

1620

Three wild cats inhabit the forests of the Pacific Northwest: the bobcat, the lynx, and largest of all, the puma, also called mountain lion or cougar. The puma's coloration is such that it readily blends into the ancient forest, through which it travels and in which it hunts. The puma's head, back, sides, and the outsides of its legs are dark tannish to reddish brown. The top of the tail is darker brown than the back, darkening to a relatively long, blackish tip. The backs of the ears and each side of the nose are also black. The throat, chest, belly, and insides of the legs are whitish.

A puma's normal gait is a rather long-strided walk, but the cat can cover twenty-five feet or more in long, graceful leaps. Regardless of what a puma is doing, it is always the epitome of grace and strength welded into fluid beauty.

Although most resident, adult pumas confine their movements to specific areas year after year, a contingent of younger, transient adults also roam throughout the areas of the resident adults. Resident pumas occupy fairly distinct, contiguous winter-spring and summer-autumn home ranges; use of these areas, however, varies not only with season but also with time and individuals. Generally speaking, resident pu-

mas use larger areas in summer than they do in winter, and males tend
to travel more widely than females. The tendency of pumas to increase
their movements during late winter is a result of the scarcity of food.
Pumas hunt almost continuously, rarely spending more than one day
in the same location. Except for the longer periods of heavy rain in
spring and autumn, the activity of pumas seems largely independent
of the weather.

During winter, a male puma ranges over a minimum area of about
sixty-four square miles, whereas a female ranges over a minimum area
of about thirteen square miles and a maximum area of about fifty
square miles. Although resident males occupy areas that are distinct
from one another, a male's area overlaps those of females. Females, on
the other hand, share common areas, and transients of both sexes move
freely through occupied areas. Pumas have a high degree of tolerance
for other pumas in their areas but are decidedly unsocial in that they
avoid contact with another individual. That pumas seldom defend an
area is a behavioral mechanism of mutual avoidance that keeps them
distributed without injury.

Pumas use all their senses in maintaining adequate distances from
one another. Urine, scrapes, feces, and scent from anal or other glands
advertise a puma's presence, either bringing pumas together or maintaining the distance between them. Puma scrapes are areas where the
cats scrape soil or litter or both into a pile in one to six places usually
less than three feet apart. The cats may deposit feces or urine or both
in or on the pile.

Among pumas, land tenure is based on prior rights, and home
ranges are well covered. Home ranges change after deaths or movements of the residents. Young adults establish home ranges only as vacancies occur. The land tenure system acts to maintain the density of
breeding adults below the carrying capacity of the available supply of
food. (Carrying capacity is the maximum number of pumas that their
prey base can sustain.)

In the short term, a puma's home range is in a state of constant
change created by the availability of prey. Over the long term, however, the conditions in certain parts of the home range are such that a
cat tends to be more successful there in making kills and as a result will
spend more time in those parts. For a puma to be thoroughly familiar

with its home range is definitely advantageous, especially for a female rearing kittens.

Pumas' staple diets in the vicinity of the spring are deer, elk, and porcupines, although pumas also eat snowshoe hares, flying squirrels, mountain beaver, and other animals. The male whose home range encompasses the high ridge and the basin of the spring as well as the meadow and much of the burn normally zigzags back and forth through the thickets, around the large openings, and under the overhang of the cliff. He goes up and down the small draws and back and forth across the creeks. This method of travel better enables him to detect prey and to stage a successful attack. He does not indiscriminately try to capture prey wherever he finds it, but being a stalker, he must find prey in a location where he can stealthily approach it close enough for a successful attack, which may require more than an hour of patient stalking on his part.

This resident male of 165 pounds can kill adult elk, which he stalks as they are bedded down in their favorite thickets. The resident females and the transient adult males and females who share his home range are not large enough and heavy enough to kill adult elk, but a few of them are large enough, if conditions are just right, to kill large elk calves. Deer are considerably smaller than elk, and the cats are more versatile in hunting them.

Each large animal that is killed has some physical or behavioral defect with respect to its long-term survival that also makes it more vulnerable to predation by the cats, which ultimately cull these weaker animals from the herd. In addition, predation by the pumas keeps the deer and elk moving, especially on the winter range. The mere presence of a puma does not usually alarm deer or elk, but when a kill is made, the reaction is striking. The deer and elk immediately leave the area, crossing to the far side, or even move into a different drainage. This forced redistribution of deer and elk helps prevent their overpopulating an area and causing severe damage to their habitat.

Having killed a deer or elk, the male drags it to a protected place and eats as much as nine pounds of meat in a meal; the smaller cats eat from four to six pounds. The male remains in the immediate vicinity of his kill, guarding it against scavengers while he eats it over a period of one to nineteen days, depending on its size and age. He eats almost entirely any young prey that he kills, including the spinal column, skull, and feet, but he eats only about 70 percent of older prey. The 30 percent that is left includes the rumen (stomach), some viscera, bones, feet, and some of the hide.

The cats of the burn each kill a deer about every ten to fourteen days in winter, and the big male, if he is eating elk, kills one every twelve days or so. In summer, however, the interval between large kills is greater when other prey, such as porcupines, is more abundant.

Pumas are variously adept at killing and eating porcupines. They often manage to avoid most of the quills but sometimes get them in their paws, shoulders, face, and mouth. A female puma whose home range includes the high ridge and the spring catches a wandering porcupine on the 10th of May and eats everything except the head. Once eaten, however, the quills begin to soften in her stomach within an hour.

Reproduction is confined to the resident pumas. The male breeds two of the females whose home ranges overlap his. Since the transient pumas are nomads, the reproductive phase of their lives is restricted until they find vacancies and establish their own home ranges. Because the land tenure system of the pumas is dynamic and flexible, a home range is not inherited intact but involves a re-sorting of living space. This re-sorting takes place first among the older cats, so the younger ones must accept what is left.

Although the pumas breed at any time of the year, individual females breed only every other year. Just before and just after the young become independent, a female associates with, or perhaps only tolerates, adult males and even adult females more frequently and for longer periods than at any other time. Such tolerance reaches its peak during estrus, when a pair remain in one another's company, traveling together for eight to sixteen days.

One female whose home range includes the high ridge is bred by the male on the 28th of March, shortly after she left her three kittens that had been born in mid-July of 1618. On the 1st of July, after a gestation period of ninety-five days, she goes to a shallow cave in the base of the cliff and gives birth to four kittens, each weighing between fourteen and sixteen ounces. Her newly born kittens are covered with short, soft hair that is dull tannish with darker blotches on the body and bands on the tail. Their eyes are closed and will not open for nine to fourteen days.

The kittens grow rapidly and weigh between eight and ten pounds by early September as a ship named *Mayflower* sets sail from England with 100 passengers aboard. Even though the kittens are weaned by the 1st of October, the mother cat will be restricted in the use of her home range, and her pattern of movement will be more complex until the kittens are one year old. She leaves her kittens in a protected place for a day or two at a time while she hunts in a loop away from them and back again. When she moves with her family, she seldom moves more than a mile at a time. As the kittens mature, the family wanders proportionately farther, and during the kittens' second year of life, they will begin to cover their mother's home range. They will become independent during their second winter, and the family ties will finally be broken in March 1622 in a portion of their mother's home range where they will have spent considerable time earlier in the winter. The mother will leave them at a kill and simply not return. In turn, the siblings will remain together for a while and then meet for short periods before going their separate ways. The young independents will become transients and wander about until they find a vacancy, take up residence, and thus achieve breeding status.

While the puma kittens have been learning of life, 100 English settlers leave port and begin their journey across the Atlantic to the New World. On the 1st of December, as the young pumas reach six months of age and a weight of about forty pounds, the 101 English settlers (of two babies born during the trip, one died) are nearing a boulder, Plimouth Rock, just north of Cape Cod on the coast of Massachusetts. Here they will land and spend their first Christmas in a struggle to survive and establish Plimouth Plantation. (Plimouth is the old spelling of Plymouth.)

This is a year of coming together. Until this year of 1620, a continent and an ocean separated the ancient forest from the Europeans. Now that is forever changed. Now only a continent separates the ancient forest from the Europeans, and now the Europeans have become invaders in another's land.

1621

Winter has set in by the time the English settlers land, and it is too late to plant crops. They build their homes with timber frames and plank siding and spend their first hard winter in the New World. (Log cabins were brought to the New World much later by Swedish settlers who colonized Delaware.) Across the continent near the spring an ancient Douglas-fir, carrying the obsidian head of an arrow shot into it by a sixteen-year-old boy who missed an elk in 1020, topples under the uneven weight of wet snow. In falling, it strikes another old fir weakened by a root rot fungus, and they both crash to the earth. Thus two more of the original trees from the burn of 987, now 634 years ago, give way to time and the ever-changing cycles of the forest.

By spring, harsh weather and illness take half the English settlement. No one would have been left alive, and certainly no harvest home festival—which we now call Thanksgiving—would have been celebrated were it not for Samoset, a friendly native chief from what is now Maine, who stuns the settlers by walking out of the forest into their midst saying, "Welcome, Englishmen, welcome," and asks for beer.

Samoset learned English, and about beer, from English fishermen working the rich Atlantic waters as they had for the previous hundred years. Samoset tells the settlers he has a friend who speaks even better English and with whom he will later return. His friend turns out to be Squanto, a member of the Pawtuxet tribe, whose English is good because he had been shanghaied by fishermen and taken to England. He was then sold into slavery in Spain, escaped back to England, and finally jumped ship near Cape Cod. He eventually found his way back home only to discover that his entire tribe had died of plague.

A man without family or kin, Squanto befriends the English and takes them into his care. He explains that Plimouth Plantation has been cleared for crops by natives who lived in the area but who have all died of plague. He shows the settlers how to tap some of the nearby forest trees for maple syrup, how to hunt, where to fish, and how to plant and grow corn by placing the kernels in little hills fertilized with fish. Squanto also arranges peace treaties between the English and local and distant tribes of natives, and prevents the natives from overpowering the few settlers by whispering into the ear of Massasoit, a powerful and respected Wampanoag chief, that the English have imprisoned the plague in their warehouse and, if angered, will release it. This threat frightens the native tribes into a peace that will last fifty years.

Spring becomes summer, and life for the settlers begins to take on an established rhythm. They are essentially lusty Elizabethans who value wit and humor and know how to have fun. They drink goodly amounts of alcohol because they consider drinking water to be bad for their health, so a weekly duty of every housewife is the making of beer. Hard cider and a liquor that tastes something like brandy is also available.

The settlers' clothes are colorfully dyed with vegetable juices. They wear multihued capes, velvet vests with brass buttons, lace and quilted caps, and soft boots that today would be recognized as suede. They only wear their best black and white clothing to "thanksgiving"—which is not a holiday but a day spent in church praying—because the black dye, the most expensive, quickly fades to purple. (We think of these early settlers as pilgrims in black and white because they put on their best clothing when they had their portraits painted.)

Summer wanes into autumn, and the time of the harvest home festival, held since the Middle Ages to celebrate a good crop, draws near and seems in order. The festival, usually held in late September or early October, is a three-day affair of eating and making merry. Had it not been for Squanto, however, there would not have been any harvest home festival because the English had caught only one codfish in their first month at Plimouth in the winter of 1620, and their European seeds had failed in the soil of the New World. When the first harvest home festival in the New World is held at Plimouth Plantation in the autumn of this year 1621, the main course is eel, which the natives teach the settlers how to catch by stomping in the mud to drive the eel to the surface, where they are easily captured. The natives, who outnumber the settlers ninety to fifty, bring venison, rabbits, ducks, geese, fish, clams, and lobster. The table is also graced with soups, meat pies, skillet-fried breads made of corn, dried fruit, and wild berries of several kinds. (Cranberries will not become part of the harvest home festival until 1650, probably because they require too much sugar to make them tasty, and turkey will not become part of Thanks-giving until Abraham Lincoln makes the holiday a national one in 1863.)

Far to the west, somewhere in the burn, three young pumas are getting ready to experience their second winter of life in preparation for entering the transient population. The fourth died as an eight-month-old kitten in February when two ancient Douglas-firs crashed to the ground. The kitten, startled by the sudden, loud, sharp, crack-ing noises of the falling trees, simply crouched in place and was hit by the butt of a large branch that was broken and hurled through the air as the top of the first tree struck the second.

1691

The last vestige of the ancient tree that had survived the fire of 987 and that fell in 1187 enters the soil after 504 years and, through the soil, becomes the living vegetation of the new forest. And the seedling that germinated in 988 following the great fire of 987, and which died standing as a snag at the age of 424 years in 1412 and fell in 1492, is incorporated into the floor of the forest after 199 years on the ground. The great burn of 987 is now 704 years old; the burn of 1451 is 240 years old; and Plimouth Plantation, 71 years old, becomes part of the Massachusetts Bay Colony. Thus, from the joining of male and female cells that make a seed that falls to the earth and grows into a tree that dies and changes its elements back into soil that supports the birth of yet another tree, the forest becomes another forest. This is a year of completions and a year of beginnings in the ever-changing cycles of the forest. And the energy of the sun, the circulation of the air and water of the world, and the gravitational pull of the moon together de-fine and orchestrate the ever-expanding cycles of beginnings and end-ings and beginnings in the cosmic dance between the forest and the Universe.

1787

Although the American Revolution began in 1775 with "the shot heard around the world" and ended in 1783 with the independence of the European Americans from British rule, the soul of the new nation was not to be born until the summer of 1787. It is a hot summer in Philadelphia when the the great labor pains of the Constitutional Convention begin—pains that are destined to bring forth the Constitution of the United States of America.

In 1787, the United States of America already has a working document that provides some governmental structure: the Articles of Confederation, ratified by Congress in 1871 as a formal recognition of the authority Congress has already been exercising for over five years. But the authority of Congress to raise and maintain an army and negotiate loans and treaties is limited to the necessities of the war for independence from Great Britain.

In essence, Congress *is* the federal government. It is also the permanent legislative body and executive body of government, and it can establish, as necessary, a temporary judiciary body. Prior to 1787, Congress has had a secretary, Charles Thompson, several clerks to help organize its work and record its decisions, and a president who is elected annually from among its members and housed and supported by Congress as the nation's titular head of state. The rudimentary executive branch consists of a secretary of foreign affairs, a secretary of war, a postmaster general, a treasury board, and a few ministers abroad. Still, every significant action has to be initialed and approved by the Congress.

No nation could have had better representation abroad than John Adams, minister to Great Britain and the Netherlands, and Thomas Jefferson, minister to France. Indeed, few secretaries of state have had a clearer perception of relations abroad than did John Jay, secretary of foreign affairs for the "United States in Congress Assembled." But the Articles of Confederation give Congress no authority over the people, such as the federal government has today. In 1787, Congress has authority only over the governments of the thirteen states, each of which in turn has authority over the people of its state. As of May 1787, Congress cannot levy taxes, only ask the state leaders to give it money; it cannot enforce provisions of a treaty unless it wishes to be at war with the state or states that violate the treaty.

These weaknesses distress many European Americans—and states. The leaders of Virginia early in 1786 invite all thirteen states to send delegates to Annapolis, Maryland, to discuss the problems of trade. Although the delegates of only five states arrive in time, they decide to call for a convention "to meet at Philadelphia on the second Monday of May next, to take into consideration the situation of the United States, to devise such further provisions as shall appear to them necessary to render the constitution of the Federal Government adequate to the urgencies of the Union, and to report . . . to the United States in Congress Assembled."

Without legal provision for such a convention and without the agreement of members of Congress that such a convention was even necessary, delegates from New Jersey, Virginia, and Pennsylvania are appointed, and Philadelphia is chosen as the site of the Federal Convention.

In 1787 Philadelphia has 40,000 inhabitants and is the nation's largest city. It is also the most accessible and has the best convention facilities—large public meeting rooms, taverns, boarding houses, amusements, and a notoriously hospitable upper class to entertain delegates at dinner and tea. It has been the host city for the First Continental Congress and the Second Continental Congress, and the city leaders intend to reclaim the federal government later this year.

Like all cities, Philadelphia is a hopeless mix of land uses, with stables, breweries, blacksmith shops, soap boilers, and tanning yards intermixed with taverns, offices, shops, and opulent residences. But unlike other cities, Philadelphia is planned, and its streets follow a regular grid pattern that strikes some visitors as monotonous. A center for foreign trade, Philadelphia is a wonderful place to shop for china, silks, stays, and wine, for wimble bits and pickled mangoes, for weathervanes, stoves, and venetian blinds. It is also a center of medicine, the arts and sciences, and literature, and among its temporary residents this year are inventor John Fitch and lexicographer Noah Webster.

The Federal Convention begins on Friday the 25th of May, a cool, overcast day with occasional light rain and variable winds. It begins because diminutive, thirty-six-year-old James Madison, a giant in intellect, convinces twelve of the squabbling states (Rhode Island declines) to send representatives to "form a more perfect Union." James Madison, architect of the Constitution, comes to the convention with a plan for a national government as yet untried in the world. His Virginia Plan is based on three separate branches of government with power emanating from the people.

Sessions are held six days a week and usually vary from 10:00 or 11:00 A.M. to 3:00 or 4:00 P.M. The only exceptions are Saturday the 26th of May and two adjournments, the 3rd and 4th of July and the 26th of July through the 6th of August. Otherwise, the expenditure of time sitting in committees, drafting papers and speeches, and preparing for the sessions creates long, intense working days for most of the group. Finally, the Constitution nears completion, and the preamble reads, "We the people of the States of New Hampshire, Massachusetts. . . ." The haggling continues until, after days and weeks of intellectual battles, and a last stroke of the pen, the world is given, "We the People of the United States . . . ." A final eloquent speech by Benjamin Franklin sways the members assembled to accept the Constitution as written, and the Convention ends on the 17th of September 1787.

How the people are to interpret the document as new situations arise remains a nagging question. Even the founders of the Constitution cannot agree. Alexander Hamilton believes in a loose construction, expanding on unspecified powers, but Thomas Jefferson and James Madison prefer strict adherence. Herein lie the seeds of the two-party system.

The document's adaptability resides in Congressional power to amend it with the consent of three-fourths of the states. (About 10,000 amendments have been proposed; 26 have been ratified.) To this end, James Madison writes, "If the will of the majority cannot be trusted where there are diversified and conflicting interests, it can be trusted nowhere."

The Constitution of the United States is not the first, however, to be based on specific checks and balances of power for the good of the people. There is one "constitution" whose seeds were planted in the forest two centuries earlier through the efforts of the Indian prophet Deganawidah, known as the Peacemaker. Born on the northwest shore of Lake Ontario, the Peacemaker was a luminous figure who journeyed in a canoe of white stone—a sign the Creator had sent him—among the Iroquois at a time when endless wars had nearly reduced the Five Nations to anarchy and despair. "Think not forever of yourselves, O Chiefs, nor of your own generation," he counseled. "Think of continuing generations of our families, think of our grandchildren and of those yet unborn, whose faces are coming from beneath the ground." As the Peacemaker traveled among the Mohawk, he met an Onondaga exile named Ayawentha, or Hiawatha (an Iroquois name mistakenly used by Henry Wadsworth Longfellow for the Ojibwa hero in his *Song of Hiawatha*). Together, in 1570, the Peacemaker and Hiawatha persuaded the warring Five Nations to join in a "Great Peace" based on a "great binding law."

Only one fearsome Onondaga—the original Tadodaho, a wizard with snakes in his hair—stood in the way, but he too ultimately was won over by the Peacemaker and Hiawatha. Then, with all fifty chiefs of the first Grand Council assembled on the shore of Lake Onondaga, the Peacemaker planted the original Tree of Peace, a magnificent white pine—their metaphor of unconditional spiritual unity and social integration—beneath which the Five Nations buried their weapons of war. Four long roots, the "white roots of peace," stretched from the tree in the four sacred directions, and the Peacemaker proclaimed: "If any man or any nation outside of the Five Nations shall show a desire to obey the laws of the Great Peace . . . they may trace the roots to their source . . . and they shall be welcomed to take shelter beneath the Tree. . . ." Thus the Great Law of Peace, based on strength through union, and which embodies Iroquois notions of free expression and representative government with checks and balances, became "The Fire That Never Dies," the unquenchable tradition of today's Six Nation Iroquois Confederacy.

Both James Madison and Benjamin Franklin not only knew about but also were profoundly impressed with the "great binding law" of the Iroquois Confederacy. Could it be that the Constitution of the United States had its beginning in centuries past under the original Tree of Peace? Could it be that our Constitution is lighted by "The Fire That Never Dies," an ancient gift of the forest through the Peacemaker and the people of the Iroquois Confederacy to the peoples of the world?

While the men on the East Coast are debating what form of national government shall guide the fledgling United States of America,
a small, robin-size seabird, nine to ten inches long and weighing about
twelve ounces, rides on the gentle swells just beyond the breakers of
the Pacific Ocean off the coast that in seventy-two years from now
(1859) will be called Oregon. A chunky little bird in breeding plumage
that is a marbled blend of brown, reddish brown, or gray on the back
and brown and white on the underparts, the marbled murrelet neither
knows nor cares about the affairs of human government.

Although the marbled murrelet occurs throughout the North Pacific, it ranges along the west coast of North America from the Aleu-
tian Islands of Alaska south to central California, and a few individuals
even winter as far south as southern California. Like some of its relatives the guillemots, puffins, and murres, the marbled murrelet has
short wings with which it propels itself underwater. Its head is large,
its neck and tail short. Its legs, attached far back on its compact body,
allow the marbled murrelet to excel in underwater maneuvering in
pursuit of fish, such as Pacific herring and sand lance, its main fare.
This arrangement, along with the small surface area of its stubby
wings, makes flight inefficient; its takeoffs and landings are difficult
because its legs are so far back on the body.

With the onset of the breeding season in mid-April, pairs of adult
marbled murrelets are feeding amidst last year's subadults, who are
feeding singly and who will remain at sea and not breed until their
second summer. On the 26th of May, a pair of adult marbled murrelets
is feeding off the mouth of the Yaquina River. Although it is midnight
on the Atlantic Coast and members of the Constitutional Convention
are sleeping, here as twilight deepens, the pair suddenly takes flight
and heads toward land. Approaching the forested shore, they abruptly
fly skyward at an angle approaching 90 degrees and climb to nearly a
thousand feet of elevation in about one minute before leveling off and
disappearing over the forest. The pair flies inland thirty-four miles to
a 600-year-old grove of Douglas-firs seventy miles west by the flight of
the crow from the spring in the ancient forest of the burn. The birds
fly to a tree over 200 feet tall with an open crown. They land on the
open side of a southward-projecting branch next to the trunk of the
tree. The large, moss-covered, horizontal branch measures 16 inches

in diameter 150 feet above the floor of the forest. Here in the moss is a simple depression that is protected by the slanting trunk of the ancient tree and by an overhanging branch. Having used this nest in bygone years, the birds did not have to search for a nesting site as other pairs do.

Before dawn, the female lays her single egg. And as the first light shows in the eastern sky, she drops vertically from the branch to attain flying speed. (Although marbled murrelets can easily attain flight from the surface of the water, they cannot do so on land.) They call softly to one another in a buzzy sound as they head toward the open water of the Pacific. Once over the top of the forest, their call becomes a *keer-keer* that can be heard by the creatures of the night as they head to their daylight retreats. On reaching open water, the pair go into a high-speed, steep dive and level out only when a few feet above the water.

Both parents share the task of incubating their egg in shifts of twenty-four hours that change each evening until the egg hatches on the 26th of June. Thereafter, the downy chick is normally fed once a night with one fish until it fledges on the 24th of July, at which time it flies from its nest high in the ancient tree to the open water of the Pacific Ocean. Many do not make it, however, and either starve or are eaten on the floor of the ancient forest.

The parents have been feeding in a loose aggregation of mixed adults and subadults since early July. Now, for a short time, the juveniles join the aggregation and are easily distinguished by their juvenile plumage and the egg tooth, used by the baby bird to peck its way out of the egg, that is retained longer than in most species of their relatives. As summer becomes autumn and early winter, however, the murrelets don their winter plumage of brownish gray upperparts, except for a white band below the back of the head that extends up from their underparts.

Thought of as birds of the sea, marbled murrelets begin their life high in ancient Douglas-firs and, therefore, are also birds of the forest. Our Constitution is thought of as a product of the 1787 Constitutional Convention held in Philadelphia, yet it too may have had its beginnings in the forest as a spark from "The Fire That Never Dies."

1803–1806

The history of human events in the New World begins to change drastically with the Louisiana Purchase during the presidency of Thomas Jefferson (1801–1809). On the 30th of April 1803, Jefferson purchases from France for $15 million the territory west of the Mississippi River extending westward to the Rocky Mountains and northward from the Mexican border to the Canadian border.

With this event, President Jefferson sends his private secretary, Captain Meriwether Lewis, and Captain William Clark, officers in the army of the United States, to explore the newly acquired territory and to find both the source of the Missouri River and "the most convenient water communication thence to the Pacific Ocean." Captain Lewis leaves the new seat of government in Washington, D.C. on the 5th of July 1803 and joins Captain Clark at Louisville, Kentucky. From there, they travel to La Charrette, the highest settlement on the Missouri River, where they arrive in December and intend to spend the winter. The Spanish commandant of the province, however, has not received an official account of its transfer to the United States, so he is obliged by the general policy of his government to prevent strangers from passing through Spanish territory. Thus Captains Lewis and Clark spend the winter out of his jurisdiction, camping at the mouth of Wood (Du Bois) River, where they train their men and make the necessary preparations for an early spring departure. The party consists of forty-five men, including nine young men from Kentucky, fourteen soldiers of the United States Army who have volunteered their services, two French watermen, an interpreter and hunter, and a black servant belonging to Captain Clark.

All preparations complete, they leave their camp at the mouth of Wood River on the 14th of May 1804. And on the 7th of November 1805, after a long and arduous journey, they finally see the Pacific Ocean. While Lewis and Clark and their men are on the ocean shore enjoying the fruits of their long labor, the annual mating flight of the rain beetle, a brown to nearly black, hairy scarab about an inch long, is taking place in the ancient forest miles to the south and east.

The mating flight of the male rain beetle begins with the onset of heavy autumn rains in October and usually terminates toward the latter part of November. Only the males fly, and the greatest flight takes place shortly after dawn. Male rain beetles skim along the surface of the forest floor about four to twelve inches off the ground in search of females, which are lighter colored than males, an inch and a half long with small, useless wings. The distribution of rain beetles is spotty because females seldom leave their subterranean burrows, so dispersal is slow.

An unmated female is usually two to six inches down in her burrow in a vertical, head-down position. Although a female's burrow is open from the surface of the soil to a depth of one or two inches, a layer of pulverized soil always lies just above the female, through which the male must dig to reach her. Two or three males are often attracted to the same burrow by the chemical odors (pheromones) given off as an attractant by the female. Soon after mating, a female burrows down vertically in the soil to pass the winter.

On the 23rd of March 1806, Lewis and Clark and their men take their final leave of Fort Clatsop on their homeward journey to the East Coast. Fort Clatsop is siutated near the mouth of the Columbia River in what is now the state of Oregon. On the 24th of May, while Lewis and Clark are camped on the Kooskooskee River in what is now Idaho, trying to nurse the child of Sacajawea, their female Shoshone Indian guide, back to health, a female rain beetle digs her way down in the soil to a depth of twenty-nine inches. There, beginning at the bottom of her burrow, she lays her eggs one at a time in a spiral as she ascends her burrow, covering each egg with soil that she pulverizes until she finally comes to rest twelve inches below the mouth of her burrow. Below her, protected by pulverized soil, are her fifty dull white, ellipsoidal eggs.

The eggs hatch on the 1st of September, when Lewis and Clark and their men are only twenty-three days away from St. Louis, Missouri, and the end of their two-year exploration of the Louisiana Purchase and beyond. Once hatched, the larvae (often called white grubs) burrow through the soil at depths from two inches to three feet, sometimes even to eight feet, below the surface and begin to feed on woody forest plants, among which are the small roots of trees now 817 years old. Some larvae girdle roots too large to chew off, but most just sever small ones and consume the entire root. Many of the small feeder roots have mycorrhizal fungi colonizing them as in the seedlings that germinated in 988 following the great fire. The larvae cease feeding on roots for at least two months, between June and September, during which time they molt—shed their skins so they can grow.

The beetles live below the ground as larvae for eight to twelve years. Then, in late July or early August, they begin to transform (pupate) into adults in a special chamber they dig in the soil, called a pupal cell. Thus, in 1818 as the fur trappers are entering the Rocky Mountains in search of beaver, the larvae that hatched in 1806 will emerge as adults with the autumn rains and begin the cycle once again. They will emerge into a forest whose structure is gradually changing, for as the old firs die they are replaced primarily by western hemlock, with some grand fir and a few western redcedar as the forest moves slowly toward its climax.

1812–1815

Early European and American explorers sailing along the coast of the Pacific Northwest found two very different waterways leading into the interior. One of them, off the northwest coast of what is now the state of Washington, is the Strait of Juan de Fuca, which opens into an immense deep-water harbor with many small streams but no large rivers emptying into it. The other is the Columbia River, which affords access a thousand miles into the interior with only occasional falls and rapids for the boats that can negotiate the difficult and often dangerous entry at the river's mouth.

George Vancouver, a midshipman with Captain Cook, first saw the coast of Oregon in 1778. He came back fourteen years later in command of two ships sent by the British Admiralty to explore the area claimed by the Spanish. By chance, he met the American sea captain Robert Gray off the coast of Washington. Gray told him that he thought he had found the mouth of the "River of the West," and that he was going back to see if he could navigate it.

While Vancouver went on to explore the Strait of Juan de Fuca, sending his sailing master Lt. Peter Puget to map the inland waterway that bears his name, Captain Gray sailed his ship, *Columbia Rediviva*, into the river and named it Columbia after his vessel. In the fall of that year, Lt. William R. Broughton, Vancouver's second in command, also entered the Columbia and took two small boats upriver a hundred miles beyond the reach of his master's heavier-burdened vessel. Peering through the haze of late October, Broughton was the first European to see and to enter the Willamette River and its history.

These early explorers discovered that the furs of wild animals, purchased for very little, could be sold in China for immense profit or traded for spices, teas, and silks that brought high prices in both Europe and New England. A competitive trade arose, with ships from England, France, Belgium, Russia, and New England vying for profits. The Americans eventually dominated the trade, partly because the Europeans were busy contending with Napoleon.

Lewis and Clark brought additional information about the Columbia River Country and encouraged American settlement. In May 1810, Capt. Nathan Winship and a brother from Boston enter the Columbia River in the ship *Albatross*. They find a beautiful expanse of lowland forty-five miles up the Columbia where they plant crops and start to build a fort, but the normal June flood forces them to higher ground. The natives, friendly at first, become hostile, so Nathan decides it is time to leave.

In New York, meanwhile, John Jacob Astor, an American, and his five Canadian partners in the Pacific Fur Company select the Columbia River for the site of their first western trading post. To them it seems possible that the Columbia River occupies the same position on the Pacific coast as does the Hudson River on the Atlantic.

Their ship, *Tonquin*, stops in the Sandwich Islands (Hawaii) to load supplies and add native boatmen to the crew. While sounding for the channel through the breakers across the bar at the mouth of the Columbia River by dropping weights attached to a rope, eight men in two small boats, including some of the Hawaiians, overturn, and the men drown. Later in March 1811, the *Tonquin* successfully makes its way into a bay inside the mouth of the Columbia, where the fur traders land on a site above the flood level on the south shore and build Fort Astoria—the first permanent settlement in the Oregon Country. Trading posts also are built along the Columbia and its tributaries—two of them in the Willamette Valley, one near Champoeg and the other north of Salem.

In 1812, the Russians establish a colony, Fort Ross, atop a remote headland in what is now Sonoma County in northern California. They have come to California to hunt seals and sea otters, to grow vegetables and fruits, and to raise livestock to support their outpost in Alaska. Their scientists have come to study the natives, the plants, and the animals. Port Rumiantsev, now known as Bodega Bay, twenty miles south of Fort Ross, becomes their principal port in California, and the deepest eastward penetration of imperial Russia.

While the Russians are establishing their colony in California, Congress is declaring war on Britain to end interference with "Free Trade and Sailor's Rights," in the words of a popular slogan. The War of 1812 is a war fought over the rights of neutrals on the high seas and issues related to American westward expansion. Before the war is over, American troops will burn York (now Toronto), the British capital of Upper Canada, and the British will retaliate by burning Washington on the 24th of August 1814. Finally, in 1815, in Ghent, Belgium, negotiators for both sides agree to end the battle and return to the status quo.

The War of 1812 brings to an end America's early lead in the settlement of the Pacific Northwest. In January 1813, John George McTavish of the North West Company, a Canadian firm, comes down the Columbia from Spokane House with the news that war has been declared and that a British gunboat is sailing to take Fort Astoria. He and his men wait at Fort Astoria for the British navy.

Wilson Price Hunt, the American partner in charge of the fort, is in Alaska on a long trading trip, leaving Duncan McDougal and Donald McKenzie, two of the Canadian partners, in charge. They listen to an offer from the North West Company to buy the fort, the trading posts, and the furs on hand. Being afraid they may lose everything if the British take the fort by force, and being unable to communicate swiftly with the other partners, McDougal and McKenzie sell the Pacific Fur Company's assets to the North West Company. They eventually receive $58,291.02, and as part of the deal, all employees are offered jobs with the new company. Many stay, and McDougal becomes head man at Fort George, as the fort is now called.

The 1815 Treaty of Ghent between Great Britain and the United States provides that all property, so far as possible, is to be returned to its prewar owners. John Jacob Astor, the principal partner in the Pacific Fur Company, is free to resume control of Fort Astoria, but he has lost interest in it, and no other American comes forth to claim it. Thus, over the next two decades, the British will retain control of the Oregon Country.

An agreement seems to have been reached between the British and the Americans in the Oregon Country regarding land ownership, an agreement that does not immediately affect the forest by the spring. No agreement will be reached, however, about protecting the 827-year-old forest because whoever claims the land will see the forest only as a commodity to exploit.

1832–1834

Numerous fires have again and again flared up throughout the burn of 987, but with the exception of the fire in 1451, they have been creeping ground fires that have merely added another physical process to nature's canvas of ever-changing forest.

Now, in 1832, a new agent of change has been added to the forest, a portent of things to come. Although not yet everywhere, a heaviness of disharmony has come to the West Coast with the influx of European settlers, who see not the land but only the commodities it produces in rich abundance. The disharmony hangs over the European settlements, extending up the valleys, along the rivers and streams, into the sacred heart of the mountains. The marten hunting along the high ridge above the spring does not feel the impending doom, nor does the short-tailed weasel hunting the western red-backed vole in its burrows beneath the floor of the ancient forest. But a pall hangs heavy nonetheless, and it is felt even by some of the Europeans who, seeking to escape it, unknowingly bring it with them into the primordial silence of the unknown forest.

One such group is the fur trappers and mountain men, one of

whom is even now on the 6th of June preparing for a day's travel somewhere along the spine of the New World, the Rocky Mountains, a little
more than a thousand miles to the east and south of the spring and high
ridge.

The mountains lie cold in predawn, silent, still. A tiny flame
pierces the darkness, that element of the unknown that dies with the
fading stars as the eastern sky slowly pales, then grays, then kaleido-
scopes from pink to orange to gold as the sun rises.

Blue smoke sifts upward through the boughs of balsam fir and shatters against the slanting line of sun. Warmth begins to soak into the
land, but under the guardianship of trees, patches of dirty snow cling
to north slopes. The hard-crusted snow slowly begins to soften and
drip submissively to the rising sun.

Somewhere a red squirrel chatters. A syrphid fly whines in the
sun. The odor of slowly roasting venison competes with that of wood
smoke in the breezeless air. Tree-whiskered ridges, marching down to
the small lake, are mirrored in profile. A trout lips the surface as mist
rises off the lake. The fire sputters quiet defiance to the dripping juice
of meat. In this cirque-protected meadow, deer and elk graze, listening
and watching in turn.

The fire tender—one of the many mountain men whom history
will not know by name but who will nonetheless help to shape history—having completed his simple meal, stands up and stretches,
shivering as warmth from the sun drives cramping cold from his body.
From a small leather pouch on his belt, he takes out enough tobacco to
fill his clay pipe, which he lights with a burning stick. Then, while the
fire spends itself, he sits in the sun at the base of a fir watching the
growing day, letting the happenings of bygone years wander through
his mind. Other days, other places, other sights, sounds, and smells
all drift across his remembering mind. These fragments of yesteryear
are the riches of life, the source of life's value guarded deep in the heart.

A puff of aspen-scented air brings an instant flashback of a smoky,
frosty morning on a late autumn day when icy water numbs the hands,
legs, and feet as the first beaver traps of the fall hunt are set. A soft
breeze swells, fingers the face, waves the grasses of the meadow, and
is gone.

Wind is the breath of the world. It carries the fragrance of South

Sea islands to the polar ice, the dankness of steaming jungles to the baking deserts. Wind caresses the land and buffets it, moistens the land and parches it. Wind, the messenger, is never still. It follows the sun westward, then leads the sun eastward. It pushes spring northward, then pulls winter southward. Free since the birth of the land, wind has blown through all the eons—never to be still.

A sweet, musky odor, a rattle of quills, heralds a passing porcupine. The porcupine and the man look at one another, and in that instant the vital question of life is asked and answered by both—friend or foe?

The porcupine clatters on.

It is strange how only part of the mind remembers while the rest is always alert, watching, studying, seeking the unusual, the out-of-place. Were it not so, life in the forest would be shorter than it already is.

The pipe goes out and is replaced with a piece of grass.

Swallows dip and wave. A raven croaks.

A deep quietness settles over the man, for somewhere within his heart and loins is an aloneness, a primordial aloneness, subtle, profound, ageless. It is known to all solitary men of the mountains. Without this aloneness, they are not free. Such freedom is a mental state, a blending into the land, an understanding born of the wilds and carried by each man.

After a time of remembering, the man must emerge from the past. It is not a gentle thing to part ways with memory. It is a sudden wrench from past to present, sometimes causing the body to jerk involuntarily as though running from memories turned predator. Thus the man jerks back to full consciousness. Closing the door on memory, he spreads his hands to the sun and warms himself. A squirrel scolds from a limb five feet overhead. The man smiles, winks at the squirrel, and ambles toward camp.

The fire out, the man gathers his things and stows them in his possibles sack. He carefully cleans the pipe and puts it away. He checks the priming on his rifle, then walks through a thin fringe of trees to the picketed horses. They raise their heads, ears forward, and watch. Talking softly, he strokes their necks and leads them into camp. They are good horses, small, delicately boned, but strong and enduring.

They are the most sure-footed horses he has ever owned, and they blend in with the country. He puts his packsaddle and a few belongings on the smaller of the two, then saddles and mounts the other.

Deer and elk lift their heads and watch as he crosses the meadow. The sun is well up as he reaches the far side. Little spider webs, gleaming in the grasses, suddenly become dull and disappear as he passes. At the timber's edge is a game trail. He guides the horses to it and starts to climb through the firs toward the top of the first ridge. The horses, shod native style with rawhide, make little noise. Nevertheless, a whiskeyjack (gray jay) whistles and a squirrel scolds. Chipmunks dart across the trail, tails in the air. A cold breeze comes off a hidden patch of snow and teases with winter's dying breath. They move into a lesser cold of the shadows and then into the warmth of the sun on the crest of the ridge. The man rides over an alpine tundra–covered swale and, reaching a huge slope of talus, reins in.

Here and there amongst the rocks comes the *waaa, waaa, waaa, oink, waaa* of rock rabbits (today they are known by their Tibetan name, pika). Looking carefully, the man sees a small curve on a sun-drenched boulder; a pair of tiny black eyes watch him. He notes that the winter haypiles of the rock rabbits are almost depleted. Some of the droppings on the rocks are soft, indicating that the rock rabbits have been feeding on fresh, succulent vegetation, such as stonecrop.

The man watches the world for several minutes. From a cliff comes a piercing whistle. The sound is that of a yellow-bellied marmot. The marmot, or whistle-pig, as the mountain men call them, is known to him. On occasion, he has had to hunt them for food.

A sudden commotion erupts in the talus. A large weasel is chasing a rock rabbit. The rabbit runs in and out amongst the boulders, the weasel in close pursuit. Seemingly tireless, the long-bodied, bounding weasel closes in for the kill. Alarm calls from rabbits in various parts of the slope accompany the chase, but hunter and hunted are silent. A granite boulder looms massively in front of the rabbit; it turns to the right—the cost, precious distance. A pained, panic-stricken squeal— then silence. The sole acknowledgement of death, this brief intrusion into the background of silence.

The weasel moves toward the man, the rabbit limp in its mouth. The rabbit is no longer a rabbit. Just as a venison steak is no longer a deer, so the rabbit has suddenly become a meal. And though the essence of the rabbit's mortal being has fled with the snap of jaws and the ensuing silence, it will, in some ageless way, live on in the weasel and in the weasel's weasel. This particular rabbit will influence the lives of all animals that come into contact with this weasel and the generations of weasels to come from the consummation of this life and this death. Thus, from the first breath of life until the last, all living things are part of one another.

The wind shifts slightly. The weasel, smelling the man and horses, stops, stamps its front feet in agitation, and disappears into the talus.

A marmot's whistle drifts on the swelling breeze. The sighing of the timberline rises on warm air from below. The man squeezes his knees together slightly, and the horses move up the narrow, rocky trail toward a small gap in the cirque's solemn, stony rim.

Three hours pass. The summit of the gap just ahead, the man guides his horses behind a mammoth slab of granite, dismounts, and ground-hitches the horses. He listens to the high wind, becoming aware of the cold, thin, lung-piercing air. Moving slowly to the summit, being careful not to skyline himself, he lies down, his head between two rocks, both larger than he. His eyes miss little, and what they miss on one sweep of the land, they will find on the next. He remains thus for a hour, scrutinizing the area through which he will travel.

The only soft, round curves that indicate living animals in this land of jags and angles appear half a mile below as a group of five bighorn sheep. He studies them for several minutes. He has spotted them by shape, not color; shape is the first principal of survival in the untamed land.

Being sure that no movement or sound of danger has gone unseen or unheard, the man moves carefully back down the slope to his horses, mounts, and urges them upward. Just below the summit, he pauses, studying the trail behind him. He then quickens the pace and crosses the sharp crest. A hundred feet down, he stops and studies the land falling away below. After a few minutes, he continues down the slope toward the singing line of stunted trees. The sun is warm on his back. Dust puffs in little swirls under the horses' hooves. The saddle squeaks. The man and horses are part of this land.

Shrew (*Sorex* sp.).

He sees the bighorn sheep once, but they are instantly lost to view by a dip in the trail. He crosses a small, rocky stream and rides toward the sun-dappled shade of the firs and spruces. As the man and horses descend, the sky, a deep blue, closely follows the contours of the land. Out of a frame of rocky grays and snowy whites they move into a swaying, nodding color-splattered meadow of yellow alpine lilies, orange-red paintbrushes, and purple and blue lupines. Serenity surrounds even the mantled ground squirrel watching from her rock and the unnoticing shrew hunting along the trail. Serenity flows into the man. He slows the horses. They stop. Eternity seeps through him. The world becomes a lullaby of solitude. He slips into the unsoundable well of peace. He sees everything, yet nothing. Peace has no fragmentation. It is singular unto itself.

A cloud shades the land. Serenity condenses to awareness. The cloud draws his eyes skyward, and with a deep intake of breath, he rides into the lowering gray. He reaches timberline as fog shrouds the trees. Around him is a wall at once comfortable and impenetrable. The sun is a round, yellow ball behind a curtain of blue-gray fog as a patch of clear sky opens momentarily. He stops. The wind grows in strength; the hole in the fog closes like a corkscrew, its point boring towards him.

Entering timberline, he rides enveloped in aloneness through mur-

muring, ghostly trees. The droplets of fog part, letting him pass, then close in behind. The trees, gathering moisture, begin to drip. The air is heavy with dampness. It starts to drizzle. The man turns off the trail and rides north for half an hour, stopping at the edge of a small meadow. He sits motionless, straining his eyes and ears into the fog and watching the horses' ears. Fifteen minutes pass. The only sound is the wind and dripping trees. He is about to move when something felt rather than seen causes him to focus his attention on the right side of the meadow. The horses, with ears forward, look also. Out of the dimensionless gray come a buck and two does. They move in delicate unison, pausing now and then to listen. The buck suddenly looks at them. The does take a few more steps, then stop and look also. The buck cannot make up his mind. He quivers, stamps a forefoot, then all three catapult from sight. The void is instantly filled with swirling fog.

The man rides around the meadow to the far side, dismounts, unsaddles the horses, and stakes them near the edge of the meadow. He carries his gear to a clump of firs and puts it against their trunks. He studies the position of the clump and decides the trees are growing out of an old seed cache stored and forgotten by one of the mantled ground squirrels.

To the left of the clump is a large solitary fir with branches sweeping the ground. Selecting a branch directed away from the meadow, he weights its free end down with a heavy rock. Going deeper into the trees away from the meadow, he draws his war hatchet and commences to lop off fir boughs. He takes them to the weighted branch and leans them against it with their cut ends up and the upper surfaces of their needles down. Within an hour has has a weatherproof brush den with walls a foot thick. From his pack, he takes a tanned, well-oiled elk skin and a woven rabbit-skin blanket that he tosses into the shelter. Placing his gear next to the entrance of the shelter within easy reach, he covers it with the elk hide. He then collects dry wood and large pieces of bark from underneath a number of fallen trees. He also finds pitch around wounds in some of the lodgepole pines. He carries the firewood and pitch to the shelter and puts it inside.

Taking the hobbles off his saddle, he walks to the horses. He moves them so they are in direct view from the shelter. In addition to hobbling them, he stakes them. Walking back toward camp, he fades into the growing dusk and carefully starts to circle the meadow with rifle in readiness. The drizzle ceases. The gathering night is a soft cadence of drops falling from the trees.

An hour passes, and no unusual sound interrupts the dripping of the trees. The drizzle starts again, then turns to light rain. The forest is bound in a strained silence. The wind tugs gently at his long hair as he reaches the shelter. He crawls in and builds a small fire. Then, sitting crosslegged, he arranges the blanket over his shoulders. Taking a small, oily piece of thin buckskin from its container made out of the tip of a buffalo horn, he carefully wipes his rifle clean. Placing his rifle and war hatchet within easy grasp, he makes two stacks out of the pine bark and places them in a V at the outside of the fire. They not only will burn for a long time but also will reflect the fire's heat into the shelter. He rolls up in the blanket on a deep bed of pine and fir boughs and, lying on his back, slowly chews on a piece of jerked venison as he listens to the growing storm.

The wind blows through the darkness. The man sleeps.

Dawn. Dripping trees. Rising mist. An empty shelter, cropped grass, horse dung. Man and horses are gone.

Sometimes rocky, sometimes soft, the trail occasionally displays the print of a horse's shod hoof. An invisible sun nears its zenith. Two horses and a man move cloaked in damp silence.

Night stalks the land, only to give way to gray dawn. Rain scatters like quail and stings the face like hornets. Water drips from the man's hair and runs down his spine. The world huddles in gloom. Night. The man lies wet and cold under a rock ledge. Clouds drift through darkness. A small wind gropes the man's face. Moonlight softens the world, which grows cold with its cloud cover removed. The man shivers violently in the gentle light. He sits up, drawing the robe tighter, and waits out the night.

The east grays, then reddens. Red melts to orange, then gold. The sun comes up. Small clouds rise from the rocks. The air warms. The world sparkles. Rainbow drops are suspended from the grasses, flowers, and trees.

The sun nears its zenith. Two horses and a man move in warm silence.

Pine forests give way to groves of quaking aspen. Yellow balsam-

root, blue and white columbines, and red-orange paintbushes surround white trunks. The aspen groves thin into sage-covered hills
where a clear river snakes its way down a long valley. The sky is deep
blue. A shadow drifts over the man and horses. A golden eagle
screams. Magpies chatter. The man studies the valley and watches his
horses' ears.

The man moves into a thicket of willows at the river's edge, ties
and hobbles the horses, then studies the river shore fifty feet away. A
cliff on the far side of the river blots out the sun, and the shade is cold.
A pebble clatters down the cliff. A small, quick movement! The skyline
is empty!

The man strains his eyes and ears; the movement was too quick,
too certain. He moves cautiously to the horses, frees them, mounts,
and rides back into the grove of aspen. He stops the horses fifty yards
from the river and looks back at the cliff's skyline. At the base of a large
sagebrush he sees a smooth, round rock—or is it a rock? He looks
away, then looks back. No movement. The rock is still there. He deliberately surveys another part of the cliff, since animals and people
can sense when they are being watched intently. The man rides away
from the river toward the edge of the valley. The rock weighs on his
mind.

Heat parches the land. There is no shade in the valley large
enough for horse or man. Distance shimmers in waves. Time hangs
agelessly. Hot and cold, hot and cold, day and night, he rides north-
westward toward a small group of mountains.

Game seems to have vanished. Seven days, and the man has not
seen a single animal, not even a fresh track. Neither a cloud nor a wisp
of a breeze disturbs the vacuum of silent heat. Having been without
food for four days, his mind is periodically shrouded with dizziness.

From the crest of a high ridge, he sees a small blue-green lake.
Guiding his horses to a thicket he dismounts, ties, and hobbles them.
Checking his rifle, he climbs to the crest and worms his way into another thicket. On his belly, he can look down at the lake. He studies
the lake and its surroundings for an hour. Nothing moves. The lake's
glassy surface looks solid. The silent heat has become a seeming constant in a world of variables.

Crawling out of the thicket, he walks back to his horses, which are

The lake as it might have appeared in 1832.

standing three-legged with heads hanging. He takes the hobbles off and hangs them from the saddle. Mounting, he heads the horses down a trail toward the lake.

The man, sitting on a fallen tree, studies the stars reflected in the water. The night, like most nights in this mountain world, is bursting with stars, and in the lake, the light of a million years is reflected in the smooth surface of the water. Rising slowly and quietly, he walks toward a small clump of aspen in a grassy opening in the forest. A faint odor of horse is in the night breeze. He rolls up in his rabbit-skin blanket and lies for a time smoking his pipe. Then he puts the pipe on a rock and lies on his back, hands clasped under his head. He watches the stars as his eyelids grow heavy. The stars swim, and the breeze carries his last waking thoughts into the night: "I've never figured out where the game goes. . . . Was it a rock? . . ."

Darkness slips westward. At the lake's edge, water drips from a soft, black muzzle. The breeze shifts, head and ears jerk toward camp. A sharp, stinging crack, a cloud of smoke, the deer drops, its life bleeding into the lake. The man, lying behind a fallen tree, reloads his rifle and watches, listening. Silence. He walks to the deer, cuts it open, and slices the top off the liver. He stands up facing camp, holding the liver to his mouth. The rock! Hot, searing pain strikes through his chest. The ground leaps upward. His life bleeds into the lake. The crack of a rifle disappears into space. A cloud of bluish smoke rises from a clump of aspens. A lone native steps out from behind the trees and with an air of detachment observes the fallen trapper and mountain man as silence again settles over the land.

These men of solitude who choose to disengage themselves from the "civilized world," who choose to know the ancient forests of the West, are unknowingly opening the West to those who will change it forever—the settler, the preacher, the farmer, the cattleman, the sheepman, the miner, the logger, the timber baron, the military. Of those who go into the shining mountains in search of furs and adventure, many simply vanish as does the trapper in our story; and like the natives whose lives they often mimic, they become part of the cycle of all things. Yet in this unknowing act of seeking and exploration, they too are part of the change that will one day lead timber companies and their loggers to the heart of the ancient forest by the spring. And a few, such as a trapper named Osborne Russell, live to see the change and take part in it.

With the fur trade near its peak, the Montreal-based North West Company and the London-based Hudson's Bay Company—rivals for decades in the fur country—combine under the name of the latter. The company selects Dr. John McLoughlin to take charge of western operations, and he moves the base of operations up the Columbia River to the north bank opposite the mouth of the Willamette River. Fort Vancouver, the site of the present-day city of Vancouver, Washington, becomes the commercial, industrial, agricultural, social, and political center of the Oregon Country. Its influence spreads from Mexican California to Russian Alaska.

During this year of 1831, Hall J. Kelley, a one-time Boston school-teacher, succeeds after years of effort in organizing the Oregon Colonization Society on the East Coast. He also interests one Nathaniel J. Wyeth in the business possibilities in the Oregon Country, and Wyeth agrees to attach himself to Kelley's society with a company of his own. Although Kelley's plans for an overland expedition to the Oregon Country fail, Wyeth goes ahead and leads his party across the country in 1832 along the route that is to become the Oregon Trail.

Wyeth pushes his expedition to Oregon with resourcefulness, but inexperience, desertion, sickness, and the loss of his supply ship, *Sultana*, on a South American reef, completely defeat his efforts. Although he returns home empty-handed, he has new plans and a contract to deliver $3,000 worth of supplies to the Rocky Mountain Fur Company, at the rendezvous of 1834—a prearranged meeting place where all the trappers of the Rocky Mountain Fur Company gather to sell their furs, purchase supplies, and have fun. In this manner, he hopes to partially finance a second expedition to the Oregon Country to establish a salmon-fishing and fur-trading business. Three Boston merchants join him, and the Columbia River Fishing and Trading Company is formed.

A second supply vessel is dispatched on its voyage to the mouth of the Columbia River to meet the overland expedition that has been organized to fulfill the supply contract. Men for this second expedition are recruited at the frontier towns of St. Louis and Independence, Missouri. Among those who join in Independence is Osborne Russell, who agrees to serve the Columbia River Fishing and Trading Company for eighteen months for a wage of $250. Russell, born on the 12th of June 1814 in the little village of Bowdoinham, Maine, on the estuary of the Kennebec River, runs away to sea at the age of sixteen but soon gives up his maritime career by jumping ship at New York. He spends the next three years in the service of the Northwest Fur Trapping and Trading Company operating in Wisconsin and Minnesota, and in 1834 he joins Nathaniel J. Wyeth's second expedition to the Rocky Mountains and the mouth of the Columbia River.

On reaching the rendezvous on Ham's Fork of the Green River, Wyeth finds the old Rocky Mountain Fur Company to have been dissolved and a new company created by the same partners in its place.

As a consequence, Wyeth's supply contract is not fully honored, and he is left with much of the freight on his hands. The decision of the partners of the Rocky Mountain Fur Company to escape their financial obligations through reorganization is the result of several years of fierce competition with the American Fur Company. The brigades of the American Fur Company have been determined interlopers who have continually tried to follow the men of the Rocky Mountain Fur Company to the best trapping grounds, but the latter have been equally determined to lead the newcomers on a fruitless chase. Neither company profits from the struggle. The Rocky Mountain Fur Company is brought to the verge of ruin when they arrive at the rendezvous without the wages for their men. The easiest way out of their financial difficulty is to default on the contract with Wyeth, who then has to alter his plans to save his own enterprise.

Accordingly, Wyeth proposes to build a fort on the plains of the Snake River and enter into the fur trade with the goods not purchased by the men of the old Rocky Mountain Fur Company. The fort is built and named Fort Hall, after Henry Hall, a partner of Wyeth's Columbia River Fishing and Trading Company. Wyeth leaves Fort Hall in the care of a garrison of twelve men, among whom is Osborne Russell.

Despite the settlement by Americans and the Ghent Treaty of 1815, the question remains: Who will own the Oregon Country from 42 degrees to 54 degrees, 40 minutes, north latitude? Who will eventually be responsible for the 846-year-old forest by the spring?

1840–1849

The Oregon Trail, blazed by trappers and fur traders, remains in use from the early 1830s to the mid 1880s. In 1841, however, fewer than one hundred American settlers follow the trail to the Oregon Country, which is still claimed by both the United States and Britain.

As American settlers are beginning to move over the Oregon Trail, the seals and sea otters along the Pacific Northwest Coast are being depleted by the Aleut hunters brought to Fort Ross by the Russians, and farming around Fort Ross is marginal at best. In addition, the United States, Spain, France, and Britain are objecting to the Russian presence in California, so in 1841, Czar Nicholas I orders his colonists home.

Many of the Russian soldiers have native Kashaya Pomo wives with whom they live in the villages near Fort Ross, and they take their wives and children with them when they return home. Others will leave Russian-native offspring in California. To this day, Kashaya Pomo natives in California have Russian words in their language and Russian-native bloodlines, and Russian architecture is still evident along parts of the northern coast of California.

Between the years 1835 and 1841, a change comes over Osborne Russell. In 1835, he joins a brigade of old Rocky Mountain Fur Company men and continues with them after a merger leaves the American Fur Company in control of the fur trade. It is an empty victory for the American Fur Company, however, because beaver are scarce, almost trapped out, and the price for their fur is declining because of a change in fashion—hats of silk have replaced those of clipped beaver fur.

It is rumored at the rendezvous of 1838 that the company is going to abandon the trade in the Rocky Mountains, so the rendezvous is not as carefree as in years gone by. Although one more rendezvous is held, Russell is not there; he becomes a free trapper operating out of Fort Hall, which passes into the hands of the Hudson's Bay Company in 1837.

Like so many trappers, Russell is reluctant to give up the old life and stays in the mountains doing a little trapping and trading until the great westward migration begins. It is an easy life with plenty of time to read the books he borrows from Fort Hall. They are good books sent to this faraway post of the Hudson's Bay Company by Chief Factor Dr. John McLoughlin out of his circulating library at Fort Vancouver.

From his reading comes a deep religious conviction that changes Russell's life. During months spent trapping, he carefully studies the Bible. He becomes convinced of its truth and feels that he has not lived according to its principles. His conversion leads him to abandon his life as a mountain man, and in 1842 he accompanies the Elijah White wagon train to the Willamette Valley.

By 1843, the American settlers are again pressing for provisional government while they wait for the United States to take over control of the Oregon Country. Three meetings are held, and at the third one at Champoeg on the 2nd of May 1843, a decision to organize a "civil community" is reached by a narrow margin. Osborne Russell is present and votes to organize a provisional government but does not take a prominent part.

On the 6th of June 1843, Russell loses his right eye while blasting rock in a millrace at Oregon City. He studies law during his convalescence and prepares himself for an active part in the new government.

The provisional government of Oregon becomes a reality, albeit a feeble one, on the 5th of July, at which time a constitution and code of laws is approved and the elected officers are sworn in. But the chosen judge will not serve, so Osborne Russell is appointed on the 2nd of October by the executive committee to fill the office.

On the 30th of October, Russell gives G. W. LeBreton a receipt for a copy of the "written laws of Oregon Territory." The title of Judge Russell, by which he is known, is given to him in recognition of his service on the Oregon bench. Russell, although included on the 1843 list of settlers in the Willamette Valley, does not become a settler in the real sense until he takes a land claim on the Luckiamute River in what is now Polk County. Russell will continue to be a prominent citizen of Oregon until 1848, when he will move to California, to die in Placerville on the 26th of August 1892 at the age of seventy-eight.

Osborne Russell is symbolic of an era that dies with him, that of the fur trapper and mountain man. The value of furs, particularly beaver, on the European fashion market had introduced a unique phenomenon into the wilds of the Rocky Mountains, a highly competitive, mobile fur trade by trappers-turned-traders. This phenomenon embodied within it the seeds of its own destruction because it was these very men who, seeking solitude in the untamed mountainous West, ultimately furthered the capitalist tradition of seeing the land and its wealth, including its creatures, simply as commodities to be exploited, often to extinction, as almost happened with the beaver.

But Osborne Russell's life is symbolic of more than the fur trade that opened the West; it is symbolic of the malleability of the human spirit so seldom seen amongst the masses of humanity. Russell had left the "civilized world" to explore and trap in an unknown, untamed land of hot valleys and massive, towering mountains. He was part of a brief, unique era of human history, and like humanity throughout its history, he was loathe to give up his cherished way of life. But times were changing, and through an inner transcendence of his old beliefs, Russell took up the challenge of change. He gave up his old way of life and accepted the new. He completed the mythic hero's journey: he left the security of the tame world as a youth of sixteen and went to sea for a time, then worked his way into the wilds of the Rocky Mountains where he grew to know himself, and he returned as a man to offer what he had learned to a growing nation.

Unlike Osborne Russell, many of us have yet to complete the hero's journey. We are still clinging desperately to an old and dying way of life, one that is based on the exploitation of seemingly unlimited natural resources, such as the ancient forests of the world. And in so doing, we are not only shrinking from Self-knowledge but also dying with the resources we are destroying because we have not the courage to face the challenge of changing times.

In 1847, with the Canadian-American boundary dispute settled, emigration along the Oregon Trail swells to 4,000. Caravans roll 2,000 miles from the Missouri River to a settlement on the Columbia River now known as The Dalles. To reach the Willamette Valley, emigrants raft down the river through the Columbia River Gorge.

Dr. John McLoughlin, who took care of thousands of newcomers to the Oregon Country and the Willamette Valley, is forced to resign as Chief Factor of the Hudson's Bay Company at Fort Vancouver in January of 1846. He moves to his home in Oregon City only to find that the Methodist missionaries, whom he fed and clothed, directed to the Willamette Valley, and supplied with transportation, oxen, cattle, and a cash subscription, have been nibbling away at his land claim.

As the human drama unfolds in the Oregon Country, one of Nature's tiny dramas unfolds on a foggy day in the forest by the spring where five bird's-nest fungi are clustered on a fallen branch under an ancient Douglas-fir dripping with condensed fog. Bird's-nest fungi have funnel-shaped or vase-shaped fruiting bodies that are splash cups from which the reproductive spores are ejected to a distance of three to four feet by the force of raindrops that land in the open-mouthed cups.

The mouth of a cup is about a quarter of an inch in diameter, and a large raindrop is about half that. The walls of the fruiting body are elastic and resist being deformed by the battering of raindrops or the large drops of condensed fog that drip from the trees. Also, the fruiting body is provided with a large, solid base that prevents the splash cup from being knocked over by rain or fog drip.

When large raindrops, having an impact velocity of about twenty feet per second, fall into the fruiting body, the displacement of the water in the cup creates a strong upward thrust along the inclined sides of the cup, forcibly ejecting the reproductive spores. The splash cup has sides that form an angle of 60 to 70 degrees with the horizontal, which allows a falling drop to create the maximum sideways ejection of a spore from the cup.

Each individual spore is held within a thin container attached to the wall of the cup. A falling raindrop strikes the spore container and ruptures it, casting the spore out of the cup. The rupturing of the spore container triggers almost instantaneous expansion of a special mass of threadlike hyphae that have been coiled under tension within the lower part of the container. These hyphae are highly adhesive and loosely interwoven and form an attachment organ that becomes entangled on plant stems and leaves or anything it touches as it flies through the air after having been ejected by a falling raindrop. Once attached, the base of the hyphae is like an anchor that causes the flying spore to snap back in a sideways motion toward whatever its base has become attached to. The backward and sideways snap of the spore on its tiny cable of twisted hyphae causes it to wrap around whatever the adhesive base is anchored to. This motion is so violent that the spore may extend three inches on its hyphal cable before it is snapped back.

Once the adhesive base is dried in place, it is not easily washed off. If the plant to which the spore is attached is eaten by a deer or some other animal, then the spore can pass through the intestinal tract and be dispersed into some other part of the forest when the animal defecates, and if the conditions are right, the cycle of growth of the bird's-nest fungus begins again.

As the 1840s close, forests are being cleared for farmland and game is becoming scarce in parts of the Willamette Valley. The forest by the spring, now 861 years old, is fifty air miles from the nearest settlement, and so is still spared from the frenzy of human activity.

1850–1869

Not until 1850—long after the settlement of the territorial dispute between Britain and the United States and the organization of Oregon as a United States territory in 1847—does Congress pass the Oregon Donation Land Law, free land for settlement.

In 1855, the European Americans are still stealing land from the Native Americans by rounding them up and forcing them onto reservations. When confronted with the foreseeable and inevitable demise of his people, Chief Sealth (corrupted to Seattle) of the Duwamish tribe in the state of Washington sent this letter to President Franklin Pierce concerning the proposed purchase of the tribe's land (the chief's letter was delivered orally and was written down and translated by more than one person, so while the translation may not be entirely accurate, the heart is intact):

> The Great Chief in Washington sends word that he wishes to buy our land. The Great Chief also sends us words of friendship and good will. This is kind of him, since we know he has little need of our friendship in return. But we will consider your offer, for we know if we do not [do] so, the white man may come with guns and take our land. What Chief Sealth says, the Great Chief in Washington can count on as truly as our white brother can count on the return of the seasons. My words are like the stars—they do not set.
>
> How can you buy or sell the sky—the warmth of the land? The idea is strange to us. Yet we do not own the freshness of the air or the sparkle of the water. How can you buy them from us? We will decide in our time. Every part of this earth is sacred to my people. Every shining pine needle, every sandy shore, every mist in the dark woods, every clearing and humming insect is holy in the memory and experience of my people.
>
> We know that the white man does not understand our ways. One portion of the land is the same to him as the next, for he is a stranger who comes in the night and takes from the land whatever he needs. The earth is not his brother, but his enemy, and when he has conquered it, he moves on. He leaves his father's graves, and his children's birthright is forgotten. The sight of your cities pains the eyes of the redman. But perhaps it is because the redman is a savage and does not understand . . .

There is no quiet place in the white man's cities. No place to hear the leaves of spring or the rustle of insect's wings. But perhaps because I am a savage and do not understand—the clatter only seems to insult the ears. And what is there to life if a man cannot hear the lovely cry of a whippoorwill or the arguments of the frogs around a pond at night? The Indian prefers the soft sound of the wind darting over the face of the pond, and the smell of the wind itself cleansed by a mid-day rain, or scented with a piñon pine. The air is precious to the redman. For all things share the same breath—the beasts, the trees, the man. The white man does not seem to notice the air he breathes. Like a man dying for many days, he is numb to the stench.

If I decide to accept, I will make one condition. The white man must treat the beasts of this land as his brothers. I am a savage and I do not understand any other way. I have seen a thousand rotting buffaloes on the prairies left by the white man who shot them from a passing train. I am a savage and I do not understand how the smoking iron horse can be more important than the buffalo that we kill only to stay alive. What is man without the beasts? If all the beasts were gone, men would die from great loneliness of spirit, for whatever happens to the beast also happens to man. All things are connected. Whatever befalls the earth befalls the sons of the earth.

Our children have seen their fathers humbled in defeat. Our warriors have felt shame. And after defeat, they turn their days in idleness and contaminate their bodies with sweet food and strong drink. It matters little where we pass the rest of our days—they are not many. A few more hours, a few more winters, and none of the children of the great tribes that once lived on this earth, or that roamed in small bands in the woods, will be left to mourn the graves of a people once as powerful and hopeful as yours.

One thing we know which the white man may one day discover. Our God is the same God. You may think now that you own him as you wish to own our land. But you cannot. He is the Body of man. And his compassion is equal for the redman and the white. This earth is precious to him. And to harm the earth is to heap contempt on its Creator. The whites, too, shall pass—perhaps sooner than other tribes. Continue to contaminate your bed, and you will one night suffocate in your own waste. When the buffalo are all slaughtered, the wild horses all tamed, the secret corners of the forest heavy with the scent of many men, and the view of the ripe hills blotted by talking wires, where is the thicket? Gone. Where is the eagle? Gone. And what is it to say goodby to the swift and the hunt? The end of living and the beginning of survival.

We might understand if we knew what it was that the white man dreams, what hopes he describes to his children on long winter nights, what visions he burns into their minds, so they will wish for tomorrow. But we are savages. The white man's dreams are hidden from us. And because they are hidden, we will go our own way. If we agree, it will be to secure your reservation you have promised. There perhaps we may live out our brief days as we wish. When the last redman has vanished from the earth, and the memory is only the shadow of a cloud moving across the prairie, these shores and forest will still hold the spirits of my people, for they love this earth as the newborn loves its mother's heartbeat. If we sell you our land, love it as we've loved it. Care for it, as we've cared for it. Hold in your mind the memory of the land, as it is when you take it. And with all your strength, with all your might, and with all your heart—preserve it for your children, and love it as God loves us all. One thing we know—our God is the same. This earth is precious to him. Even the white man cannot be exempt from the common destiny.

In 1859, Oregon finally becomes a state, which encompasses 96,981 square miles and has 300 miles of coastline. The year that Oregon becomes a state, the forest of 988 is 871 years old.

Abraham Lincoln becomes the sixteenth president of the United States in 1861, the year the Civil War breaks out over the issue of slavery. The war lasts until 1865. Abraham Lincoln is assassinated in this year, and the forest by the spring is 877 years old.

1870–1899

The mountain men used to say, "To know a country follow her rivers." In 1870, the Willamette River between Corvallis and Eugene still flows in five separate channels, and the river's banks are heavily forested for half a mile on either side. Drastic changes begin in 1871. Between 1871 and 1899, more than 5,500 dead trees that have drifted down tributary streams and rivers swollen with floodwaters are pulled from a fifty-mile stretch of the Willamette River in one ten-year period. The trees range from 5 to 9 feet in diameter and from 90 to 120 feet long. The U.S. Army Corps of Engineers also confines the Willamette River to one channel. The rivers are cleaned of their life-giving driftwood so that river travel is possible, and riverbanks are logged off to keep the trees from falling into the waterways and becoming obstructions for river traffic. In other rivers, such as the Clackamas, the rock creating waterfalls is blasted out so that boats can navigate. In addition, swamps and marshes, which abounded in the early years, are drained, and forests continue to be cut and burned and converted to farmland. It is the same all over western Oregon and western Washington. And there is much talk of "clearing the land" and of "busting the sod," of "harnessing the rivers" and of "taming the wilds." By 1899, these processes are well under way as the great forests are being cut out of the river bottoms and on those slopes with access to water, where the wood is floated to the mills. As yet, the 911-year-old forest of 988 is still too remote in distance and topography for human technology and is, for the time being, safe from the axes and saws of men.

1900–1929

The year 1900 is a tame year. The rivers are increasingly being harnessed, the forests are being cut faster, the land is continually being cleared for farming, and roads are penetrating more and more into the sacred heart of the land. The Native Americans are on "reservations." The People Of The Land are gone, imprisoned without dignity, without hope, and the forest, its human heart torn from its bosom, is empty. The last Native Americans to camp in the meadow above the burn of 987 were a seventy-five-year-old man, He-Who-Remembers, and his three sons.

He-Who-Remembers had first seen the meadow in the summer of 1820 when he was fifteen summers old and the forest by the spring was 832 years old. He, his older brother, his father, and his uncle had been searching for elk. They had camped along the edge of the meadow for two nights, and He-Who-Remembers had caught fish in the stream as had many other boys of his tribe before him. In 1880, at the age of seventy-five, he had been drawn back to the meadow in a dream.

He told his sons that in his dream, "I was in a beautiful meadow of my youth with the wide arc of the sky above, a noble forest stretching unbroken from mountain to mountain as far as my eye could see into the blue distance, and there was a carpet of wildflowers surrounding my feet. As I stood in the meadow facing the rising sun, my arms outstretched in surrender to the Great Spirit, I saw an intense white light come out of the sun and move slowly toward me. As the light drew nearer and nearer, the wrinkles of age fled from my body and my skin became smooth, flowing with the grace of youth. Finally, completely surrounded by the white light, I was gently lifted and drawn into the sun." He-Who-Remembers was silent for a time somewhere deep within himself. Finally he said, "My sons, my time to walk on the wind is near and I must prepare for my journey to the spirit land of my ancestors," a journey Rising Star, his wife of fifty years, had already made.

Although his sons had never been to the meadow and He-Who-Remembers had been there only twice in his youth, he knew the way. His photographic memory for places and events, even to small details, was recognized early in his childhood and had always been respected among his people. He-Who-Remembers had long been the tribal historian. So the next day, before the last stars had faded in the growing dawn, the four men quietly left the reservation and started southward toward the meadow above the ancient forest by the spring.

They traveled for some days and arrived late on a warm, clear September afternoon. They made a simple camp as in the days of old and slept under the watchful twinkling of the stars. They spent the next day together remembering the freedom and the dignity of the past.

Now ready for his journey, He-Who-Remembers began to let go of the bonds of life on the second day at the meadow. That evening he said, "My sons, you have filled my heart for many seasons. Never was a man more proud of his children than is this man. My time is now very near, please help me to the large rock near the upper right edge of the meadow." At his request, they seated him wrapped in his blanket with his back against the rock, facing the east. Then each in his turn said, "Farewell, my father; may your journey be swift and good," and in silence they returned to camp.

He-Who-Remembers sat in the quiet peace and dignity of one who knows he is at one with the Universe, with the Spirit that moves through all things, as he watched the cycle of the stars whose light had been traveling through space for thousands of years and reached his eyes on this night. And during this night, the last light of a star that burned out thousands of years ago reached earth—never to be seen again. He-Who-Remembers sat in the quiet peace and dignity of one who knows and accepts that his years spent on earth are completed and that his next journey is at hand. His old eyes had seen much of beauty and much of sadness, and his heart went out to those of his people who were yet to walk Mother Earth, for theirs would be a difficult journey indeed. As the golden sphere cleared the horizon, the old eyes dimmed, and He-Who-Remembers gently let go of life to begin his journey into the light of the sun, to the land of his ancestors where Rising Star waited to greet him. He-Who-Remembers completed his earthly pilgrimage when the forest by the spring was 892 years old.

By midmorning, the brothers, knowing that their father had left on his journey, went to the big rock. Looking out over the meadow from the rock, the youngest son saw a small mound of soil in the upper portion of the meadow and went to investigate it. In so doing, he found six rocks next to one another, forming part of a circle. Tracing the rocks with his hand, he discovered the stone fire circle made in the year 1000, and he knew that this was the place to bury his father, a place in touch with the Ancient Ones. He told his brothers what he had found. They took their father's body to the fire circle and buried him in the rich, gentle earth just uphill from it so that his feet could rest against the stone circle, the symbol of completion. They scattered the earth and replanted the grasses, making it look as natural as possible. They spent one more night in the meadow and before leaving the next day, bade their father a final farewell.

In 1914, when the forest by the spring is 926 years old, the dark shadow of humanity erupts into World War I, a war that changes humanity's relation with itself. By the end of the war in 1918, the world is forever and inextricably changed. Somehow it is no longer innocent because "the war to end all wars" shows humanity its power to destroy, and preoccupation with destruction becomes a global pastime.

By 1929, the seeds of World War II are incubating in Europe under the auspices of Adolf Hitler's Nazi movement in Germany and Benito Mussolini's Fascist movement in Italy. Their rise to power is aided by the stock market crash in the United States and the ensuing Depression, the worst downturn ever experienced by the capitalist economies.

As Hitler and Mussolini guide the world toward war in Europe, small, brilliant, silvery flashes dart back and forth through a May sunbeam penetrating the shadows of the forest canopy along the edge of the marshy area near the 941-year-old forest by the spring. At other times, the silvery flashes stop, seemingly suspended in the air, or drift lazily up and down and hither and yon only to suddenly disappear from the sunbeam. This is the mating ritual of the dance fly, also called balloon fly.

Dance flies are generally predaceous, and the females of some species, apparently being more hungry than amorous, at least during the early stages of courtship, are likely to eat their mates. The male, therefore, makes a bubble or balloon that to the naked eye appears to be made up of fine, shiny, white fibers that are wound spirally into a thin-walled hollow sphere. Covering the front of the bubble (front in the sense that the fly normally carries the bubble with this end forward) and somewhat entangled in its threads and globules is the prey, which may be a small insect, such as a midge or a psocid, or a tiny spider. The bubble is open behind and resembles a tiny, filmy white wasp's nest with the legs of the prey entangled in the middle. This bubble-entangled prey serves three functions: to provide a "come hither" invitation to the female instead of a warning "you might be eaten"; to distract the female from her predaceous tendencies once she and her mate have embraced; and to serve as a stimulus for mating.

The ritual begins with the male catching its prey and enclosing it in a bubble. He then attracts a female, and copulation begins when the pair embraces in the air and he transfers the bubble to the female. She does not feed on the prey, however, during this first stage of mating. During mating, the pair gradually flies lower and lower and settles on the twig of a shrub about a foot off the ground. Here the male, who has been astride the female in flight, grasps the stem and supports himself and the female while she holds her bubble with her feet.

Once settled on the stem, the female begins to probe the prey with her mouthparts, turning the bubble over and over between thrusts of her piercing mouth. She seems to be trying to suck the juices from all parts of the prey by piercing it in many places through the bubble. The bubble becomes very ragged as a result of this constant manipulation.

The female, concluding her meal in about thirty minutes, abruptly drops the mauled bubble and terminates mating. The male has survived!

The female will lay her eggs in the soil, and the dance of the flies will continue in the sunbeams of the forest in years to come.

1930–1949

The 1930s in the United States are years of hardship; the Depression is in full swing as the environmental tragedy of the Dust Bowl is being played out in the southern Great Plains.

In Europe, the Great Depression begins in 1931. Hitler comes to power in January 1933. On the 14th of August, the forest in the northwestern corner of Oregon catches fire, a forest that in 1902 is said to have been made up of trees from 8 to 30 feet in circumference and 150 to 300 feet tall, a forest that marched unbroken from the crest of the Coast Range to the shores of the Pacific Ocean. The humidity drops to 26 percent on the 24th of August, and the two already-raging fires blow up. When the fire is finally out, 239,695 acres have been burned. One of the two fires that began what is called the Tillamook Burn is said to have been started by a logging company trying to get "just one more log" out after being told to shut down because of the extreme fire danger. In October, Hitler withdraws Germany from both an international disarmament conference and from the League of Nations.

In March 1938, Hitler marches into Austria and takes over, uniting Germany and Austria without a struggle. I am born in Bronxville, New York, on the 13th of October 1938 but my first memory is in 1940 in Winterpark, Florida, when I am two years old. I find a "sand crab" along the water's edge, and my mother, Kim, puts it into a glass milk bottle with sand and sea water so I can watch it burrow its way out of sight into the sand.

Hitler occupies Prague, Czechoslovakia, in March 1939 and invades Poland on the 1st of September. On the 3rd of September 1939, Britain and France declare war on Germany, and World War II begins. In Oregon, a major forest fire again strikes the northwestern corner of the state, burning 189,660 acres, and the forest by the spring becomes 951 years old.

On Sunday the 7th of December 1941, even while representatives of Japan are discussing a settlement of differences in Washington, D.C., the Japanese launch an air raid on Pearl Harbor, Hawaii, the chief American naval base in the Pacific. The next day the United States and Britain declare war on Japan. Three days later Germany and Italy declare war on the United States, and global conflict erupts once again.

My father, Cliff, takes the position of dean of business at Oregon State College in 1942, and we move from New York to Corvallis, Oregon.

After years of terror and brutality, the war draws to a close in 1945. Hitler and his intimates commit suicide in an underground hideaway in Berlin on the 1st of May, and the war in Europe ends on the 8th of May. On the 6th of August, an American plane drops an atomic bomb on the Japanese city of Hiroshima, destroying the city and killing more than seventy thousand of its two hundred thousand residents. The Soviet Union declares war on Japan two days later and invades Manchuria. The next day a second atomic bomb falls from an American plane, this time on Nagasaki. The war with Japan ends on the 14th of August, and peace is formally signed on the 2nd of September. While we dream about and talk about a world without war, the mere absence of war does not mean peace—it only means the absence of strife on a scale that we define as war.

Again the northwestern corner of Oregon is engulfed in a raging forest fire that burns 180,130 acres. On the 13th of October I am seven and in the second grade, and the forest by the spring is 957 years old.

By the end of World War II, most of the ancient Sitka spruce along the Oregon and Washington coasts are gone, cut down during the World Wars to make airplanes to kill human beings and to lay waste the bounty of Mother Earth. With the end of World War II, two innovations enter the ancient forest of the Pacific Northwest, the portable sawmill and the chain saw. And the forest falls faster and faster.

In early October 1949 a deer walks up the old game trail through the forest by the spring. On its way, it steps on a small branch that moves under its foot and nudges the fruiting body of a ripe puff-ball fungus. The sudden contact with the branch is sufficient to cause a brownish puff of mature spores to explode from the opening atop the puff-ball and be whisked away over the forest floor by the breeze.

Although other animals also brush against the ripe fruiting bodies of puff-balls and cause them to cast their spores to the wind, this is not the only mechanism that causes the fungi to release their spores. A sudden gust of wind may be strong enough to cause a release of spores, but that does not happen often enough to ensure their thorough dissemination into the surrounding forest. Large drops from a hard rain, such as those in a thunderstorm, that strike a puff-ball to one side of its opening on the flattened, papery top are instantly followed by the ejection of a small puff of spores to a height of about an inch. And two days from now, the crowns of the ancient trees will catch moisture from fog that will fall in large drops, causing the mature puff-balls to "smoke" as though on fire in a forest that is 961 years old.

1950–1957

I have a close friend since the first grade, Billy Savage, who lives about a mile and a half from me. Billy lives along a small finger of water called Squaw Creek, south of Corvallis just below the golf course of the Corvallis Country Club. Billy loves peanut butter and hates bananas, and "Santa Claus Is Coming to Town" is his favorite song. He also loves fish, any kind of fish. They fascinate him. So we spend most of our time together either fishing in Squaw Creek, or capturing grasshoppers in the meadows near its banks with which to catch the fish. We also spend inordinate amounts of time searching for tree frogs in the roadside ditches and for horsehair worms in the old concrete watering trough just over the fence from his house.

In September 1950, at the age of twelve, Billy and I start the seventh grade. But Billy does not complete it. He kills himself late on the first day of school, and I have my first lesson about human death and the suddenness of loss. I had seen many things die in my young years. After all, Billy and I had killed worms and grasshoppers on fish hooks and then had killed the fish we caught so we could eat them. But this is different; I don't understand. I had just seen Billy at 4:30 in the afternoon when I had left him at the creek by his house to go home. Now his mother, Madge, a beautiful woman who had struggled hard to raise her family of three girls and Billy after the death of her husband in 1945, calls and tells my mother that Billy is dead. Gone, just like the snap of fingers. I see Billy one more time—in his casket—and I still do not understand that his desk is suddenly, unexpectedly empty, that I will never fish with him again. Had Billy lived, I'm sure he would have become an ichthyologist.

I spend the school years of 1951 and 1952 in boarding schools in Germany and Switzerland and gain my first impressions of other forests. Although I am largely miserable in these boarding schools, my first concepts of ecological common denominators are beginning to form. The songs of some birds and the eggs of others, for example, are very similar to those along Squaw Creek at home, and the frogs look very much alike.

I start the tenth grade at Corvallis High School in the autumn of 1953. I hate high school, and, except for biology and English, I am a poor student. I spend almost all my time planning where I will move my trapline, inventing new and better traps, reading about Native Americans, and practicing their teachings and methods of survival in the forest. I spend countless hours wandering alone through the forest and along streams and rivers, lying on my back watching the clouds, tracking deer, rabbits, squirrels, mice, and shrews to unravel the mysteries of their lives, and just sitting quietly watching Mother Earth.

In those early years, fire was my only constant companion, as it was to my childhood heroes, the mountain men. My first fire was intensely spiritual and private, known only to me and to the silent forest. The wisp of fir smoke, the heat, the tiny licking flame became part of my spirit. It still is. Since the days of my youth, fire has warmed me during cold winter nights of interior Alaska and during chilly desert nights in North Africa. Fire has cooked my food in the jungle of northern India and in the Himalaya of Nepal. Fire has lifted my spirit on days of seemingly endless rain and shrouding fog. Eons of fire have molded the spirit of the land, each fire a reflection of the past, of the beginning, of the dawn of humanity when the first human-made fire removed the darkness and its terror.

I finally graduate from high school in 1956. I spend July wandering through the mountains of the Olympic Peninsula of Washington State, living off the land as I travel. The 16th of August, however, finds a bewildered youth of seventeen in the United States Army, in which the rule of life is mindless obedience. I spend the first two months in the army learning how to "kill the enemy," and I am told that there is always an enemy even if I don't know who it is. Military wisdom is trying to teach me to look another human being in the eye and stick my bayonet into his gut for "the good of God and Country." My military service is mercifully short, and I am discharged on the 3rd of July 1957, when the ancient forest by the spring is 969 years old.

1958

It is mid-June 1958. I am almost twenty when I ease the heavy back-pack off my shoulders in an ancient forest by a spring of sweet water at the base of a high, rocky ridge. The day is hot, and the cool of the forest floor is inviting, so I lie on the ground and rest my back and shoulders against the punky remains of a fallen tree. While watching the dead needles of western hemlock spin down from the canopy to the ground, where they will be recycled into the soil, I idly dig in the rotten wood of the fallen tree against which I rest. Suddenly I jerk my hand back to find my right index finger bleeding from a clean cut. The cut is not particularly painful, but it is relatively deep. "What on earth could have done that?" After wrapping my finger with my handkerchief, I begin carefully to dig into the rotten wood. After about fifteen minutes of searching, I feel something hard and dig it out. There in my hand is a perfect obsidian arrowhead. I stare at it for some time wondering how it happened to be so deeply embedded in the old tree. Could I but see into the past, I would know that a native youth of sixteen had shot at an elk calf in September of 1020 and, overshooting, lost his arrow in the trunk of a young Douglas-fir when the forest was but thirty-two years old, and I would know that the old tree had fallen in the year 1621, at the age of 633 years, the first year the English lived at Plimouth Plantation. Now, in June 1958, the old tree gives up the arrowhead after having held it safely in its wood for 938 years.

As the sun begins to sink toward the western horizon, I get up, put on my backpack, and start up the well-used elk trail toward the meadow above the forest. Climbing up the side of the mountain, I pass from Douglas-fir and western hemlock into a mixed forest of Douglas-fir and mountain hemlock with interspersed silver fir, noble fir, sub-alpine fir, and whitebark pine.

Here and there snags of whitebark pine stand gleaming in the low-ering sun, their plated bark scattered about their bases like the shed scales of dragons.

I reach the lower end of the meadow and stop by the stream to get a drink. Then I survey the meadow for a place to camp. In the upper part of the meadow is a small clump of subalpine firs. It looks like a good place, so I go to it. My simple camp is completely hidden inside the clump of trees, and the smoke from my tiny fire is dissipated as it goes through the branches of the firs. Having eaten the four trout that I caught in the stream with my handline and grasshoppers, I sit at the lower edge of the firs and watch the day give way to night.

The next day dawns clear and crisp. By midmorning the sun has warmed the land, and I lie in the meadow on my back watching the clouds until my gaze is arrested by the dark speck of an eagle sailing effortlessly in and out of cloud canyons and around cloud peaks. In my mind I journey to the great golden eagle riding the currents of warm air reflected from the earth into the sky, into the immensity and free-dom of space where there is no beginning and no end.

I soar wingtip to wingtip with the great bird. One with the eagle, one with the air, the warmth, the earth, the clouds, the sun, one with the Spirit that is the unity of all things, I am the Spirit and the Spirit is I.

Looking down, I see that the meadow on which I was lying has become a riot of color surrounded above by the whiteness of snow, and along its sides and below by the dark green of forest that is broken in the distance by clearcuts that every year march closer and closer to the ancient forest as humanity, like termites, gobbles up the land. And in-stead of seeing the pattern of the streams that from above appeared like the naked branches of a maple tree in winter, connecting the forest within itself, connecting it with the river of the lowland, and ulti-mately with the oceans of the world as did the native youth in the year

Clearcuts and logging roads.

1000, I in 1958 see the meanderings of logging roads penetrating ever deeper into the heart of the land, leaving nothing sacred, nothing inviolate.

Hidden in the grasses and flowers of the meadow, not far from where I am lying, is a fire ring of stone, a silent testimony to the ageless spirit of humanity, to the daydreams of a youth, and to the wisdom of an old man, for the atoms borrowed by He-Who-Remembers have long since passed to the meadow and smile in its flowers and wave in its grasses. This ageless spirit of youth and of old age and beyond causes each person in his or her own way to seek out the heights of the soul that life may have meaning in the greater context of the Universe.

With these thoughts in my mind, I realize how closely my life is linked by my love for and by my common years on Earth with and in the ancient forest by the spring, now 970 years old.

1960

It is the 13th of October and I have just turned twenty-two. The sky is blue and without clouds. The snow atop Mount St. Helens glistens in the sun across Spirit Lake. I stop eating the sun-ripened, sun-warmed black huckleberries and stand for a long time, an eternity, on a pass overlooking Spirit Lake. I have been in the mountains for three agonizing weeks, and in my heart I now know that I will never go back to the mountains of my youth. I will never again know the mountains as I have known them.

I have spent three weeks struggling within myself, trying to figure out what I must do. I have seen many of the places that I love fall to the chain saw. The last one I just left—the valley of the Green River.

I can remember the trail along the river that flowed through an ancient forest that was unbroken for fifty miles in any direction. The trail was dappled with soft green, and bright yellow light filtered through a canopy of vine maples. The forest was cool and deep with western redcedar trees so big that I could not climb over them when they lay on the ground across the old trail, so I either had to find a way under them or go around them. There was a soda spring that the band-tailed pigeons liked to drink from and around whose edge they ate the ripe blue elderberries. The river had so many native cutthroat trout in it that I caught them by dangling a dry fly an inch over the surface of the water. Deer, elk, black bear, marten, mink, blue grouse, and an occasional ruffed grouse used to share the river with me as I fished for my supper. Now all this is gone. As far as the eye can see is one giant clearcut with human garbage scattered along the miles of logging roads. I caught one fish, and it had a hook in its mouth.

Are all the forests of the world to be felled by the chain saw? Is nothing sacred from the human animal's lust for material wealth? What do I do now? Shall I turn my back on civilization, if it can be called that, and live with and off the land in Canada or Alaska? Or do I leave the mountains and go into the cities that I despise and fight for the survival of Mother Earth? Will I ever again feel the clean, cold wind on my face as I sleep under the stars winking in the black vault of the night sky?

> To sleep with the wind blowing over my face is to have
> my Spirit take wing . . .
> In spring, it dances over the land on the fresh winds of
> renewal—the season of birth and change.
> In summer, it soars to the stars on the gusty winds of
> youth—the season of exuberance and dreams.

In autumn, it floats in moonlight on the mellow winds of maturity—the season of fulfillment and reflection.

In winter, it whirls through dark nights on the tempestuous winds of old age—the season of senility and death.

And in spring, it dances over the land on the fresh winds of renewal—the season of birth and change.

To sleep with the wind blowing over my face is to have my Spirit take wing . . .

These are the questions with which I have been struggling for days. And now I stand on the pass, the crossroad of my life, and I must make a choice. I don't know how long I have been standing here, but the sun is setting over Mount St. Helens, and I still have miles to go. Like the native youths who have gone before me into the sacred heart of the ancient forest, I leave behind my youth. Unlike those youths of old, however, I also leave my heart in the care of the land, for where I must travel there are no sacred forests left. From that day in 1960–when I watched the sun set over Mount St. Helens—to this, in 1988, I have never been back to the high, wild country of my youth, but I have spent the better part of twenty years as a scientist studying the ancient forest.

1963–1964

My 25th birthday dawns over the Atlantic Ocean, and that evening I land in Cairo, Egypt, where I spend the next several months as a vertebrate zoologist for the Peabody Museum of Yale University, surveying the vertebrate wildlife to be killed as a part of the completion of the Aswan High Dam and the formation of Lake Nasser. During the months in Egypt, along the Gulf of Suez, in the desert south of Alexandria, at Kurkur Oasis west of Aswan, and along the Nile between Aswan and the Sudanese border, I begin to learn about myself as a human being in a way not possible for me elsewhere.

I am suddenly thrust together with six other men of whom I know nothing and with whom I must either learn to communicate and get

Desert pavement in the Western Desert, Egypt.

along or be totally miserable. And I, a noncommunicative introvert, accept the struggle of learning to deal with other people—a challenge with which I still struggle daily.

I return from a field trip to the Red Sea on the 22nd of November 1963. It is late evening, and I am sitting in the Simerimis Hotel in Cairo having supper with some of the other men from the Yale expedition when one of the group comes in late with tears in his eyes and says, "President Kennedy has just been shot!" There is a stunned silence as though the world has suddenly stopped while each of us takes personal account of the news and processes it in our own way. We leave the hotel and go to the United States embassy to find out what has happened, but everywhere it seems are riots. We get to the embassy only to find it being mobbed by Egyptians, so we go to our hotel, the Garden City Hotel, turn on the radio, and watch the world from the safety of our second-story windows. This night my world stands still for it seems the impossible has happened—reality has gone mad! I feel alone and frightened, isolated and ungrounded in a foreign land.

I spend much time in the desert studying the plants and animals. The Western or Libyan Desert west of the Nile River is largely sand, desert pavement, and desert varnish as far as the eye can see in any direction. The day may be still as a tomb or howling with wind and stinging sand. The Eastern or Nubian Desert east of the Nile and west

Kurkur Oasis in the Western Desert, Egypt.

of the Red Sea Hills, on the other hand, is largely ironstone with comparatively little sand and seems simply hot, very hot. In a sense, the desert is changeless and yet, like a forest or the sea, is constantly changing. It is perhaps not so much the desert that is changing but rather I that am being changed by the desert.

I spend Christmas 1963 many miles out in the Western Desert from Aswan at Kurkur Oasis. The temperature is 94 degrees Fahrenheit, and the wind blows through the dry fronds of the doum palm, which rustle as though inhabited by small demons.

Kurkur Oasis is a tiny world of life clinging tenaciously to existence around a small supply of water, which in turn is surrounded by many miles of scorching sandy, pebbly desert. This is the home of the Dorcas gazelle and Ruppel's sand fox, where the miracle of cattails seems impossibly out of place, and yet they are here. This is where I learn about the hot, suffocating closeness and unrelenting sting of a desert sandstorm, when to breathe seems like sure death and everywhere the sun is blotted out in a brown pall. This is where I learn how precious water is, and this is where I learn that the desert has its own language, its own rhythm, which only silence and time will reveal to the patient heart.

I spend the 1st of January 1964 camped along the shore of the Red Sea. There is magic along the Red Sea as the little waves quietly caress the shore and the rising sun plays on the water and casts its glow on the Red Sea Hills before the world becomes distorted by the shimmering waves of heat as the day matures. I have a feeling of eternity along the Red Sea as though the gentle water, the soft wind, and the ancient, knowing land are putting a cloak of peace over my shoulders and bidding me stay.

One day in March 1964 while walking along a low hill, or gebel, in the Nubian Desert not far from the Nile and about a hundred miles north of the Sudanese border, I sit down on a large boulder of ironstone to rest. As I survey the magnificence of the desert, watching the waves of heat shimmer in the distance, I have a deep sense of company. Looking around, I find that I am sitting on the same rock where a Paleolithic man must have sat more than 25,000 years ago and chipped hand axes from the ironstone. One of his finished axes lies at my feet. I pick it up and find the tip broken off; I can almost feel his frustration at breaking the tip just when he thought he had a finished product. I feel a kinship with this man of ancient times, and I know that time is only a trap of my mind. Because I feel the Ancient One's presence, I also feel the roots of all of humanity embodied in the craftsmanship of one man stored in the seemingly timeless silence of the desert. Today, the 10th of March 1964, I am sitting where my Paleolithic brother sat, and I know that today I stand on the shoulders—the foundation—of what he learned and passed on when to me time seemed younger and the world seemed newer.

Red Sea Hills, Egypt.

Although several kinds of lizards live along the shores of the Nile, one of the more interesting is the Egyptian skink, the young of which have bright blue tails. The lizard looks a lot like the western skink that lives halfway around the world under pieces of wood along the big river near the 976-year-old forest.

Western skinks are small, shiny lizards that have an attractive pattern of two cream-colored longitudinal stripes that extend from the head along each side of their rich, brown backs onto the base of the tail. Young lizards have bright blue tails that gradually fade to bluish gray or brownish gray as they mature.

Western skinks are most often found under large, flat rocks or pieces of Douglas-fir bark and rotting wood along the shores of the big river. Here they remain cool next to the moist earth. Although secretive and seldom seen, these skinks are active during the day, getting about with rapid, jerky movements. But when stalking insects, such as the grasshoppers, beetles, crickets, moths, and flies on which they feed, they strike with catlike speed.

An occasional chance meeting occurs between a skink and a would-be predator, such as the ravens that continuously patrol the river. Should a raven, for example, grab at the bright blue tail, it breaks off and jumps and wiggles for several minutes, often holding the raven's attention while the skink escapes under the nearest cover.

Female western skinks lay from two to six eggs in burrows or in cavities that they excavate under stones or large pieces of wood. The females remain with their eggs until they hatch and even remain with the hatchlings until they leave the nest. During this time, the mother skinks will attack predators that threaten their young and will repair any disturbance to their nests, thus ensuring the survival of generations of western skinks along the big river.

1965

June 1965, I am in the old tin natural history building at Oregon State University in the last throes of completing my master's degree. My thesis is on the natural history of the red tree vole, and I have had to climb more than two hundred trees, some 80 to 100 feet above the ground, to get enough animals for study. The work is intense, and the heat that in summer frequently reaches over 100 degrees Fahrenheit in my office feels like an oven that is cooking my brains. I dignify my space with the word *office*, but it is really more like a small closet in an attic under a metal roof. And if that is not enough, my desk is in the herp collection, which means that I am mostly surrounded by jars of dead salamanders, toads, frogs, lizards, and snakes, all of which subject me to a constant, silent stare. Moreover, the jars are filled with isopropyl alcohol, which diffuses into the room, giving me a perpetual splitting headache, and making me wonder at times about my sanity. So, periodically I flee to the ancient forest.

Sitting along the edge of the stream near the marshy area one afternoon, I notice a small, blackish mammal scurrying along the water's edge amidst the skunk cabbages. The mammal is a marsh shrew. To me, this little-known mammal is one of the most fascinating animals in the forest.

The marsh shrew is the largest of the long-tailed shrews in North America. It has a pointed nose that seems forever to be busy going this way and that; its minute eyes are not noticeable without close scrutiny, and its teeth are tipped with a reddish brown. The fur on its back is dark brown to blackish, and its underside is only a little lighter, as is the tail, which is hairy in young animals and naked in old individuals.

Like its cousin the northern water shrew, which lives in the swift, cold streams of the meadow above the forest, the marsh shrew has fringes of short, stiff hairs on the margins of its feet, including the toes. The fringe, usually called swimming fringe, is most noticeable on young animals. It appears to sustain much wear during the shrew's life and is not replaced by new hair in old animals.

Although this shrew is active throughout the twenty-four-hour cycle, it is most active at twilight and during the night. Being aquatic, it spends much time in the water. From where I am sitting on a fallen tree, the shrew suddenly disappears amidst a skunk cabbage plant, then reappears and enters the water from a sloping area of the bank. Sculling quickly around the surface, it rapidly submerges, using its long snout and whiskers to explore underwater. It swims with hind legs in almost constant motion but is quiet when it pauses to rest briefly at the surface. Underwater, most of the propulsion is provided by its hind legs, which are used alternately, not simultaneously like a frog's. Air trapped in the shrew's fur gives it not only buoyancy but also a silvery appearance that, along with the small bubbles rising in its wake, allows me to follow its progress underwater.

After a few seconds, the shrew swims to the surface and, springing two to three inches out of the water, grasps the the steep bank with its claws, climbs out, and explores along the water's edge for a minute or so. Suddenly startled by something that I do not detect, it runs over the surface of the water for about five seconds with with its belly just barely above the surface, then dives and disappears.

Marsh shrews feed primarily on aquatic insects, such as nymphal stoneflies, mayflies, and alderflies. Other prey taken along the water's edge include phantom crane flies, ground beetles, snails, slugs, spiders, and harvestmen or daddy-longlegs. Watching a shrew eat an earthworm is an interesting experience; the shrew attacks the worm with a lightning-swift series of bites along its body. Large worms are usually eaten from the rear end to the front; small worms, however, are consumed from either end. Worms encountered underwater are attacked, seized in the teeth, and carried to land before they are eaten. Worms may also be immobilized with a rapid series of bites along their bodies and carried to a special area on land to be stored for a later meal.

In August, with the completion of my master's of science degree in zoology, I leave for Alaska to work at the University of Alaska at the village of College, just outside Fairbanks. The quaking aspen and the birch are goblets of yellow on white stems by September, and the clear nights are painted with the northern lights. Such a feeling of oneness, of primordial connectedness with the Universe, I have never felt before. The night sky over the northern roof of the world is indeed where the Eternal fingerpaints, and it is the movement of the Eternal that I feel within my heart.

As winter approaches and the sun migrates southward, the great vault of the night sky stares and winks with myriad illumined planets and stars while the soft light of the moon blends earth and heaven into the union of all life. And the warmth, migrating south with the sun, leaves in its place a dry cold that wrings every drop of moisture from the air as the temperature drops to 50 degrees below zero Fahrenheit. During the brief period of winter daylight, each droplet of moisture

Ice crystal.

squeezed from the air comes drifting as tiny silvery flakes out of a windless sky to settle unnoticed on the ground, to be lost amidst the billions upon billions of snowflakes that already cover the earth.

As winter's grip tightens, and the nights grow longer and seemingly colder, I wonder whether, during the last great ice age, the place where the ancient forest by the spring now stands was like this Alaskan winter, perhaps while my Paleolithic brother sat chipping his hand axe in the Nubian Desert.

1966–1967

In September 1966, I leave for Nepal, where I stay until August 1967 studying the wildlife and collecting ectoparasites (ticks, fleas, and lice), which are sent to the Naval Medical Research Unit Three in Cairo, Egypt, for studies of any diseases they may carry. Here, in Nepal, are forests such as none I have ever seen, and yet they are somehow similar to forests all over the world.

I spend the month of May 1967 working out of a field camp at Phu-

Langtang Mountain from Phulang Ghyang, Nepal.

lang Ghyang, Newakot District, between 11,000 and 12,000 feet above sea level. My camp is surrounded by mountains whose perpetually snow-clad peaks rise more than 20,000 feet into the air and whose shoulders are at once defined and separated by deep valleys of blue and amber. I am in the home of the clouded leopard and the snow leopard, which is a forest of true firs and of rhododendrons that grow 20 to 30 feet tall.

Every afternoon about four o'clock, the thunderstorms rise with the warm, moist air from the valleys, and the sizzling crackle of lightning and the instantaneous crescendo of thunder seem loud enough to shatter my eardrums. The monsoon season is beginning below, and on the 1st of June I descend into the torrential rains.

The paths to the valleys are sometimes alive with red wriggling earthworms and are lined with the splendor of orchids; the valley floors are crawling with land leaches that get to me from the vegetation along the trails through the eyelets of my boots, down my neck, and up my shirt sleeves. It rains so hard that a fine mist falls into my tent, and everywhere the mold grows and the water stands in puddles. The rivers swell and carry Nepal's topsoil southward into India—soil from their forests that we, U.S. AID, helped to clear with our technology

Looking into the Trisuli Valley from Phulang Ghyang, Nepal.

and our lack of wisdom. And I wonder how long the Nepalese forests will last, for surely we are doing them a great disservice and stealing their dignity with our arrogance.

I have amoebic dysentery and forget what it is like to feel good. I also have a job to do, however, so I continue to work as best I can. At one point, I ask Willi Unsoeld if he will help me with logistics for a field trip. He does, and I tell him "Thank you." Willi says, "You can't thank me but you can pass it on to someone else as someone once did for me." I endeavor always to live by that rule.

I learned about human dignity in Nepal and India. Many of the people with whom I interact are sick; in fact, my house in Kathmandu is next to an old building that seemingly houses every type of human affliction I can imagine, and I never hear the afflicted complain. They accept life as it is, a lesson in humility that I am still struggling to learn.

One day while in the Trisuli Valley I hear the clear, distinct notes of the green barbat, a Nepalese forest bird that sounds much like the western tanager of the 979-year-old forest halfway around the world. While listening to the barbat, I watch an Old World otter that reminds me of the otters that live in the big river and its tributaries.

The otters of the big river are long, cylindrical carnivores with low bodies. They range from thirty-three to fifty-two inches long and weigh from almost one and a half up to almost six pounds. Their legs are short, and their long, tapering tails are somewhat flattened horizontally. Their heads are small, as are their eyes and ears. The feet are webbed between the toes, and the soles are naked and may have what appear to be warts. The thick, silky underfur is wholly concealed by short, glossy guard hairs that vary from dark brown to dark reddish brown on the back and slightly paler below. The throat and cheeks are grayish brown. The pelage fades to a lighter, more reddish brown in summer.

Although the otters are primarily active in the big river at dusk and throughout the night, they are often abroad during daylight hours. To be fortunate enough to observe the otters as they frolic in the bounding, rushing water, or for that matter in a placid mountain lake, is to behold the epitome of aquatic grace and beauty among forest mammals. Moreover, the otters' frequent chirping gives the distinct impression that they are thoroughly enjoying a good time.

The otters are excellent, versatile swimmers. They can swim either by paddling with their limbs in any combination or by holding their limbs stretched toward the rear and close to their sides while they undulate their powerful bodies. The strong undulating motion is used when swimming in earnest, and during such times they swim alternately on the surface of the water and beneath it.

When moving on land, the otters have three gaits—walking, running, and bounding. When walking, the whole body is held rigidly with the head and neck outstretched, and since the hind limbs are a little longer than the front ones, the body is inclined slightly downward. The end one-third of the tail may drag on the ground. A running otter holds its tail above the ground by slightly arching the end one-fourth of it. Bounding is an otter's fastest gait; when bounding, the front and hind feet are brought toward each other, causing the back to arch and the tail to be lifted off the ground.

In winter, the otters travel overland on the snow and ice by combining running and sliding. They alternately run, then tuck their front feet under their bodies and slide, run again and slide again. In fact, they enjoy sliding in the snow to the fullest extent. Finding a hill with good snow cover near the water and clear of debris, they climb up the slope and coast to the bottom, do an Immelmann turn, and immediately run to the top to repeat the performance. (An Immelmann turn is a maneuver in which an airplane first completes half a loop then half a roll in order to simultaneously gain altitude and change direction in flight.) The otters toboggan again and again even though the slide may be slightly rough, so they may get repeated bumps on their stomachs. An occasional otter may not like the excessive speed on a particularly steep and slippery slide, so it will thrust its forepaws forward to slow the pace or even stop itself. But it usually does not take long before the timid one joins the others with reckless abandon. The otters seem to love nothing more than playing in the water and romping and sliding across the countryside.

The otters are great travelers. Some individuals may travel 130 to 150 miles of the big river and its tributaries in a single year, and a family may range from 8 to 25 miles in a single season. A lone male or a pair may even travel 20 to 30 miles from its den and return after an absence of several days. The distances that the otters travel varies greatly and is related to the available supply of food, the general suitability of the habitat, and perhaps to an innate wanderlust.

Regardless of how far the otters travel, they have particular areas where they emerge to roll and rub themselves. They nearly always choose sandy areas when these are available, but they will use grass, leaves, and even snow. They are particular about their rolling areas in that they use the bank farthest from nearby, well-used trails or, in the lower part of the big river, roads. It seems that human activity along trails and roads makes them "nervous," particularly when such activity is some distance above the water and therefore out of their view. Spending so much time in water makes it imperative that they keep their fur clean to maintain its insulating properties. The frequent rolling and rubbing appears to serve this purpose.

The otters invariably leave their sign at these rolling areas—both their urine and black, tarlike feces. In fact, when several otters travel together, each tries to be the last to leave its mark, even if it is only a dribble.

Otters have more than their share of curiosity. If something unusual catches their attention in the water, they will stop and watch it, or if on the bank, they may sit up full length, brace themselves with their tails, and watch. They often accompany their observations with a running commentary of chirps.

The big river and its tributaries provide ample food for the otters. During winter and spring, they subsist primarily on a variety of fishes, whereas during summer and autumn, crayfish are their staple, augmented with such tasty morsels as frogs, salamanders, large aquatic beetles, a few mammals and birds, some carrion, and occasionally blueberries or huckleberries.

The breeding season occurs from November through early April. Though sociable much of the year, males fight among themselves during the breeding season, particularly when a sexually active female is in the vicinity. Some males become very rough when attempting to mate and will not tolerate the interference of another male. A few males go "berserk" when they sense interference and will charge whatever they deem the disturbance to be. Others, however, remain unaggressive throughout the breeding season.

Females come into heat immediately after giving birth, and unless bred, they remain in heat for about 45 days. Because they have delayed implantation, the gestation period ranges from 288 to 375 days. (Delayed implantation means that a fertilized egg floats around in the uterus for some time before it becomes implanted or attached to the wall of the uterus and begins to grow.) Implantation of the embryos occurs about the 1st of February. Since the embryos grow actively for only about the last two months before birth, the young are born during March and April.

The young are born in dens, cavities among the roots of trees, or in thickets of vegetation. Dens may be as much as five hundred feet above the high-water mark and up to one-half mile away from water, or they may be at the water's edge. Dens normally are burrows that have been appropriated from some other animal and renovated by the otter. The otters' dens are well hidden; those located at the water's edge have the main entrance far enough below the surface to prevent it from being frozen shut.

Otters normally breed every other year and produce a single litter that ranges from one to five young but is usually two or three. The process of birth lasts from three to eight hours, depending in part on the size of the litter. As soon as the newborn are cleaned, their mother curls tightly around them so that they are almost completely protected from cold air.

Babies weigh about four ounces at birth. They are fully covered with hair that is about one-fourth of an inch long. The hair is uniformly blackish brown on the back and is lighter and more grayish on the underside. The lips, cheeks, chin, and throat are paler than they are in the adult. The babies are born toothless and with closed eyes. They are helpless for five or six weeks. Although adult otters defecate and urinate outside their dens, the babies have to be cleaned by their mother until they are about seven weeks old. Their eyes open in about thirty-five days, and when they are five or six weeks old, they begin to play with one another and with their mother. The mother allows her youngsters to go outside the den for the first time when they are ten to twelve weeks old.

The young have to be coaxed into the water the first time; in fact, a mother sometimes has to drag one of her offspring into the water by the scruff of its neck. They seem to be head-heavy when first learning to swim and have trouble keeping their heads above water. Swimming lessons, therefore, are accompanied by much struggling and sputtering.

In the beginning, the mother catches food and calls her young to come and get it. At their arrival, she releases the prey alive, which usually escapes into the water, followed by the floundering youngsters trying to find it. Through repetition, however, they learn to catch and hold onto their food.

The mother generally leads the way in traveling, calling her young. Should they become too adventuresome and try to rush ahead of her, she nips their noses. When so punished, a youngster drops to the ground and lies very quietly. When punished severely, a young otter remains lying on its back and will not move forward until the mother returns and caresses it.

Otters become sexually mature in two years, but males, for some unknown reason, usually do not breed successfully until they are between five and seven years old. The otters of the big river in the valley below the high ridge may live to become at least eleven years old, and during their lifetime may travel far enough down the big river to meet the logging roads advancing steadily along its banks toward the ancient forest by the spring.

1969–1973

On the 20th of July 1969, the first human being walks on the moon, and humanity takes another step into technological history. On that day, one man sees, for the first time, the humility, the frailty of the human condition as he looks back from space and beholds the tiny, shining sphere of Mother Earth suspended amongst the stars.

In June 1970, I move to Bandon, Oregon, to begin field work for an ecological survey of the mammals of the Oregon coast. The field work lasts until September 1973, when the forest by the spring is 985 years old.

The work along the coast is intense and time consuming and is rewarded in the end by uncovering some of the secrets of the ancient forest, such as the phenomenon of small forest-dwelling rodents that eat truffles and inoculate the soil with viable spores that are vital to the survival of the forest trees. It also becomes clear, however, that the human alterations of the Pacific Northwest, begun in the 1840s with simple clearings for farmland in the valleys, have reached massive proportions and are escalating. Little driftwood, for example, is left on the coastal beaches, or in the estuaries or saltmarshes. In fact, many saltmarshes have been diked, and most of the magnificent shifting coastal sand dunes have been stabilized with European beachgrass. The ancient forests of the Pacific Northwest are being cut faster and faster for short-term profits without regard for their biological sustainability, but the ancient forest by the spring is still inaccessible.

The field work completed, I begin writing the final report, *Natural History of Oregon Coast Mammals*, in October 1973 and finally finish it in February 1975. The word *History* in the title is significant to me because history signifies past tense, and the rate at which the ancient forest is being liquidated in the Coast Range of Oregon makes a study such as mine historical in habitat loss even before the field work is completed.

While working on the coast, I have the opportunity to study the beaver, which more than any other animal has had a drastic effect on North American history. The quest for its valuable pelt (often called a blanket) stimulated exploration; the fur trade was born; battles were fought; fortunes were made and lost; a unique way of life evolved— the solitary trapper and mountain man. Overexploitation rapidly exterminated beaver from much of their geographical distribution and severely reduced the populations. Today, through the efforts of federal and state agencies, the beaver has increased in numbers and is once again found throughout most of its former range, including the big river and its tributaries.

Beaver are among the largest rodents in the world; they are the largest, living rodent in North America. Beaver are compact, thick-set animals with small eyes and ears. They have short legs and a large, broad, scaly, paddlelike tail. Adults range from two and a half to four feet in length and often weigh more than sixty pounds.

Beaver are well adapted to aquatic life and are excellent swimmers and divers. They use oxygen economically and can remain submerged more than fifteen minutes. Their small eyes are protected by nictitating membranes. (The word *nictitate* means "to wink" and refers to an inner eyelid that helps keep a beaver's eyes clean.) A beaver's nostrils and ears are valvular and can be closed underwater. Beavers have large hind feet that are webbed between the toes, and the claws of the second and third toes are split, presumably as an aid to grooming.

Beaver have unusually dense coats that consist of fine underfur overlaid with coarse guard hairs. The soft, short underfur is gray, whereas the coarse, shiny guard hairs vary from rich glossy brown, to yellowish brown, to reddish brown. The guard hairs on the underside are not as long or as close together as they are on the top. The underparts, therefore, are lighter in color. The feet and the tail are black.

These large rodents are usually thought of as the engineers of the animal world because of their ability to cut down good-sized trees and because of the complex dams and abodes they construct in streams and lakes. Beaver do not hibernate but store food underwater for use during winter.

Although beaver dams may be large, over six feet high and occasionally as much as six hundred yards long, the dams in the tributaries of the big river are usually small and inconspicuous. Beaver dams impound water that may form ponds covering many acres. In mountainous regions, these ponds gradually fill in with sediment and vegetation and ultimately form meadows.

The dams are closely inspected by the beaver and are often maintained for years. Along some of the tributaries of the big river such dams are built with sticks (normally after the animal has eaten the bark off) shoved into an appropriate soft spot in the bottom of a stream or into a "foundation" of mud carried to the damsite by the beaver. To the foundation of sticks (butt ends facing upstream), the beaver adds mud, vegetation, shrubs, and more sticks. As the dam grows, the sticks become crisscrossed and the dam becomes securely anchored; such a dam is often extremely difficult to remove by hand. Severe winter floods sometimes wash out a dam, even a securely anchored one.

Beaver construct three types of abodes: a standing lodge in open water away from the bank, a bank lodge with a burrow extending into the bank, or a simple burrow dug into the bank without a lodge of any type. The bank lodge is most frequently used in the streams of the forest along the big river.

Beaver have paired anal scent glands known as castors or beaver pods. They occur in both sexes but are slightly larger in the male. The content of the castors is called castoreum and is used in marking territorial limits. The castoreum, a musk with a pleasant, rather sweet odor, is deposited on scent mounds, also called beaver mud pies or simply beaver pies. These scent mounds are made with piles of mud, occasionally mud and vegetation, rarely vegetation without mud. The beaver obtains these materials from the stream and places them on the shore along the water's edge.

Scent mounds vary in size from barely perceptible to piles of mud two feet high and in number from two to seven per colony. Although most scent mounds are located along the edge of a colony, some are located near the dwelling, especially if the abode has been recently constructed. Young and old beaver, both males and females, regularly and frequently visit the scent mounds to deposit mud and castoreum. Since a typical beaver colony consists of two parents and the young of the year, as well as the yearlings born the previous year, such behavior eliminates the necessity of actively defending territories by removing antagonism between adjacent colonies while retaining the integrity of the resident colony. Strange castoreum on a scent mound causes a resident beaver to immediately deposit its own castoreum, the emission of which produces a sound that can be heard about sixteen yards away. Strange castoreum on a scent mound may also elicit aggressive behavior in the resident beaver as indicated by loud hissing.

Beaver are social and somewhat placid animals, a calmness that can be attributed to their familial and colonial characteristics. For example, other than untrained young, which might vocalize while outside the lodge, vocalization occurs chiefly within the lodge and is related to those behaviors in which sound or communication is of little survival value. Sound production in beaver does not seem to have the same usefulness it does in animals less secretive that roam at will. Vocalization is associated more with familial and colonial behavior than with social control. Beaver do, however, produce one sound with which many people are familiar—slapping their tails on the surface of the water just prior to quickly diving beneath it. Tail slapping, which produces a resounding *smack*!, is usually considered a warning given to another beaver by a startled or frightened individual. The normal dive of an undisturbed beaver is quiet.

Beaver are vegetarians and eat a wide variety of plants. In the big river and its tributaries they eat the bark of red alder and willow as their main diet, as well as salmonberry, salal, deer fern, swordfern, sedges, and during the spring and early summer, skunk cabbage. They also eat small quantities of bark from Douglas-fir and western hemlock.

Although beaver may travel a mile or more from water to obtain a desired food, along the big river, they seldom travel more than two hundred yards from the water. Beaver also construct canal systems inland from their ponds; in these they float food, such as small, trimmed trees, from the cutting sites to the pond. The canals are usually filled with water from about fifteen to twenty-five inches deep. Underground chambers are frequently constructed into the sides of a canal, and a chamber often has a large hole penetrating the roof to the surface of the ground above. During winter, the hole normally has food (cut sticks with bark still attached) protruding from it; by spring, the sticks are usually gone. Beaver also store food on the bottom of a pond, where it remains fresh and is available when the pond freezes over.

Perhaps the most visible signs of beavers' feeding activity are the stumps of trees they fell to obtain the bark. The trees are cut by the beavers' sharp incisor (front) teeth, which keep growing. In fact, if the front teeth are not constantly worn down, they grow so fast that the upper and lower teeth grow beyond each other, and the beaver, unable to open its mouth wide enough to eat, starves to death.

Female beaver probably reach sexual maturity in their second summer; although males also reach sexual maturity in their second summer, they may be capable of reproduction late in their first summer.

The breeding season for beaver is normally from January through March; breeding activity peaks in early February. A single litter is born per year, ranging from one to nine offspring, but the usual litter consists of two to four young called kits. Kits are born well haired and with their eyes open. At birth they weigh from eight to twenty-four ounces. They nurse for about six weeks and remain part of the family group until sexual maturity is attained. For animals, beaver are long-lived inhabitants of the streams and the big river of the ancient forest and may approach twenty years of age.

Unlike most animals of the big river and its tributaries, however, the beaver may actually be helped if the ancient forest is one day cut because removal of the conifers will stimulate a sudden increase in red alder and willows—the beavers' main food—along the water's edge.

1974–1987

In late 1974, I am asked if I will work for the U.S. Department of the Interior, Bureau of Land Management (BLM), and make a survey of vertebrate wildlife in the rangelands of the Vale District of southeastern Oregon. I agree and move to La Grande, Oregon, in March 1975, where I have an office and laboratory in the USDA Forest Service Range and Wildlife Habitat Laboratory of the Pacific Northwest Forest and Range Experiment Station.

Although I am working most of the time in southeastern Oregon, my friend and colleague, Jack Ward Thomas, who runs the Forest Service research laboratory in La Grande, asks me to lend him three days of my time to help outline a book on wildlife and forestry. That was in March 1975. The book, *Wildlife Habitats in Managed Forests: The Blue Mountains of Oregon and Washington*, is finally finished in September 1979. This is the longest three days I've ever spent, but then Jack is not only a Texan but also an Aggie!

As work on *The Blue Mountains*, as the book is usually called, draws to a close, we begin writing a book called *Wildlife Habitats in Managed Rangelands: The Great Basin of Southeastern Oregon* to conclude my work for the Vale District of the Bureau of Land Management. This time, however, we publish the book a chapter at a time as each gets done. While the book will not be finished until 1985, I have completed everything I set out to do in the Vale District and am asked by personnel in both the Forest Service and the Bureau of Land Management to move to western Oregon and work on some of the emerging issues in the cutting of ancient forests. So, on the 2nd of October 1980, I move to Corvallis, where I have an office and a laboratory in the Forestry Sciences Laboratory of the U.S. Forest Service on the Oregon State University campus.

While still in La Grande, however, I am called back to Washington, D.C., to testify at the Environmental Protection Agency hearings on the herbicide 2,4,5-T. After my testimony on the 12th of May 1980, I take the train to Princeton, New Jersey, to visit friends, Jim and Carol Applegate and their children. I am planning to fly to Seattle, Washington, on the 17th of May for a meeting on the 19th, but the Applegate children ask me to stay one more day. I agree and fly to Seattle on the 18th of May, just in time to see the eruption of Mount St. Helens from the air. What I see is both a cataclysmic and a miniscule change in the Universe. The scale is relative and is defined by the observer and the observer's perception of space and time. People in the Pacific Northwest cry disaster, but I see Mother Earth's change as a benefit; after all, the soil over which the volcanic ash falls is nurtured as it was after the eruption of 1800. And in my mind's eye, I see a reenactment of, a flashback to, the beginning when the earth was young and life was new, and I feel the unity of all things and the puniness of time.

While in Corvallis, I study the ancient forest—mainly the function of large, fallen trees, mycorrhizal fungi, and small mammal relations—from 1981 until the 1st of October 1986, when the research phase of the project is completed. From October 1986 until I resign from the Bureau of Land Management on the 30th of September 1987, I once again, as senior editor, struggle with all the human failings that arise from producing a multiauthored book, such as the final report from this project, *From the Forest to the Sea: A Story of Fallen Trees*, to be published in 1988, when the ancient forest is 1,000 years old.

With the end of my career as a research scientist at hand, I feel a whole way of life slipping into the past, and I realize how much I learned as a youth in the ancient forest by the spring, in the meadow, on the high ridge, and along the streams and the big river. I realize what a priceless gift has been bestowed on me, and I am grateful.

1988

The ancient forest is warm. A gentle breeze caresses giant Douglas-firs. Insects whine and buzz in small, sun-drenched areas that dapple the floor of the forest. Somewhere a squirrel chatters, a raven croaks. Somewhere a brown creeper *wee-wonks* its way up a tree trunk. Swainson's thrushes add melody as the sun glides slowly, inexorably westward.

Shadows begin to claim the world, and as the forest cools, giving up its warmth to the undefinable space of the Universe, forest odors change. Warm fragrances of day mix in twilight with cool scents of night. The sun is gone. Evening settles quietly over the land; and odors begin to wend through the forest.

Odors, a common language, change with the seasons. Indelibly stamped in my mind, they are trails to the past, a chemical link to memory. Somewhere in the past, in my youth, I have stood in an ancient forest such as this—yet different. Different because I was young. Different because no white person before me had been within the forest. Different because the odor that tonight leads me through time was, in the past, new to my senses. Different because tonight I remember with greater maturity what I learned from the forest in my youth.

My youth is of yesteryear, for today, the 13th of October 1988, I

Nature's ancient forest.

have lived fifty years, one-half a century, and I marvel and I shudder at how much we human beings have changed the earth in my few years. As I begin my next fifty years, I am acutely aware that I stand at a vantage point in human history and see the imminent liquidation of most of Nature's ancient forests, not only in the Pacific Northwest but also throughout the rest of the world, through the purposeful practice of the "economics of extinction" for short-term profits. And I wonder, What will the world be like without these regal forests? What will the future lose when the irretrievable artistry of millennia falls under the chain saw?

As I think about the ancient forest by the spring, I cannot help but marvel that a single 1,000-year-old Douglas-fir has an unbroken line of ancestry going back at least to the beginning of the Pleistocene, 1.5 million years ago. This means that if each tree in the line of ancestry were to have lived 1,000 years, an unbroken chain of 1,500 generations would have produced the Douglas-fir I see today. If the average life span of the trees were 700 years, there would have been 2,143 generations; 500 years, 3,000 generations: and if only 300 years, 5,000 generations. In addition to the continual genetic changing of the trees, the forest has been changing, has been different each hour of each day,

Humanity's economic plantation next to a small remnant of Nature's forest in the Siuslaw National Forest of western Oregon.

each day of each month, year, century, and millennium. Yet all of this Creation, all of this history can be forever severed in mere minutes with a chain saw.

If I take my ancestral lineage back to the time when the ancient peoples crossed the Bering-Chukchi platform some 20,000 years ago, and if during those 20,000 years the average life span of my ancestors were 50 years, then I am the culmination of an unbroken chain of 400 generations. If I take my ancestry back to the days of Moses, I would be looking at about 66 generations; and back to the days of Jesus Christ, at 40 generations. Today, even a single 1,000-year-old Douglas-fir would encompass 20 human generations if the average human life span were 50 years, or 14 generations if it were 70 years.

Around the world through all of human history our roots have developed with those of the forest; our roots grow from the same soil. So, when we destroy the forests of the world—as we are doing today—we also destroy the soil in which the seed of our heritage lies. How short is our life, how arrogant is our ego compared with the human struggle and suffering that is paralleled in the life of even a single 1,000-year-old Douglas-fir.

Forgive us, for we know not what we do.

Consider our present knowledge of the world, what we think we know. Then consider that a "scientific fact" is only a fact by consensus. Thus, whatever we think the world is at any moment in history—that is not what it is. Our every concept is only a working hypothesis. Is it not wise, therefore, to retain, so long as biologically possible, the living archives of our humanity, the living forests of the world?

Today I have been on earth fifty years, and the forest by the spring is a thousand years old; although it is now more of a western hemlock forest than one of Douglas-fir, a number of the ancient Douglas-firs still live. When will a logging road pierce the heart of this ancient forest? When will chain saws sever the ancestral artery of time and history? Will I ever see it again? Will I ever again stand where so many of my Native American brothers have stood in reverence and awe of Nature's masterpiece, the ancient forest by the spring? What will future generations have as the spiritual center of their history when only stumps and sawdust remain, and Nature's forest is replaced by the simplistic plantations of economic design? What will happen when the soils of the ancient forests, which have been carried over from one forest to the next, are robbed of their historic continuity and are drastically simplified and altered, perhaps irreversibly forever?

I can feel the eternal spring of my soul in the ancient forest, a sense of place and a feeling of well-being in the Universe. Am I the last person ever to know the peace, the sacred heart of the ancient forest by the spring, for even now its silence and its birdsong are sometimes shattered by the wind-borne sounds of logging equipment over a ridge but a scant ten miles away.

Of late, as I fly over the Pacific Northwest and look down from the airplane at the ever-spreading clearcuts, I think of the unconscionable act of crucifixion, for surely we are crucifying the Earth that sustains us, and all I can say is, "Mother Earth, forgive us, for we know not what we do."

Epilogue

Traveling back in time, looking over the history of forests, I marvel at their biological resiliency, even before the advent of human beings. Forests have persisted through tremendous geological upheavals, catastrophic climatic changes, and the severe impact of people changing the face of the earth. It began with the discovery of fire as a tool by Paleolithic peoples, and much growing evidence suggests that such preagricultural peoples had a major effect on the environment through burning, both deliberately and accidentally. The earth's strata with thick layers of charcoal and even carbonized trunks of trees at several sites in the Netherlands and in northern Germany document great forest fires, and these strata also frequently contain artifacts, fireplaces, and other refuse from the camps of Stone Age hunters. Human use of fire probably caused major changes in vegetation, changes that were beneficial to humans. For Paleolithic peoples, the problems of conservation—beyond maintaining one's life—did not exist, because the destructive changes wrought by people that reduce basic resources and impair the capacity of the earth to provide for humanity had to wait for the development of culture.

The most dramatic change in the relation of humans to forests came first with the use of fire; second with the domestication of plants and animals and the rise of agriculture somewhere between 7,000 and 5,000 B.C.; third with the invention of the ox yoke and horse collar, which allowed people to use animals for pulling heavy loads; and fourth with the invention of the wheel. Human activities through the subsequent millennia have reduced the area of the world's forests by at least one-third, and perhaps by more than one-half, to about 8 billion acres, and the destruction continues. The reason is fourfold: the demand for fuel, the demand for agricultural lands, the demand for industrial timber, and the demand for maximum profit from resources perceived to be free for the taking. As we destroy the forests of the world, for whatever rational reason, we are, as a global society, simultaneously destroying our historical roots and grossly impairing our spiritual well-being. Consider, for example, that without forests there would have been no wood for the ships of olden days or for the first airplanes. The peoples of the great continents would still be separated from one another; the oceanic islands, such as Hawaii, New Zealand, and Australia, would be barren of people; and the oceans and the skies of the world would still be unknown. Without heat from wood there could be no metal, and the face of the moon would still be without the footprints of humanity.

I did not, however, set out to write a litany of human blunders or about the future of forestry. (I have written about the latter, however, in *The Redesigned Forest*.) I set out on a journey through a forest of a thousand years so that you may see that the ancient forests represent our spiritual and historical roots as human beings, not just those of the Native Americans, or of the European invaders, or of the African slaves brought to the New World first by the Spanish in the 1500s and then by the European Americans two centuries later. As a masterpiece by a great painter or sculptor belongs to all of humanity in all generations, not just to the individual or museum in whose privileged trust and care it momentarily rests, so the ancient forest, the masterpiece of Creation, the historical accounting of our human struggle for consciousness through the centuries, belongs to all of humanity in all generations, not just to one special group or another who would secure it for narrow interests through lack of understanding.

It is now 133 years since Chief Sealth wrote his letter to President

Franklin Pierce. Is Chief Sealth's prediction coming true—much sooner than even he imagined? Are we suffocating in our own waste? Are we now beginning to fight for environmental survival because we have little environmental consciousness? Bear in mind that *since World War II we humans, for the first time in the history of the world, have the capacity to irreparably disarrange and disarticulate Planet Earth, which supports us. We must, therefore, in humility remember that Planet Earth does not need us. We need Planet Earth!*

If our Constitution was in any way influenced by "The Fire That Never Dies," then the Native Americans, such as the Peacemaker, Hiawatha, and Chief Sealth are our ancestors—perhaps not our immediate, genetic ancestors, but rather our ideological and spiritual ancestors, our forefathers of wisdom.

Today the environmental scale is poised in the balance, and humanity stands at the crossroad between the end of living and the beginning of survival. And for those who can hear, the Peacemaker's words ring out of the ancient forest of the past even as he spoke to the Five Nations of the Iroquois: "Think not forever of yourselves, O Chiefs, nor of your own generation. Think of continuing generations of our families, think of our grandchildren and of those yet unborn, whose faces are coming from beneath the ground." We will be wise to heed these words, for they speak to all ages—those of the past, those of today, and those yet to come. We cannot put a recall on a nonfunctional forest as we can on a defective automobile, but we can learn how to grow and sustain a healthy forest if we act now while there is still time.

Yet if we as separate nations cannot see that we are united in a global society and that our national "renewable natural resources" collectively form the world's supply of renewable natural resources, such as forests that produce the wood fiber and most of the world's supply of water and oxygen on which all people must depend for survival, then the time has come to seriously consider a world consensus to administer the wise use of our renewable natural resources. I say "renewable natural resources" because our present concept of "management" *assumes* that "renewable" and "resource" are synonymous and that "renewable" and "sustainable" are synonymous, and they are not! Just because something can be renewed does not mean that it will be renewed or renewed on a sustainable—nondeclining—basis. Witness humanity's deforestation of the world.

Further, as Meeker points out in his book *Minding the Earth*, the term *resource* is sadly misused. *Resource* originally meant a reciprocal gift between humans and the Earth, but today's dictionaries define *resource* as "the collective wealth of a country or its means of producing wealth; any property that can be converted into money." And as Meeker has correctly noted, "Converting the natural world—resources—into money has become the theme of our time." Thus we transform spirited and lively mutual gifts into lifeless commodities, including ourselves— the human resource.

And just as surely as Albert Einstein's formulation of $E = mc^2$ was the key that unlocked the mystery of the atom, so understanding the ancient forest is the key to unlocking the mystery of how to sustain the temperate coniferous forests, and in time the forests of the world, for each is a masterpiece of Creation that holds a thread in common with all. If we understand the threads and how each is woven, we can learn not only how to maintain the health and order of but also how to repair the fabric of the forests of the world through restoration forestry.

Restoration is the thought and act of putting something back in a prior position, place, or condition. That much is clear enough. But why should we humans bother putting something back the way it was? Why try to go backward in time when society's push is forward, always forward, faster and faster?

In our drive to maximize the yield of wood fiber, we strive only for a sustained harvest of timber, and we are intensively altering more and more acres to that end. We are trading our forests in on European-style plantations that are really nothing more than economic tree farms. We cannot have a sustainable yield of anything, however, until we first have a sustainable forest to produce the yield. In practice, we tend to think it a tragic, economic waste if wood fiber is not somehow used by humans but is allowed to recycle in the ecosystem. And because of our paranoia over "lost profits"—defined as economic waste—we extract far more from the forest than we replace. We will, for example, invest capital in the next crop of trees, but we will not reinvest capital to maintain the health of the forest that produces the crop. This scenario is in the tradition of our western culture, and through it much of the biosphere has been and is being degraded. Take, for example, the newspaper article in *The Sunday Oregonian* on 15 May 1988:

> Deforested Himalayas become staggering ecological disaster. . . . Today, satellite photography has shown that little more than 10 percent of the mountain land has good tree coverage. In Nepal, less than one quarter of the country is believed to be under forest cover. As late as 1970, it was estimated that half of the country was forested. . . . The environmental consequences are staggering.

Anil Agarwal, director of the Center for Science and the Environment in New Delhi, is quoted in the same article as saying, "Already, the consequences are bad. But in 10, 15 years, we will be seeing unimaginable floods, terrible droughts and so much more if the mountains continue to get worse."

This brings us directly to the value of restoration as a means of changing the way we think and a means of changing the way we relate to the forests of the world. Basically, restoration helps us understand how a given portion of the ecosystem functions: as we put it back together, as we go backward in time to reconstruct what was, we learn how to sustain the system's processes and their ability to produce the products we desire now and in the future. Similarly, restoration helps us to understand the limitations of a given portion of the ecosystem. As we put it back together, as we slow down and take the time to reconstruct what was, we learn how fast we can push the system to produce products on a sustainable basis without impairing it.

Thus, the very process of restoring the land to health is the process through which we become attuned to Nature and, through Nature, with ourselves. Restoration forestry, therefore, is both the means and the end, for as we learn how to restore the forest, we heal the forest, and as we heal the forest, we heal ourselves. We also simultaneously restore both our options for products and amenities from the forest and the options of future generations. This is crucial because our moral obligation as human beings is to maintain options for future generations but not to judge how those options are used. Ours must be an unconditional gift. It is the only gift we have.

In restoration forestry lies the hope of the world and of humanity.

We must be prepared to make mistakes, misjudgments, as we learn how to restore the forests of the world, but mistakes will be forgiven if we learn from them. The key to and the value of restoration is in the thought process it implies. *And part of this process is saving as much of Nature's ancient forest as humanly possible so that we and future generations can learn how to restore and sustain the forests of the world for all of humanity.*

You have no doubt noticed that few women are mentioned in this book. It is not because women have not been important in history; it is because few women have started wars and none that I know of have been responsible for the dismantling of the world's forest. That has been the work of men. Further, until recently, few women have been allowed to participate in government. Now, however, it is my fervent hope that women will come forward and bring their healing vision to the task of repairing the damage we have done. It takes far less vision and far less skill to destroy the forests of the world than it does to repair them. To heal the land will require the wise and gentle touch of women, from whom we men have much to learn.

Before you close this book, I would like you to close your eyes and visualize the most beautiful forest, mountain, desert, lake, or beach, or any special place you have ever seen. Hold this picture in your mind and imagine that you are the last person on earth, and there is no one with whom to share this beauty. What value does it have? What value would it have if you had one other person to share it with? two other people? three other people? Nothing of value can exist for us as human beings that is not defined by its and our relationship to other human beings—someone with whom to share.

What we are doing to the forests of the world is but a mirror reflection of what we are doing to ourselves and to one another, and as Gandhi said, "An eye for an eye only makes the whole world blind." In the last analysis, all we have as human beings is each other, and if we lose sight of each other we have nothing—not even a forest.

Glossary

ALGA (s.), ALGAE (pl.)—any of various primitive, chiefly aquatic, one-celled or multicellular plants lacking true stems, roots, and leaves but usually containing the green pigment chlorophyll.

ANAEROBIC—the ability of a microorganism, such as a bacterium, to live in the absence of oxygen.

ANCIENT FOREST—a forest that is past full maturity; the last stage in forest succession; a forest with two or more levels of canopy, heart rot, and other signs of obvious physiological deterioration.

ANGIOSPERMAE—any of a class of plants whose seeds are enclosed in an ovary, as distinguished from plants having naked seeds (Gymnospermae).

ANNUAL—a plant that completes its life cycle in one growing season.

AUTOGENIC SUCCESSION—self-generating or self-imposing change.

BACTERIUM (s.), BACTERIA (pl.)—any of numerous one-celled microorganisms of the class Schizomycetes, occurring in a wide variety of forms, existing as free-living organisms or as parasites.

BARK—the outer, protective layer of woody branches, stems, and roots of trees, and other woody plants.

BASAL SHOOTS—stems that sprout from the base of some woody plants.

BIENNIAL—a plant that grows vegetatively during the first year and blooms, fruits, and dies during the second year.

BINOMIAL—the two-word Latinized scientific name of an organism; the first word describes the genus, the second the species.

BROAD-LEAVED—any evergreen tree or shrub that has relatively broad leaves, such as rhododendron and holly, as distinguished from needle-bearing evergreens, such as firs, pines, hemlocks, and spruces.

CAMBIUM—in woody vegetation, the layer of cells that lies between the secondary xylem and secondary phloem cell layers; through a process of cell division, the cambium produces the secondary xylem and the secondary phloem, which are also known, respectively, as the wood and the innermost living bark.

CANOPY—the more or less continuous cover of branches and foliage formed collectively by the crowns of adjacent trees and other woody vegetation; layers of canopy may be called stories.

CARBOHYDRATE—any of a group of chemical compounds, including sugars, starches, and cellulose, containing carbon, hydrogen, and oxygen only.

CASTOREUM—the material from the anal scent glands of beaver (*Castor canadensis*).

CATASTROPHIC EVENTS—events that result from a great and sudden calamity or disaster; in the case of a forest, these include windstorms, wildfire, floods, snowslides, volcanic eruptions, and insect outbreaks.

CAVITY—the hollow excavated in snags by birds; used for roosting and reproduction by many birds and mammals.

CAVITY EXCAVATION—the process of digging or chipping a cavity in dead wood.

CAVITY EXCAVATOR—an animal that excavates a cavity in wood for nesting or roosting.

CAVITY NESTER—a species of wildlife that nests in a cavity.

CELLULOSE—the main constituent of all plant tissues and fibers—an amorphous carbohydrate polymer used in the manufacture of many fibrous products, including paper, textiles, and explosives.

CHAR—to burn the surface of; scorch; to reduce to charcoal by incomplete combustion.

CHLOROPHYLL—any of a group of related green pigments found in organisms possessing photosynthesis.

CLIMAX—the culminating stage in plant succession for a given site, at which the vegetation is self-reproducing and thus has reached a stable condition through time.

CLIMAX FOREST—a forest plant community that represents the culminating stage of forest succession for a particular site.

CLOACA—a single chamber through which the contents of the digestive, excretory, and reproductive systems pass.

CLOSED CANOPY—the condition that exists when the canopy created by trees, shrubs, or both is dense enough to exclude most of the direct sunlight from the forest floor.

COLONIZATION— the process or act of establishing a colony or colonies.

COLONY—a group of the same kind of plants or animals living together.

COMMUNITY—a group of one or more populations of plants and/or animals using a common area; an ecological term used in a broad sense to include groups of plants and animals of various sizes and degrees of integration.

COMPOUND—a substance composed of two or more chemical elements.

CONIFER—the most important order of the Gymnospermae, comprising a wide range of trees, mostly evergreens that bear cones and have needle-shaped or scalelike leaves; timber commercially identified as softwood.

CONIFEROUS — cone bearing.

CONIFEROUS FOREST — a forest dominated by cone-bearing trees.

CORTEX — a layer of tissue in roots and stems lying between the outermost layer of cells or protective covering of a plant and the vascular tissue.

CROP — the vegetation growing on an area; in forestry it is thought of as the major woody growth forming the forest crop—any wood fiber that is harvestable.

CROWN — the upper part of a tree or other woody plant that carries the main branching system and foliage and that surmounts at the crown's base a more or less clean stem.

CYCLING — to occur in or pass through a cycle; to move in, or as if in, a circle.

DECAY — in wood, the decomposition by fungi or other microorganisms resulting in softening, progressive loss of strength and weight, and changes in texture and color.

DECIDUOUS — pertaining to any plant organ, such as a leaf, that is shed naturally; perennial plants that shed their leaves and are therefore leafless for some time during the year.

DECOMPOSE, DECOMPOSITION — to separate into component parts or elements; to break down; to decay or putrefy.

DELAYED IMPLANTATION — a fertilized egg that floats around in the uterus for some time before it becomes implanted or attached to the wall of the uterus and begins to grow.

DENDRITIC — a pattern that resembles the branching of a hardwood tree.

DENSE CANOPY — a condition in which the forest canopy is essentially closed and the foliage is particularly thick or luxuriant. See also CLOSED CANOPY.

DIVERSITY — the relative degree of abundance of species of plants and animals, functions, communities, habitats, or habitat features per unit of area.

DOMINANT — species of plants or groups of plants that, by means of their numbers, coverage of an area, or size, influence or control the existence of associated species; also, individual animals that determine the behavior of one or more other animals in a way that establishes a social hierarchy.

DOMINANT TREE — see DOMINANT.

DYNAMIC — characterized by or tending to produce continuous change.

ECOLOGICAL — an adjective that identifies a relationship between living organisms and their nonliving, physical environment.

ECOSYSTEM — all the living organisms interacting with their nonliving, physical environment, considered as a unit.

ECOTOMYCORRHIZA — fungi that form a symbiotic relationship with the roots of plants in which the fungus mantles the surface of the host rootlet with mycelial tissue and grows between the cells of the rootlet cortex.

ECOTONE — the area influenced by the transition between plant communities or between successional stages or vegetative conditions within a plant community.

EDGE — the place where plant communities or where successional stages or vegetative conditions within a plant community come together.

ENDEMIC — native or confined to a certain region; having a comparatively restricted distribution.

EPIPHYTE — a plant, such as a lichen or moss, that grows on another plant and depends on it for mechanical support but not as a source of nutrients.

EVERGREEN — having foliage that remains green and functional through more than one growing season.

EXTERNAL SUCCESSION — the changes in the plant community over time that surround a snag or fallen tree.

FECAL MATERIAL — material discharged from the bowels; more generally, any discharge from the digestive tract of an organism.

FORAGE — vegetation used for food by wildlife, particularly wild ungulates, such as deer and elk.

FORB — any herbaceous species of plant other than grasses, sedges, or rushes; fleshy-leaved plants.

FOREST — generally, that portion of the ecosystem characterized by tree cover; more particularly, a plant community predominantly of trees and other woody vegetation growing close together.

FOREST FLOOR — the surface layer of soil supporting forest vegetation.

FRASS — insect feces.

FUNCTION — the natural or proper action for which an organism or habitat or behavior has evolved.

FUNGAL — caused by or associated with fungi.

FUNGAL HYPHAE — see fungi and hyphae.

FUNGI — mushrooms, truffles, molds, yeasts, rusts, etc.; simply organized plants, unicellular or made of cellular filaments or strands called hyphae; lacking chlorophyll; reproduce asexually and sexually with the formation of spores.

GENE POOL — narrowly, the genic material of a localized interbreeding population; broadly, the genetic resources or materials of a species throughout its entire geographical distribution.

GENUS — the first word in a binomial or scientific name.

GERMINATE — to begin to grow, to sprout.

GIRDLING — making more or less continuous incisions around a living stem that cut through at least the bark and cambium and which ultimately kill woody vegetation.

GRAMINAE — the taxonomic family to which grasses belong.

GRASS — any species of plant that is a member of the family Graminae, characteristically having narrow leaves; hollow, jointed stems; and spikes or clusters of membranous flowers borne in smaller spikelets. Such plants collectively.

GUARD HAIR—any of the coarse hairs covering the underfur of certain mammals.

GYMNOSPERMAE—a group of woody plants having naked seeds, as distinguished from those having seeds enclosed in an ovary (Angiospermae).

HABITAT—the sum total of environmental conditions of a specific place occupied by a plant, or animal, or a population of such species.

HARD SNAG—a snag composed primarily of sound wood, particularly sound sapwood.

HARDWOOD—the wood of broad-leaved trees, and the trees themselves, belonging to the botanical group Angiospermae; distinguished from softwoods by the presence of vessels.

HEART ROT—any rot in a tree confined to the heartwood, associated with fungi and generally originating in a live tree.

HEARTWOOD—the inner layers of wood that, in a growing tree, have ceased to contain living cells and in which the reserve materials, such as starch, have been removed or converted into more durable substances.

HERB—a seed-producing annual, biennial, or perennial that does not develop persistent woody tissue but dies down at the end of a growing season.

HERBACEOUS—pertaining to or characteristic of an herb or nonwoody plant as distinguished from a woody plant.

HOCK—the joint on the hind leg of mammals, such as deer, elk, and horses, that corresponds to the human ankle.

HOME RANGE—the area that an animal covers during its normal daily (twenty-four hour) activities and which it does not defend against others of its own kind.

HUMIDITY—see relative humidity.

HUMUS—a general term for the more or less decomposed plant and animal residues in the soil, litter being therefore excluded.

HUMUS LAYER—the surface layer of soil composed of or dominated by organic material, whether or not the organic material is incorporated with mineral soil.

HYDROPHOBIC SOIL—soil that repels water; water cannot penetrate it.

HYPHA (s.), HYPHAE (pl.)—filament or strand of a fungus thallus (nonreproductive vegetative body), which is composed of one or more cylindrical cells; increases by growth at its tip; gives rise to new hyphae by lateral branching.

INNER BARK—part of the living tissue of a tree situated just under the nonliving outer bark. See also CAMBIUM.

INOCULATION—introduction of an organism into a new environment.

INOCULUM—the material transferred by an inoculation; the act of introducing material, such as fungal spores, from one area to another or from one organism to another, such as tree to tree.

INORGANIC—involving neither organic life nor the products of organic life; not composed of organic matter; especially minerals.

INORGANIC COMPOUND—a chemical compound that does not involve organic products.

INSECTIVOROUS—an animal that eats insects and other invertebrate animals.

INTEGRATION—coordination of parts into a functioning whole, as in a plant community.

INTEGRATOR—something that expresses the combined influences of a number of interacting variables, such as a main stream, which is an integrator of all its tributaries, and the ocean is the final integrator of all its rivers.

INTEGRITY—the state of being unimpaired; soundness; completeness; unity.

INTERNAL SUCCESSION—the process of change stimulated primarily by decay and deterioration in a snag or fallen tree.

INVERTEBRATE—an animal lacking a backbone or spinal column.

LARVA (s.), LARVAE (pl.)—the general term for the newly hatched, earliest stage of any of various animals that undergo metamorphosis, such as insects, frogs, and salamanders; the larva differs markedly in form and appearance from the adult.

LARVAL FORM—the form or shape of a larva.

LICHEN—a plant that is actually two plants in one; the outer plant is a fungus housing the inner plant, an alga.

LIGNIN—the chief noncarbohydrate constituent of wood, a polymer that functions as a natural binder and support for the cellulose fibers of woody plants.

LITTER—the uppermost layer of organic debris on the forest floor; essentially the freshly fallen or slightly decomposed vegetable material, mainly foliate or leaf litter, but also twigs, fragments of bark, flowers, and fruits.

LITTER FALL—the fall of litter to the forest floor.

LOOKOUT—a structure used by an animal for a better vantage point.

MATURE FOREST—a forest primarily composed of or dominated by mature trees in vigorous condition. See also MATURITY.

MATURE TREE—see MATURITY.

MATURITY—in physiology, the stage at which a tree or other plant has attained full development and is in full production of seeds.

METABOLITES—any of various organic compounds produced by metabolism, which is the complex of physical and chemical processes involved in the maintenance of life.

METAMORPHOSIS—a marked change in appearance, character, condition, or function, such as a tadpole changing into a frog or a caterpillar changing into a butterfly.

METATARSAL GLAND—scent glands located on the insides of the hind legs of deer in the area of the hock; they are visible as tufts of long, stiff hairs.

MICROBE—microscopic organism.

MICROCLIMATE — the essentially uniform local climate of a usually small site or habitat, such as the inside of a rodent's burrow.

MICROORGANISM — a microscopic organism.

MICROSCOPIC — too small to be seen by the unaided eye, large enough to be seen with the aid of a microscope; exceedingly small; minute.

MINERAL SOIL — soil composed mainly of inorganic materials and with a relatively low amount of organic material.

MYCELIUM — the vegetative part of a fungus, consisting of a mass of branching threadlike filaments or strands called hyphae.

MYCORRHIZA — the symbiotic relationship of a fungus with the roots of certain plants.

NICTITATING MEMBRANE — the thin membrane found in many animals at the inner angle or beneath the lower lid of the eye and capable of being drawn across the eyeball.

NITROGEN FIXATION — the conversion of elemental nitrogen (N_2) from the atmosphere to organic combinations or to forms readily usable in biological processes.

NITROGEN-FIXING BACTERIA — bacteria that can take nitrogen gas out of the air and transform it into an organic compound that plants can use.

NURSERY COLONY — a congregating of bats for the purpose of giving birth and nurturing their young.

NURSE TREE — a dead, fallen tree that fosters tree seedlings by protecting them from such environmental factors as wind, insolation, or frost, or by providing appropriate conditions of rooting medium, moisture, nutrients, and microclimate.

NUTRIENT CYCLING — the circulation of elements, such as nitrogen and carbon, through specific pathways from the living and nonliving portions of the environment and back again; all mineral and nutrient cycles involving plants, animals, and humans — such as the carbon cycle, phosphorous cycle, and nitrogen cycle.

OBLIGATORY — restricted to one mode of life, necessary for survival.

OPEN CANOPY — a canopy condition that allows large amounts of direct sunlight to reach the forest floor.

ORGAN — a distinct part of a plant or animal that has one or more particular functions.

ORGANIC — of, pertaining to, or derived from living organisms; of or designating compounds containing the element carbon. See INORGANIC.

ORGANIC COMBINATIONS — mixtures of organic substances.

ORGANIC COMPOUND — a chemical compound that involves carbon and is derived from living organisms. See INORGANIC.

ORGANIC MATTER IN SOIL — material derived from plants and animals, much of it in an advanced state of decay.

ORGANISM — any living individual of any species of plant or animal.

PAEDOGENIC — individual larval salamanders that become sexually mature in the larval form.

PARASITE — an organism living in or on another organism.

PATHOGEN — any agent causing what is defined as a disease, such as a bacterium or fungus.

PELAGE — the coat of a mammal, consisting of hair, fur, wool, or other soft covering, as distinct from bare skin.

PELT — the skin of a dead animal with the fur or hair still on it; a stripped animal skin ready for tanning.

PERENNIAL — a plant that persists for several years, usually with new herbaceous growth.

PHLOEM — the food-conducting tissue of vascular plants, consisting of sieve tubes and other cellular material. Compare to xylem.

PHOTOSYNTHESIS — the process by which chlorophyll-containing cells in green plants convert sunlight to chemical energy and make organic compounds from inorganic compounds, especially carbohydrates from carbon dioxide and water, with the simultaneous release of oxygen.

PIT-AND-MOUND TOPOGRAPHY — the roughened surface of the forest floor caused by the residual pits or holes in the ground that are left when a tree is uprooted, and the accompanying root wad that forms a mound next to the pit.

POLYMER — any of numerous natural and synthetic compounds of unusually high molecular weight consisting of up to millions of repeated linked units, each a relatively light and simple molecule.

PREDATOR — any animal that kills and feeds on other animals.

PRIMARY CAVITY NESTER — any species of wildlife that excavates its own nest cavity in a snag.

PRIMARY EXCAVATOR — a species that digs or chips out cavities in wood to provide itself or its mate with a site for roosting or nesting.

RELATIVE HUMIDITY — the ratio of the amount of water vapor in the air at a specific temperature to the maximum capacity of the air to contain water vapor at that temperature.

ROOT WAD — the mass of roots, soil, and rocks that remains intact when a tree, shrub, or stump is uprooted.

SAPLING — a young tree more than a few feet high and an inch in diameter at breast height, growing vigorously and without dead bark or more than an occasional dead branch.

SAPROPHYTE — a plant that lives on and derives its nourishment from dead or decaying organic matter.

SAPWOOD — the outer layer of wood in a growing tree that contains living cells and reserve materials, such as starch.

SCIENTIFIC NAME — the binomial or two-word Latinized name of an organism; the first word describes the genus, the second the species.

SECONDARY CAVITY NESTER—a species of animal that occupies a cavity in a snag that was excavated by another species.

SEEDLING—a young tree grown from seed from the time of germination until it becomes a sapling; the division between seedling and sapling is indefinite and may be arbitrarily fixed.

SHADE-INTOLERANT PLANT—a species of plant that does not germinate or grow well in shade.

SHADE-TOLERANT PLANT—a species of plant that both germinates and grows well in shade.

SHRUB—a plant with persistent woody stems and relatively low growth form; usually produces several basal shoots as opposed to a single stem; differs from a tree by its low stature and non-treelike form.

SLOPE—the incline of the land surface measured in degrees from the horizontal; also characterized by the compass direction in which it faces.

SNAG—a standing, dead tree from which the leaves and most of the branches have fallen; such a tree broken off but still more than twenty feet tall.

SOFT SNAG—a snag composed primarily of wood in advanced stages of decay and deterioration, particularly in the sapwood portions.

SOFTWOOD—the soft wood of a coniferous tree (Gymnospermae, such as fir or pine) as distinguished from the hard wood from a deciduous tree (Angiospermae, such as oak or maple). See HARDWOOD.

SOFTWOOD EXCAVATORS—cavity-excavating birds that can excavate only in soft snags.

SOIL—earth material so modified by physical, chemical, and biological agents that it will support rooted plants.

SPECIES—a unit of classification of plants and animals consisting of the largest and most inclusive array of sexually reproducing and crossfertilizing individuals that share a common gene pool.

SPERMATOPHORE—a specialized capsule containing sperm that is deposited by the male salamander and fastened to some object in such a way that the female salamander can walk over it, pick it up with her cloaca, and fertilize her eggs.

SPORE—a single- or several-celled reproductive body that becomes detached from the parent and gives rise to a new individual; occurs in all groups of plants but particularly in bacteria and fungi.

SPOROCARP—a multicellular structure in which spores are formed and mature.

STEM—the principal axis of a plant from which buds and shoots develop; with woody species, the term applies to all ages and thicknesses.

STREAM ORDER—streams are characterized by their order. Headwater stream channels are designated first-order; two first-order streams combine to form a second-order stream; two second-order streams combine to form a third-order stream; and so forth.

STRUCTURAL DIVERSITY — in part, diversity in a forest that results from layering or tiering of the canopy; an increase in layering or tiering leads to an increase in structural diversity.

STUMP — the woody base of a tree left in the ground after the stem breaks off and falls.

SUBCLIMAX — a stage in the ecological succession of a plant or animal community immediately preceding the climax, and often persisting because of the effects of fire, flood, or other major disturbance.

SUCCESSION — the changes that take place as a plant community, and its attending animal community, evolve from bare ground to climax.

SUCCESSIONAL STAGE — a stage or recognizable condition of a plant community, and its attending animal community, that occurs during its development from bare ground to climax.

SUMMER RANGE — a range, usually at higher elevation than a winter range, used by deer and elk during the summer; a summer range is usually much more extensive than a winter range. See also HOME RANGE.

SUNNING — the process of an animal methodically exposing itself to direct sunlight; also called sunbathing.

SUPPRESSION — the process of competition between trees in a young forest for soil nutrients, water, sunlight, and space in which to grow; more vigorous trees suppress the growth of weaker ones, often leading to their death.

SYMBIOSIS — the relationship of two or more different organisms living in a close association that may be but is not necessarily of benefit to each; sometimes obligatory to one or more of the organisms in the relationship.

SYMBIOTIC — two different organisms living together in relationship.

TALUS — the accumulation of broken rock that occurs at the base of cliffs or other steep slopes.

TERRITORY — any area that an individual of a given species of animal defends against another individual of its own kind.

THALLOPHYTE — a plant in any one of the phyla of fungi and algae.

THALLUS — the body of a plant that is not differentiated into leaves, stems, and roots; one- to many-celled, such as thallophytes.

THERMAL COVER — cover used by animals to ameliorate effects of weather.

TRACHEIDS — any of the elongated, tapering, supporting, and conductive cells in woody tissue.

TRUFFLE — a general term for the fruiting body of any of various fleshy belowground fungi; some kinds are esteemed as food by humans.

UNDERFUR — the dense, soft, fine fur beneath the coarse outer hairs of certain mammals.

UNGULATE — a mammal with hooves.

VALVULAR — having valvelike parts.

VASCULAR PLANT — any plant that contains vessels.

VEGETATIVE — engaged in nutritive and growth functions as contrasted with reproductive functions.

VESSEL — one of the tubular conductive structures of woody plants, consisting of cylindrical, often-dead cells that are attached end to end.

WATER-HOLDING CAPACITY — a measure of the ability of soil, wood, or some other substance to soak up and hold water.

WHORL — the arrangement of three or more branches radiating from a single stem at a given point above the ground; characteristic of the way Douglas-fir branches.

WINTER RANGE — a range, usually at lower elevation than a summer range, used by migratory deer and elk during the winter; usually better defined and smaller than a summer range. See also HOME RANGE.

WOODY — containing wood fibers.

XYLEM — the supporting and water-conducting tissue of vascular plants, consisting primarily of tracheids and vessels; woody tissue. Compare to phloem.

YEAST — any of various one-celled fungi that reproduce by budding—dividing their bodies into new, one-celled individuals—and that are capable of fermenting carbohydrates.

YOUNG FOREST — a forest that is dominated by trees that are older than seedlings and younger than mature trees.

Common and Scientific Names of Plants and Animals Cited in the Text

PLANTS

FUNGI
bird's nest fungus, Nidulariaceae
brown cubical rot, *Laetiporus sulphureus*
laminate root rot, *Phellinus weiri*
needle-cast fungus, Hypodermataceae
puff-ball fungus, *Lycoperdon* spp.
rust fungus, Melamsoraceae

TREES AND SHRUBS
acacia, *Acacia* spp.
beech, *Fagus* spp.
bigleaf maple, *Acer macrophyllum*
birch, *Betula* spp.
bitterbrush, *Purshia tridentata*
blackcap, *Rubus leucodermis*
black huckleberry, *Vaccinium membranaceum*
blueberry, *Vaccinium ovalifolium*
blue elderberry, *Sambucus cerulea*
bristle-cone pine, *Pinus aristata*
cranberry, *Vaccinium macrocarpon*
Douglas-fir, *Pseudotsuga menziesii*
doum palm, *Hyphaene thebaica*
elm, *Ulmus* spp.
fir, *Abies* spp.
giant sequoia, *Sequoia gigantea*
grand fir, *Abies grandis*
hemlock, *Tsuga* spp.
hickory, *Carya* spp.
huckleberry, *Vaccinium* spp.
juniper, *Juniperus* spp.
Indian peach, *Osmaronia cerasiformis*
larch, *Larix* spp.
lodgepole pine, *Pinus contorta*
maple, *Acer* spp.
mountain hemlock, *Tsuga mertensiana*

mountain-mahogany, *Cercocarpus ledifolius*
mountain spiraea, *Spiraea densiflora*
noble fir, *Abies procera*
oak, *Quercus* spp.
Pacific dogwood, *Cornus nuttallii*
Pacific rhododendron, *Rhododendron macrophyllum*
Pacific yew, *Taxus brevifolia*
pine, *Pinus* spp.
pinyon pine, *Pinus monophylla*
ponderosa pine, *Pinus ponderosa*
quaking aspen, *Populus tremuloides*
red alder, *Alnus rubra*
red elderberry, *Sambucus racemosa*
sagebrush, *Artemisia* spp.
salal, *Gaultheria shallon*
salmonberry, *Rubus spectabilis*
serviceberry, *Amelanchier alnifolia*
shining Oregon grape, *Berberis nervosa*
silver fir, *Abies amabilis*
Sitka spruce, *Picea sitchensis*
snowbush, *Ceanothus velutinus*
spruce, *Picea* spp.
stink currant, *Ribes bracteosum*
subalpine fir, *Abies lasiocarpa*
sycamore, *Plantanus* spp.
tamarack, *Larix laricina*
thimbleberry, *Rubus parviflorus*
trailing blackberry, *Rubus ursinus*
vine maple, *Acer circinatum*
western hemlock, *Tsuga heterophylla*
western redcedar, *Thuja plicata*
whitebark pine, *Pinus albicaulis*
white pine (eastern), *Pinus strobus*
white spruce, *Picea glauca*
willow, *Salix* spp.

LIVERWORTS
liverwort, Hepaticae

FERNS
deer fern, *Blechnum spicant*
swordfern, *Polystichum munitum*

GRASSES AND GRASSLIKE PLANTS
California fescue, *Festuca californica*
European beachgrass, *Ammophila arenaria*
sedge, *Carex* spp.

HERBS
alpine shooting star, *Dodecatheon alpinum*
aster, *Aster* spp.
avalanche lily, *Erythronium montanum*
balsamroot, *Balsamorhiza* spp.
beargrass, *Xerophyllum tenax*
bedstraw, *Galium* spp.
beggar-tick, *Bidens* spp.
bluebells, *Mertensia paniculata*
bunchberry, *Cornus canadensis*
camas, *Camassia quamash*
cattail, *Typha* spp.
columbine, *Aquilegia formosa*
dandelion, *Taraxacum officinale*
Drummond's cinquefoil, *Potentilla drummondii*
dwarf mistletoe, *Arceuthobium* spp.
false bugbane, *Trautvetteria caroliniensis*

false Solomon's seal, *Smilacina racemosa*
fawnlily, *Erythronium grandiflorum*
gentian, *Gentiana sceptrum*
goldenrod, *Solidago canadensis*
grass-of-Parnassus, *Parnassia fimbriata*
Gray's lovage, *Ligusticum grayi*
hawksbeard, *Crepis* spp.
lily-of-the-valley, *Maianthemum dilatatum*
lupine, *Lupinus* spp.
monkeyflower, *Mimulus guttatus*
monkshood, *Aconitum columbianum*
old-man-in-the-spring, *Senecio vulgaris*
orchid, Orchidaceae
paintbrush, *Castilleja* spp.
pearly-everlasting, *Anaphalis margaritacea*
prince's pine, *Chimaphila umbellata*
skunk cabbage, *Lysichitum americanum*
spring beauty, *Claytonia lanceolata*
spring queen, *Synthyris reniformis*
stonecrop, *Sedum* spp.
subalpine buttercup, *Ranunculus eschscholtzii*
subalpine lupine, *Lupinus latifolius*
thistle, *Cirsium* spp.
tiger lily, *Lilium columbianum*
twinflower, *Linnaea borealis*
white bog orchid, *Habenaria dilatata*
wild strawberry, *Fragaria vesca*
wood violet, *Viola glabella*
yellow wood violet, *Viola sempervirens*

INVERTEBRATES

INSECTS
alderfly, Sialidae
aphid, Aphididae
bark beetles and ambrosia beetles, Scolytidae
beetles, Coleoptera
butterfly, Lepidoptera
carpenter ant, *Camponotus* spp.
Cascade tiger beetle, *Cicindela longilabris ostenta*
cricket, Gryllidae
dance fly, *Empis* spp.
Dejean tiger beetle, *Omus dejeani*
depressed tiger beetle, *Cicindela depressula*
Douglas-fir beetle, *Dendroctonus pseudotsugae*

Douglas-fir tussock moth, *Orgyia pseudotsugata*
flat-headed wood-borer, Buprestidae
flea, Siphonaptera
fly, Diptera
golden buprestid, *Buprestis aurulenta*
grasshopper, Acrididae
ground beetles, Carabidae
lacewing, Chrysopidae
leafhopper, Homoptera
louse, Anoplura
mayfly, Ephemeroptera
midge, Chironomidae
moth, Lepidoptera
mountain pine beetle, *Dendroctonus ponderosae*
Oregon tiger beetle, *Cicindela oregona*

Pacific dampwood termite, *Zootermopsis angusticollis*, *Z. nevadensis*
phantom crane fly, Ptychopteridae
pin-hole borer, Platypodidae
ponderous borer, *Ergates spiculatus*
psocid, Psocidae
rain beetle, *Pleocoma dubitalis*
redbellied checkered beetle, *Enoclerus sphegeus*
round-headed wood-borer, Cerambycidae
stonefly, Plecoptera
syrphid fly, Syrphidae
tent caterpillars, Lasiocampidae
termite, Isoptera
western spruce budworm, *Choristoneura fumiferana*, *C. occidentalis*

MILLIPEDES
millipede, Diplopoda

SNAILS
slug, Pulmonata
snail, Pulmonata

SPIDERS AND ALLIES
daddy-longlegs (harvestmen), Phalangida
mite, Acarina
pseudoscorpion, Pseudoscorpionida
spider, Araneida
tick, Ixodides

WORMS
earthworm, Annelida
horsehair worm, Nematomorpha
leach, Annelida
worm, Annelida

VERTEBRATES

FISH
carp, *Siphateles altarcus*, *S. gibbarcus*, *Notropis angustarca* (all extinct)
chinook salmon, *Oncorhynchus tschawytscha*
cutthroat trout, *Salmo clarki*
Pacific herring, *Clupea harengus*
sand lance, *Ammodytes hexapterus*
steelhead trout, *Salmo gairdneri*
sucker, *Chamistes oregonus*, *C. betrachops* (both extinct)

AMPHIBIANS
clouded salamander, *Aneides ferreus*
Oregon salamander, *Ensatina eschscholtzi*
Oregon slender salamander, *Batrachoseps wrighti*
Pacific giant salamander, *Dicamptodon ensatus*
Pacific treefrog, *Hyla regilla*
salamander, Caudata
tailed frog, *Ascaphus truei*
toad, *Bufo* spp.

REPTILES
common garter snake, *Thamnophis sirtalis*

Egyptian skink, *Chalcides ocellatus*
lizard, Lacertilia
snake, Ophidia
western skink, *Eumeces skiltonianus*

BIRDS
band-tailed pigeon, *Columba fasciata*
belted kingfisher, *Ceryle alcyon*
black-billed magpie, *Pica pica*
blue grouse, *Dendragapus obscurus*
brown creeper, *Certhia americana*
chestnut-backed chickadee, *Parus rufescens*
common raven, *Corvus corax*
dark-eyed junco, *Junco hyemalis*
guillemot, *Cepphus* spp.
golden eagle, *Aquila chrysaetos*
gray jay, *Perisoreus canadensis*
great blue heron, *Ardea herodias*
great horned owl, *Bubo virginianus*
green barbat, *Megalaima zeylanica*
hairy woodpecker, *Picoides villosus*
house wren, *Troglodytes aedon*
Lewis' woodpecker, *Melanerpes lewis*
marbled murrelet, *Brachyramphus marmoratus*
murre, *Uria* spp.
northern flicker, *Colaptes auratus*

northern goshawk, *Accipiter gentilis*
olive-sided flycatcher, *Contopus borealis*
pileated woodpecker, *Dryocopus pileatus*
puffin, *Fratercula* spp.
red-breasted nuthatch, *Sitta canadensis*
red-tailed hawk, *Buteo jamaicensis*
ruffed grouse, *Bonasa umbellus*
rufous hummingbird, *Selasphorus rufus*
sage grouse, *Centrocercus urophasianus*
sapsucker, *Sphyrapicus* spp.
spotted owl, *Strix occidentalis*
Steller's jay, *Cyanocitta stelleri*
Swainson's thrush, *Catharus ustulatus*
tree swallow, *Tachycineta bicolor*
turkey vulture, *Cathartes aura*
varied thrush, *Ixoreus naevius*
Vaux's swift, *Chaetura vauxi*
western bluebird, *Sialia mexicana*
western screech-owl, *Otus kennicottii*
western tanager, *Piranga ludoviciana*
woodpeckers, Picidae

MAMMALS
bear, *Arctotherium* spp. (extinct)
beaver, *Castor*, probably n. sp.
  (extinct), *C. canadensis*
big brown bat, *Eptesicus fuscus*
bighorn sheep, *Ovis canadensis*
bison (buffalo), *Bison bison*
black bear, *Ursus americanus*
black-tailed deer, *Odocoileus hemionus*
black-tailed jackrabbit, *Lepus
  californicus*
bobcat, *Felis rufus*
bushy-tailed woodrat, *Neotoma cinerea*
California bat, *Myotis californicus*
camel, *Camelops hesternus, Tanupolama*
  spp., *Eschatius* spp. (all extinct)
chickaree, *Tamiasciurus douglasi*
clouded leopard, *Neofelis nebulosa*
coast mole, *Scapanus orarius*
coyote, *Canis latrans*
creeping vole, *Microtus oregoni*
deer mouse, *Peromyscus maniculatus*
dire-wolf, *Canis* cf. *dirus* (extinct)
Dorcas gazelle, *Gazella dorcas*
elk, *Cervus elaphus*
gray wolf, *Canis lupus*
ground sloth, *Mylodon*, near *harlani*
  (extinct)
heather vole, *Phenacomys intermedius*
hoary bat, *Lasiurus cinereus*

horse, *Equus caballus, E. pacificus*
  (extinct), *E.* spp. minor (extinct)
little brown bat, *Myotis lucifugus*
long-eared bat, *Myotis evotis*
long-legged bat, *Myotis volans*
long-tailed weasel, *Mustela frenata*
lynx, *Felis lynx*
mammoth, *Elephas? columbi* (extinct)
mantled ground squirrel, *Spermophilus
  lateralis*
marsh shrew, *Sorex bendirei*
marten, *Martes americana*
Mazama pocket gopher, *Thomomys
  mazama*
mink, *Mustela vison*
mountain beaver, *Aplodontia rufa*
mountain cottontail, *Sylvilagus nuttalli*
mouse, Cricetidae
muskrat, *Fiber oregonus* (extinct)
northern flying squirrel, *Glaucomys
  sabrinus*
northern water shrew, *Sorex palustris*
Old World otter, *Lutra lutra*
Oregon red tree vole, *Arborimus
  longicaudus*
ox, *Bos taurus*
Pacific jumping mouse, *Zapus trinotatus*
peccary, *Platygonus* cf. *vetus, P.* spp.
  minor (both extinct)
pika, *Ochotona princeps*
porcupine, *Erethizon dorsatum*
puma, *Felis concolor*
raccoon, *Procyon lotor*
red squirrel, *Tamiasciurus hudsonicus*
river otter, *Lutra canadensis*
Ruppel's sand fox, *Vulpes ruppeli*
seal, Phocidae
sea otter, *Enhydra lutris*
short-tail weasel, *Mustela erminea*
shrew, *Sorex* spp.
shrew-mole, *Neürotrichus gibbsi*
silver-haired bat, *Lasionycteris
  noctivagans*
snow leopard, *Uncia uncia*
snowshoe hare, *Lepus americanus*
spotted skunk, *Spilogale putorius*
Townsend big-eared bat, *Plecotus
  townsendi*
Townsend chipmunk, *Eutamias
  townsendi*
Trowbridge shrew, *Sorex trowbridgei*
vole, Arvicolidae

western red-backed vole, *Clethrionomys californicus*
white-tailed jackrabbit, *Lepus townsendi*
woodrat, *Neotoma* spp.
yellow-bellied marmot, *Marmota flaviventris*

yellowpine chipmunk, *Eutamias amoenus*
Yuma bat, *Myotis yumanensis*

Bibliography

Abercrombie, T. J. 1988. When the Moors ruled Spain. Natl. Geographic 174:86–119.

Aho, P. E. 1982. Indicators of cull in western Oregon. USDA For. Serv. Gen. Tech. Rep. PNW-144. Pac. Northwest. For. and Range Exp. Sta., Portland, Ore. 17 pp.

Aho, P. E., R. J. Seidler, H. J. Evans, and P. N. Raju. 1974. Distribution, enumeration, and identification of nitrogen-fixing bacteria associated with decay in living white fir trees. Phytopathology. 64:1413–20.

Aleksiuk, M. 1968. Scent-mound communication, territoriality, and population regulation in beaver (*Castor canadensis* Kuhl). J. Mammal. 49:759–62.

Allison, I. S. 1966. Fossil Lake, Oregon, its geology and fossil faunas. Studies in Geology No. 9. Ore. State Univ., Corvallis. 48 pp.

Altig, R., and E. D. Brodie, Jr. 1972. Laboratory behavior of *Ascaphus truei* tadpoles. J. Herpetol. 6:21–24.

Amman, G. D., M. D. McGregor, D. B. Cahill, and W. H. Klein. 1977. Guidelines for reducing losses of lodgepole pine to the mountain pine beetle in unmanaged stands in the Rocky Mountains. USDA For. Serv. Gen. Tech. Rep. INT-36. Intermount. For. and Range Exp. Sta., Ogden, Utah. 19 pp.

Anderson, R. F. 1960. Forest and shade tree entomology. John Wiley & Sons, New York. 428 pp.

Anderson, S. and J. N. Jones, Jr., eds. 1967. Recent mammals of the world: a synopsis of families. Ronald Press, New York. 453 pp.

Antonelli, A. L., R. A. Nussbaum, and S. D. Smith. 1972. Comparative food habits of four species of stream-dwelling vertebrates (*Dicamptodon ensatus, D. copei, Cottus tenuis, Salmo gairdneri*). Northw. Sci. 46:277–89.

Arden, H. 1987. "The fire that never dies." Natl. Geographic 172:375–403.

Asia's population nearing 3 billion. *Corvallis Gazette-Times*, Corvallis, Ore., 2 July 1988.

Ayre, G. L. 1963. Laboratory studies on the feeding habits of seven species of ants (Hymenoptera: Formicidae) in Ontario. Can. Entomol. 95:712–15.

Bailey, V. 1923. The combing claws of the beaver. J. Mammal. 4:77–79.

———. 1926. How beavers build their houses. J. Mammal. 7:41–44.

———. 1936. The mammals and life zones of Oregon. N. Amer. Fauna 55:1–416.

Barbour, R. W., and W. H. Davis. 1969. Bats of America. Univ. Kentucky Press, Lexington. 286 pp.

Barr, D. J., and D. N. Swanston. 1970. Measurement of creep in a shallow, slide-prone till soil. Amer. J. Sci. 269:467–80.

Baumhoff, M. A., and R. F. Heizer. 1967. Postglacial climate and archaeology in the desert west. *In* The Quaternary of the United States, edited by J. E. Wright, Jr., and D. G. Frey, 697–707. Princeton Univ. Press, Princeton, N.J.

Beasley, R. S. 1976. Contribution of subsurface flow from the upper slopes of a forested watershed to channel flow. Soil Sci. Soc. Amer. J. 40:955–57.

Beatty, S. W. 1984. Influence of microtopography and canopy species on spatial patterns of forest understory plants. Ecology 66:1406–19.

Becker, G. 1971. Physiological influences on wood-destroying insects of wood compounds and substances produced by microorganisms. Wood Sci. and Tech. 5:236–46.

Bent, A. C. 1964a. Life histories of North American cuckoos, goatsuckers, hummingbirds, and their allies. Part two. Dover, New York, pp. 244–506.

———. 1964b. Life histories of North American nuthatches, wrens, thrashers, and their allies. Dover, New York. 475 pp.

———. 1964c. Life histories of North American woodpeckers. Dover, New York. 334 pp.

Binford, L. C., B. G. Elliot, and S. W. Singer. 1975. Discovery of a nest and the downy young of the marbled murrelet. Wilson Bull. 87:303–4.

Binns, A. 1967. Peter Skene Ogden: Fur trader. Binfords & Mort, Portland, Ore. 363 pp.

Bogan, M. A. 1972. Observations on parturition and development in the hoary bat, *Lasiurus cinereus*. J. Mammal. 53:611–14.

Bookhout, T. A. 1965. Breeding biology of snowshoe hares in Michigan's upper peninsula. J. Wildl. Manage. 29:296–303.

Borman, F. H., and G. E. Likens. 1979. Pattern and process in a forested ecosystem. Springer-Verlag, New York. 253 pp.

Borror, D. J., and D. M. Delong. 1964. An introduction to the study of insects. Rev. ed. Rinehart and Winston, New York. 819 pp.

Bratton, S. P. 1976. Resource division in an understory herb community: responses to temporal and microtopographic gradients. Amer. Nat. 110:679–93.

Brenner, F. J. 1964. Reproduction of the beaver in Crawford County, Pennsylvania. J. Wildl. Manage. 28:743–47.

Breznak, J. A. 1975. Symbiotic relationships between termites and their intestinal microbiota. *In* Symbiosis Symposium, edited by D. H. Jennings and D. L. Lee, 559–80. Cambridge Univ. Soc. of For. Exp. Biol. Ser. 29.

————. 1982. Intestinal microbiota of termites and other xylophagous insects. Ann. Rev. Microbiol. 36:323–43.

Brockmann, C. F. 1968. Trees of North America. Western Publ., Racine, Wis. 280 pp.

Brodie, H. J. 1951. The splash-cup dispersal mechanism in plants. Can. J. Bot. 29:224–34.

Brown, H. A. 1975. Temperature and development of the tailed frog, *Ascaphus truei*. Comp. Biochem. Physiol. 50A:397–405.

Brownlee, R. G., R. M. Silverstein, D. Müller-Schwarze, and A. G. Singer. 1969. Isolation, identification, and function of the chief component of the male tarsal scent in black-tailed deer. Nature 221:284–85.

Bull, E. L. 1975. Habitat utilization of the pileated woodpecker, Blue Mountains, Oregon. M.S. thesis. Ore. State Univ., Corvallis. 58 pp.

Bull, E. L., and E. C. Meslow. 1977. Habitat requirements of the pileated woodpecker in northeastern Oregon. J. For. 75:335–37.

Burroughs, E. R., Jr., and B. R. Thomas. 1977. Declining root strength in Douglas-fir after felling as a factor in slope stability. USDA For. Serv. Res. Pap. INT-190. Intermount. For. and Range Exp. Sta., Odgen, Utah. 27 pp.

Bury, R. B. 1972. Small mammals and other prey in the diet of the Pacific giant salamander (*Dicamptodon ensatus*). Amer. Midl. Nat. 87:524–26.

Bury, R. B., and M. Martin. 1973. Comparative studies on the distribution and foods of plethodontid salamanders in the redwood region of northern California. J. Herpetol. 7:331–35.

Call, M. O., and C. Maser. 1985. Sage grouse. *In* Wildlife habitats in managed rangelands: the Great Basin of southeastern Oregon, edited by J. W. Thomas and C. Maser. USDA For. Serv. Gen. Tech. Rep. PNW-187. Pac. Northwest. For. and Range Exp. Sta., Portland, Ore. 30 pp.

Camp, C. L. 1918. Excavations of burrows of the rodent *Aplodontia*, with observations on the habits of the animal. Univ. Calif. Publ. Zool. 17:517–36.

Camp, W. H. 1956. The forests of the past and present. *In* A world geography of forest resources, edited by S. Haden-Guest et al., 13–47. Ronald Press, New York.

Campbell, R. W., and T. R. Torgersen. 1982. Some effects of predaceous ants on western spruce budworm pupae in north central Washington. Environ. Entomol. 11:111–14.

———. 1983a. Compensatory mortality in defoliator population dynamics. Environ. Entomol. 12:630–32.

———. 1983b. Effect of branch height on predation of western spruce budworm (Lepidoptera: Tortricidae) pupae by birds and ants. Environ. Entomol. 12:697–99.

Carter, D. C. 1970. Chiropteran reproduction. *In* About bats, edited by B. H. Slaughter and D. W. Walton, 233–46. South. Methodist Univ. Press, Dallas, Tex.

Carter, H. R. 1984. At-sea biology of the marbled murrelet (*Brachyramphus marmoratus*) in Barkley Sound, British Columbia. M.S. thesis. Univ. of Manitoba, Winnipeg.

Carter, H. R., and S. G. Sealy. 1984. Marbled murrelet mortality due to gill-net fishing in Barkley Sound, British Columbia. *In* Marine birds: their feeding ecology and commercial fisheries relationships, edited by D. N. Nettleship, G. A. Sanger, and P. F. Springer, 212–20. Can. Wildl. Serv. Special Publ.

———. 1987a. Fish-holding behavior of marbled murrelets. Wilson Bull. 99:289–91.

———. 1987b. Inland records of downy young and fledgling marbled murrelets in North America. Murrelet 68:58–63.

Castello, J. D., C. G. Shaw, and M. M. Furniss. 1976. Isolation of *Cryptoporous volvatus* and *Fomes pinicola* from *Dendoctonus pseudotsugae*. Phytopathology 66:1431–34.

Cattelino, P. J., I. R. Noble, R. O. Slatyer, and S. R. Kessell. 1979. Predicting the multiple pathways of plant succession. Environ. Manage. 3:41–50.

Chamberlin, T. W. 1972. Interflow in the mountainous forest soils of coastal British Columbia. *In* Mountain geomorphology: geomorphological processes in the Canadian Cordillera, B.C., 121–27. Geogr. Soc. 14, Tantalus Res. Ltd., Vancouver, B.C.

Chamberlin, W. J. 1949. Insects affecting forest products and other materials. Ore. State Coll. Coop. Assoc., Corvallis, Ore. 159 pp.

Childs, T. W. 1963. *Poria weirii* root rot. Phytopathology 53:1124–27.

Christy, J. E., P. Sollins, and J. M. Trappe. 1982. First-year survival of *Tsuga heterophylla* without mycorrhizae and subsequent ectomycorrhizal development on decaying logs and mineral soil. Can. J. Bot. 60:1601–5.

Clark, J. G. D. 1952. Prehistoric Europe: the economic basis. Methuen & Co., London. 349 pp.

Cline, S. P., A. B. Berg, and H. M. Wight. 1980. Snag characteristics and dynamics in Douglas-fir forests, western Oregon. J. Wildl. Manage. 44:773–86.

Colbert, E. H. 1973. Wandering land and animals. E. P. Dutton, New York. 323 pp.

Conner, R. N. 1979. Seasonal changes in woodpecker foraging methods: strategies for winter survival. *In* The role of insectivorous birds in forest ecosystems, edited by J. G. Dickson, R. N. Conner, R. R. Fleet, et al., 95–105. Academic Press, New York.

Conner, R. N., R. G. Hooper, H. S. Crawford, H. S. Mosby. 1975. Woodpecker nesting habitat in cut and uncut woodlands in Virginia. J. Wildl. Manage. 39:144–50.

Conner, R. N., O. K. Miller, and C. S. Adkisson. 1976. Woodpecker dependence on trees infected by fungal heart rots. Wilson Bull. 88:575–81.

Cooper, C. F. 1961. The ecology of fire. Sci. Amer. 204:150–60.

Corning, H. M. 1947. Willamette landings: ghost towns of the river. Binfords & Mort, Portland, Ore. 201 pp.

Coues, E. 1965. History of the expedition under the command of Lewis and Clark. 3 vols. Dover, New York. 1364 pp.

Cowan, B. D., and W. P. Nagel, 1965. Predators of the Douglas-fir beetle. Ore. State. Univ. Agricul. Exp. Sta. Tech. Bull. 86:1–32.

Cowan, I. McT. 1936. Nesting habits of the flying squirrel, *Glaucomys sabrinus*. J. Mammal. 17:58–60.

Cowan, I. McT., and C. J. Guiguet, 1965. The mammals of British Columbia. B.C. Prov. Mus. 11:1–141.

Cramblet, H. M., and R. L. Ridenhour. 1956. Parturition in *Aplodontia*. J. Mammal. 37:87–90.

Dalquest, W. W. 1948. Mammals of Washington. Univ. Kans. Mus. Nat. Hist. Publ. 2:1–444.

Dalquest, W. W., and D. R. Orcutt. 1942. The biology of the least shrewmole, *Neürotrichus gibbsii minor*. Amer. Midl. Nat. 27:387–401.

Dasmann, R. F., and R. D. Taber. 1956. Behavior of Columbia black-tailed deer with reference to population ecology. J. Mammal. 37:143–64.

Deagan, K. A. 1987. La Navidad, 1492: searching for Columbus's lost colony. Natl. Geographic 172:672–75.

DeBell, D. S., and J. F. Franklin. 1987. Old-growth Douglas-fir and western hemlock: a 36-year record of growth and mortality. West. J. Appl. For. 2:111–14.

Denslow, J. S. 1980. Gap partitioning among tropical rain forest trees. Biotropica 12 (Suppl.):47–55.

de Vlaming, V. L., and R. B. Bury. 1970. Thermal selection in tadpoles of the tailed frog, *Ascaphus truei*. J. Herpetol. 4:179–89.

de Vries, J., and T. L. Chow. 1978. Hydraulic behavior of a forested mountain soil in coastal British Columbia. Water Resour. Res. 14:935–42.

Deyrup, M. A. 1975. The insect community of dead and dying Douglas-fir. 1: The Hymenoptera. Ecosyst. Anal. Stud. Bull. 6, Conif. Forest Biome, Univ. Wash., Seattle. 104 pp.

———. 1976. The insect community of dead and dying Douglas-fir: Diptera, Coleoptera, and Neuroptera. Ph.D. dissertation. Univ. Wash., Seattle. 540 pp.

———. 1981. Deadwood decomposers. Nat. Hist. 90:84–91.

Dillon, L. S. 1956. Wisconsin climate and life zones in North America. Science 123:167–76.

Dix, R. L. 1964. A history of biotic and climatic changes within the North American grassland. *In* Grazing in terrestrial and marine environments, edited by D. J. Crisp, 71–89. Blackwells Sci. Publ., Dorking, England.

Dorf, E. 1960. Climatic changes of the past and present. Amer. Sci. 48:341–46.

Downey, C. 1987. Thanksgiving myths and misconceptions. *Corvallis Gazette-Times*, Corvallis, Ore. Nov. 22.

Dyrness, C. T. 1967. Mass soil movements in the H. J. Andrews Experimental Forest. USDA For. Serv. Res. Pap. PNW-42. Pac. Northwest For. and Range Exp. Sta., Portland, Ore. 12 pp.

———. 1973. Early stages of plant succession following logging and burning in the western Cascades of Oregon. Ecology 54:57–69.

———. 1976. Effect of wildfire on soil wettability in the High Cascades of Oregon. USDA For. Serv. Res. Pap. PNW-202. Pac. Northwest For. and Range Exp. Sta., Portland, Ore. 18 pp.

Eichrodt, R. 1969. Ueber die Bedeutung von Moderholz für die natürliche Verjüngen in subalpinen Fichtenwald. Zürich: Eidg. Tech. Hochsch. Diss. No. 4261. 123 pp.

Engelhardt, N. T. 1957. Pathological deterioration of looper-killed western hemlock on southern Vancouver Island. For. Sci. 3:125–36.

Erickson, A. W., J. E. Nellor, and G. A. Petrides. 1964. The black bear in Michigan. Mich. State Univ. Res. Bull. 4. 102 pp.

Esenther, G. R., and T. K. Kirk. 1974. Catabolism of aspen sapwood in *Reticulitermes flavipes* (Isoptera: Rhinotermitidae). Ann. Entomol. Soc. Amer. 67:989–91.

Etheridge, D. E. 1973. Wound parasites causing tree decay in British Columbia. Pac. For. Res. Cent., For. Pest Leafl. No. 62. 15 pp.

Evans, K. E., and R. N. Conner. 1979. Snag management. *In* Proceedings of the workshop on management of northcentral and northeastern forests for nongame birds, edited by R. M. DeGraaf and K. E. Evans, pp. 211–225; USDA For. Serv. Gen. Tech. Rep. NC-51. North Central For. Exp. Sta., Minneapolis.

Fellin, D. G. 1975. Feeding habits of *Pleocoma* larvae in coniferous forests of western Oregon. Northw. Sci. 49:71–86.

Fellin, D. G., and P. O. Ritcher. 1967. Distribution of *Pleocoma* species in Oregon with notes on the habitat of *P. simi* and *P. carinata*. Pan-Pac. Entomol. 43:251–63.

Ferron, J. 1983. Scent marking by cheek rubbing in the northern flying squirrel (*Glaucomys sabrinus*), Can. J. Zool. 61:2377–80.

Flook, D. R. 1970. A study of sex differential in the survival of wapiti. Can. Wildl. Serv. Rep. Ser. 11:1–71.

Forsman, E. D. 1976. A preliminary investigation of the spotted owl in Oregon. M.S. thesis. Ore. State Univ., Corvallis. 127 pp.

Forsman, E. D., E. C. Melsow, and M. J. Strub. 1977. Spotted owl abundance in young versus old-growth forests, Oregon Wildl. Soc. Bull. 5:43–47.

Forsman, E. D., E. C. Melsow, and H. M. Wight. 1984. Distribution and biology of the spotted owl in Oregon. Wildl. Monogr. No. 87:1–64.

Fowler, H. G., and R. B. Roberts. 1980. Foraging behavior of the carpenter ant, *Camponotus pennsylvanicus* (Hymenoptera: Formicidae) in New Jersey. J. N.Y. Entomol. Soc. 53:295–304.

Francke-Grosmann, H. 1967. Ectosymbiosis in wood-inhabiting insects. *In* Symbiosis, vol. 2, edited by S. M. Henry, 142–205. Academic Press, New York.

Frank, A. B. 1885. Über die auf Wurzelsymbiose beruhende Ernährung gewisser Bäume durch unterirdische Pilze. Deut. Bot. Ges. Ber. 3:128–45.

Franklin, J. F., and C. T. Dyrness. 1973. Natural vegetation of Oregon and Washington. USDA For. Serv. Gen. Tech. Rep. PNW-8. Pac. Northwest For. and Range Exp. Sta., Portland, Ore. 417 pp.

Franklin, J. F., K. Cromack, Jr., W. Denison, A. McKee, C. Maser, J. Sedell, F. Swanson, and G. Judy. 1981. Ecological characteristics of old-growth Douglas-fir forests. USDA For. Serv. Gen. Tech. Rep. PNW-118. Pac. Northwest For. and Range Exp. Sta., Portland, Ore. 48 pp.

Franklin, J. F., H. H. Shugart, and M. E. Harmon. 1987. Tree death as an ecological process: the causes, consequences, and variability of tree mortality. BioScience 37:550–56.

Franklin, W. L. 1968. Herd organization, territoriality, movements and home ranges in Roosevelt elk. M.S. thesis. Humboldt State Coll., Arcata, Calif. 89 pp.

Franklin, W. L., A. S. Mossman, and M. Dole. 1975. Social organizations and home range of Roosevelt elk. J. Mammal. 56:102–18.

Furniss, M. M., and P. W. Orr. 1970. Douglas-fir beetle. USDA For. Serv. For. Pest Leafl. 5. Gov. Print. Off., Wash., D.C. 4 pp.

Furniss, R. L., and V. M. Carolin. 1977. Western forest insects. USDA For. Serv. Misc. Publ. 1339. Gov. Print. Off., Wash., D.C. 654 pp.

Gabrielson, I. N., and S. G. Jewett. 1970. Birds of the Pacific Northwest, with special reference to Oregon. Dover, New York. 650 pp.

Gaiser, R. N. 1952. Root channels and roots in forest soils. Soil Sci. Soc. Amer. Proc. 16:62–65.

Gartor, E. O., and L. A. Langelier. 1983. Effects of stand characteristics on avian predators of western spruce budworm. *In* The role of the host in the population dynamics of forest insects, edited by L. Safranyik, 65–72. IUFRO Conf., Pac. Res. Cent. Can. For. Serv., Victoria, B.C.

Gothan, W., and H. Weyland. 1954. Lehrbuch der Paläobotanik. Akademie Verlag, Berlin. 535 pp.

Gotwald, W. H., Jr. 1968. Food gathering behavior of the ant *Camponotus noveboracensis* (Fitch) (Hymenoptera: Formicidae). J. N.Y. Entomol. Soc. 76:278–96.

Graf, W. 1955. The Roosevelt elk. Port Angeles Evening News, Port Angeles, Wash. 105 pp.

———. Territorialism in deer. J. Mammal. 37:165–70.

Graham, A., and C. Heimsch. 1960. Pollen studies of some Texas peat deposits. Ecology 41:751–63.

Graham, R. 1982. Biomass dynamics of dead Douglas-fir and western hemlock boles in mid-elevation forests of the Cascade Range. Ph.D. dissertation. Ore. State Univ., Corvallis. 152 pp.

Graham, S. A. 1924. Temperature as a limiting factor in the life of subcortical insects. J. Econ. Entomol. 17:377–83.

———. 1925. The felled tree trunk as an ecological unit. Ecology 6:397–411.

Graham, S. A., and F. B. Knight. 1965. Principles of forest entomology. 4th ed. McGraw-Hill, New York. 417 pp.

Grange, W. B. 1932. Observations on the snowshoe hare, *Lepus americanus phaeonotus* Allen. J. Mammal. 13:1–19.

Grayson, D. K. 1977. On the Holocene history of some northern Great Basin lagomorphs. J. Mammal. 58:507–13.

———. 1979. Mount Mazama, climatic change, and Fort Rock Basin archaeofaunas. *In* Volcanic activity and human ecology, 427–57. Academic Press, New York.

———. 1987. The biogeographic history of small mammals in the Great Basin: observations on the last 20,000 years. J. Mammal. 68:359–75.

Green, G. W., and C. R. Sullivan. 1950. Ants attacking larvae of the forest tent caterpillar, *Malacosoma disstria* Hbn. (Lepidoptera: Lasiocampidae). Can. Entomol. 82:194–95.

Greenhall, A. M., and J. L. Paradiso. 1968. Bats and bat banding. USDI, Bur. Sport Fish. and Wildl. Resour. Publ. 72:1–48.

Gregory, P. H. 1949. The operation of the puff-ball mechanism of *Lycoperdon perlatum* by raindrops shown by ultra-high-speed schlieren cinematography. Trans. Brit. Mycol. Soc. 32:11–15.

Grier, C. C. 1975. Wildfire effects on nutrient distribution and leaching in a coniferous ecosystem. Can. J. For. Res. 5:599–607.

Griffin, J. B. 1967. Late Quaternary prehistory in the northeastern woodlands. *In* The Quaternary of the United States, edited by J. E. Wright, Jr., and D. G. Frey, 655–67. Princeton Univ. Press, Princeton, N.J.

Guilday, J. E., P. W. Parmalee, and H. W. Hamilton. 1977. The Clark's Cave bone deposits and the late Pleistocene paleoecology of the Central Appalachian Mountains of Virginia. Carnegie Mus. Nat. Hist. Bull. 2:1–87.

Guthrie, R. D. 1966. The extinct wapiti of Alaska and Yukon Territory. Can. J. Zool. 44:47–57.

Hadfield, J. S. 1985. Laminated root rot: a guide for reducing and preventing losses in Oregon and Washington forests. USDA For. Serv., PNW Region For. Pest Manage. 13 pp.

Hafsten, V. 1961. Pleistocene development of vegetation and climate in the Southern High Plains as evidenced by pollen analysis. *In* Paleoecology of the Llano Estacado, edited by F. Wendorf, 59–91. Fort Burgwin Res. Cent. Publ. No. 1. Mus. of New Mexico Press, Santa Fe.

Hall, A. J. 1987. James Madison, architect of the Constitution. Natl. Geographic 172:340–73.

Hamilton, W. J., Jr., and W. R. Eadie. 1964. Reproduction in the otter, *Lutra canadensis*. J. Mammal. 45:242–52.

Hansen, E. M. 1977. Forest pathology: fungi, forests and man. *In* Mushrooms and man: an interdisciplinary approach to mycology, edited by T. Walters, 107–24. Linn Benton Comm. Coll., Albany, Ore.

———. 1979. Survival of *Phellinus weirii* in Douglas-fir stumps after logging. Can. J. For. Res. 9:484–88.

Harley, J. L. 1969. The biology of mycorrhiza. 2nd ed. Leonard Hill, London, England. 334 pp.

Harper, J. A. 1971. Ecology of Roosevelt elk. Ore. State Game Comm., Portland, Ore. 44 pp.

Harr, R. D. 1982. Fog drip in the Bull Run Municipal Watershed, Oregon. Water Resour. Bull. 18:785–89.

Harris, L. D. 1984. The fragmented forest. Univ. Chicago Press, Chicago. 211 pp.

Harris, L. D., C. Maser, and A. McKee. 1982. Patterns of old-growth harvest and implications for Cascades wildlife. Trans. N. Amer. Wildl. Nat. Resour. Conf. 47:374–92.

Harvey, A. E., M. F. Jurgensen, and M. J. Larsen. 1978. Seasonal distribution of ectomycorrhizae in a mature Douglas-fir/larch forest soil in western Montana. For. Sci. 24:203–8.

Harvey, A. E., M. J. Larsen, and M. F. Jurgensen. 1979a. Comparative distribution of ectomycorrhizae in soils of three western Montana forest habitat types. For. Sci. 25:350–58.

———. 1979b. Fire-decay: interactive roles regulating wood accumulation and soil development in the northern Rocky Mountains. USDA For.

Serv. Res. Note INT-263. Intermount. For. and Range Exp. Sta., Ogden, Utah. 4 pp.

Hayes, J. P., S. P. Cross, and P. W. McIntire. 1986. Seasonal variation in mycophagy by the western red-backed vole, *Clethrionomys californicus*, in southwestern Oregon. Northw. Sci. 60:250–57.

Helvey, J. D., A. R. Teidemann, and W. B. Fowler. 1974. Some climatic and hydrologic effects of wildfire in Washington State. Proc. Tall Timbers Fire Ecol. Conf. 15:201–22.

Hermann, R. K. 1976. Man and forests—a prodigal relation. *In* Forest and future resource conflicts, 29–51. Northw. Area Found. For. Ser., Ore. State Univ. Dep. of Print., Corvallis.

————. 1982. The genus *Pseudotsuga*: historical records and nomenclature. For. Res. Lab., Ore. State Univ., Corvallis. Spec. Publ. 2a:1–29.

————. 1985. The genus *Pseudotsuga*: ancestral history and past distribution. For. Res. Lab., Ore. State Univ., Corvallis. Spec. Publ. 2b:1–32.

Hillinger, C. 1987. Russia's colony in America. *Corvallis Gazette-Times*, Corvallis, Ore. December 27.

Hitchcock, C. L., and A. Cronquist. 1973. Flora of the Pacific Northwest. Univ. Wash. Press, Seattle. 730 pp.

Hirsch, K. V., D. A. Woodby, and L. B. Astheimer. 1981. Growth of a nestling marbled murrelet. Condor 83:264–65.

Horn, E. L. 1972. Wildflowers 1: the Cascades. Touchstone Press, Beaverton, Ore. 159 pp.

Hornocker, M. G. 1969. Winter territoriality in mountain lions. J. Wildl. Manage. 33:457–64.

————. 1970. An analysis of mountain lion predation upon mule deer and elk in the Idaho Primitive Area. Wildl. Monogr. 21:1–39.

Hopkins, D. M. 1959. Cenozoic history of the Bering Land Bridge. Science 129:1519–28.

Hoyt, S. F. 1957. The ecology of the pileated woodpecker. Ecology 38:246–56.

Imms, A. D. 1960. A general textbook of entomology. E. P. Dutton, New York. 886 pp.

Ingles, L. G. 1961. Reingestion in the mountain beaver. J. Mammal. 42:411–12.

Jackman, S. M. 1974. Woodpeckers of the Pacific Northwest: their characteristics and their role in the forest. M.S. thesis. Ore. State Univ., Corvallis. 147 pp.

Jackson, H. H. T. 1961. Mammals of Wisconsin. Univ. Wis. Press, Madison. 504 pp.

Johnson, M. L. 1973. Characters of the heather vole, *Phenacomys*, and the red tree vole, *Arborimus*. J. Mammal. 54:239–44.

Johnson, N. E., K. R. Shea, and R. L. Johnsey. 1964. Mortality and deterioration of looper-killed hemlock in western Washington. J. For. 62:162–63.

Jones, D. 1972. "The earth is sacred." Environ. Action. Nov. 11. p. 7.

Jonkel, C. J., and I. McT. Cowan. 1971. The black bear in the spruce-fir forest. Wildl. Monogr. 27:1–57.

Judge, J. 1988. Exploring America's forgotten century. Natl. Geographic 173:330–62.

Kagan, D., S. Ozment, and F. M. Turner. 1983. The western heritage. 2nd ed. Macmillan, New York. 1078 pp.

Kaufman, M. 1988. Deforested Himalayas become staggering ecological disaster. *The Sunday Oregonian*, Portland. May 15.

Kessel, E. L. 1955. The mating activities of balloon flies. Systematic Zool. 4:97–104.

Kindschy, R. R., Jr., and E. J. Larrison. 1961. Observations on a captive mountain beaver. Murrelet 42:1–3.

Koide, R. T., and H. A. Mooney. 1987. Spatial variation in inoculum potential of vesicular-arbuscular mycorrhizal fungi caused by formation of gopher mounds. New Phytol. 107:173–82.

Koonce, A. L., and L. F. Roth. 1980. The effects of prescribed burning on dwarf mistletoe in ponderosa pine. *In* Proc. Conf. on Fire and Meteorol., Soc. Amer. For. 6., 197–203.

Kozloff, E. N. 1976. Plants and animals of the Pacific Northwest. Univ. Wash. Press, Seattle. 264 pp.

Kreisel, H. 1961. Die Entwicklung der Mykozönose an *Fagus*-Stubben auf norddeutschen Kahlschlägen. Feddes Repert. Beih. 19:227–32.

Kritzman, E. B. 1972. A captive shrew-mole and her litter. Murrelet 53:47–49.

Larsen, M. J., M. F. Jurgensen, and A. E. Harvey. 1978. N_2 fixation associated with wood decayed by some common fungi in western Montana. Can. J. For. Res. 8:341–45.

———. 1982. N_2 fixation in brown-rotted soil woods in an intermountain cedar-hemlock ecosystem. For. Sci. 28:292–96.

Li, C. Y., and M. A. Castellano. 1987. *Azospirillum* isolated from within sporocarps of the mycorrhizal fungi *Hebeloma crustuliniforme*, *Laccaria laccata*, and *Rhizopogon vinicolor*. Trans. Br. Mycol Soc. 88:563–65.

Li, C. Y., C. Maser, Z. Maser, and B. A. Caldwell. 1986. Role of three rodents in forest nitrogen fixation in western Oregon: another aspect of mammal–mycorrhizal fungus–tree mutualism. Great Basin Nat. 46:411–14.

Liers, E. E. 1951. Notes on the river otter (*Lutra canadensis*). J. Mammal. 32:1–9.

Lucia, E. 1983. Tillamook burn country: a pictorial history. Caxton Printers, Ltd. Caldwell, Idaho. 305 pp.

Maiorana, V. C. 1977. Observations of salamanders (Amphibia, Urodela, Plethodontidae) dying in the field. J. Herptol. 11:1–5.

Mannan, R. W., E. C. Meslow, and H. M. Wight. 1980. Use of snags by birds in Douglas-fir forests, western Oregon. J. Wildl. Manage. 44:787–97.

Marks, G. C. and T. T. Kozlowski, eds. 1973. Ectomycorrhizae: their ecology and physiology. Academic Press, New York. 444 pp.

Marshall, D. B. 1988. Status of the marbled murrelet in North America with special emphasis on populations in Washington, Oregon, and California. Unpublished report prepared for the Audubon Society of Portland, Ore. 42 pp.

Martin, P. 1971. Movements and activities of the mountain beaver (*Aplodontia rufa*). J. Mammal. 52:717–23.

Maser, C. 1966. Life histories and ecology of *Phenacomys albipes*, *Phenacomys longicaudus*, *Phenacomys silvicola*. M.S. thesis. Ore. State Univ., Corvallis. 221 pp.

———. 1967. Black bear damage to Douglas-fir in Oregon. Murrelet 48:34–38.

———. 1969–1983. Unpublished field notes, species accounts, and catalogs on file at Burke Museum, Univ. of Wash., Seattle.

———. 1976. Notes on the sexual behavior of *Cicindela oregona*. Cicindela 8:13–14.

———. 1977a. Notes on *Cicindela oregona* in Oregon. Cicindela 9:61–64.

———. 1977b. Notes on *Omus dejeani*. Cicindela 9:35–38.

———. 1988a. The redesigned forest. R. & E. Miles, San Pedro, Calif. 234 pp.

———. 1988b. Restoration and the future of land management. Restoration and Manage. Notes 6:28–29.

Maser, C., R. Anderson, and E. L. Bull. 1981. Aggregation and sex segregation in northern flying squirrels in northeastern Oregon: an observation. Murrelet 62:54–55.

Maser, C., R. G. Anderson, K. Cromack, Jr., J. T. Williams, and R. E. Martin. 1979. Dead and down woody material. *In* Wildlife habitats in managed forests: the Blue Mountains of Oregon and Washington, edited by J. W. Thomas, 78–95. USDA Agricul. Handb. 553. Gov. Print. Off., Wash. D.C.

Maser, C., and F. M. Beer. 1984. Notes on cicindelid habitats in Oregon. Cicindela 16:39–60.

Maser, C., and J. F. Franklin. 1974. Checklist of vertebrate animals of the Cascade Head Experimental Forest. USDA For. Serv. Resour. Bull. PNW-51. Pac. Northwest. For. and Range Exp. Sta., Portland, Ore. 32 pp.

Maser, C., and Z. Maser. 1987. Notes on mycophagy in four species of mice in the genus *Peromyscus*. Great Basin Nat. 47:308–13.

————. 1988. Interactions among squirrels, mycorrhizal fungi, and coniferous forests in Oregon. Great Basin Nat. 48:358–69.

Maser, C., B. R. Mate, J. F. Franklin, and C. T. Dyrness. 1981. Natural history of Oregon coast mammals. USDA For. Serv. Gen. Tech. Rep. PNW-133. Pac. Northwest. For. and Range. Exp. Sta., Portland, Ore. 496 pp.

Maser, C., Z. Maser, J. W. Witt, and G. Hunt. 1986. The northern flying squirrel: a mycophagist in southwestern Oregon. Can. J. Zool. 64:2086–89.

Maser, C., and R. S. Rohweder. 1983. Winter food habits of cougars from northeastern Oregon. Great Basin Nat. 43:425–28.

Maser, C., and J. M. Trappe. 1984a. The fallen tree: a source of diversity. *In* New forests for a changing world, 16–20. Proc. Soc. Amer. For. Natl. Conv., Bethesda, Md.

————, eds. 1984b. The seen and unseen world of the fallen tree. USDA For. Serv. Gen. Tech. Rep. PNW-164. Pac. Northwest. For. and Range Exp. Sta., Portland, Ore. 56 pp.

Maser, C., J. M. Trappe, and C. Y. Li. 1984. Large woody debris and long-term forest productivity. *In* Proceedings Pacific Northwest Bioenergy Systems: Policies and Applications. Bonneville Power Admin., Portland, Ore. 6 pp.

Maser, C., J. M. Trappe, and R. A. Nussbaum. 1978. Fungal–small mammal interrelationships with emphasis on Oregon coniferous forests. Ecology 59:799–809.

Maser, C., J. M. Trappe, and D. C. Ure. 1978. Implications of small mammal mycophagy to the management of western coniferous forests. Trans. North Amer. Wildl. and Nat. Resour. Conf. 43:78–88.

Maser, Z., C. Maser, and J. M. Trappe. 1985. Food habits of the northern flying squirrel (*Glaucomys sabrinus*) in Oregon. Can. J. Zool. 63:1084–88.

Matteson, F. S. 1877. Mountain boomer. Amer. Nat. 11:434–35.

McAllister, T. 1988. Marbled murrelet enters old-timber fray. *The Oregonian*, Portland, Ore. January 14.

McArthur, L. A. 1965. Oregon geographic names. 3rd ed. Binfords & Mort, Portland. 686 pp.

McCambridge, W. F., G. D. Amman, and G. C. Trostle. 1979. Mountain pine beetle. USDA For. Serv. For. Insect & Dis. Leaflet 2. Gov. Print. Off., Wash., D.C. 7 pp.

McClelland, B. R. 1979. The pileated woodpecker in forests of the northern Rocky Mountains. *In* The role of insectivorous birds in forest ecosystems, edited by J. G. Dickson, R. N. Conner, R. R. Fleet, et al., 283–99. Academic Press, New York.

McClelland, B. R. and S. S. Frissell. 1975. Identifying forest snags useful for hole-nesting birds. J. For. 73:414–17.

McComb, W. C., and R. E. Noble. 1981a. Microclimates of nest boxes and natural cavities in bottomland hardwoods. J. Wildl. Manage. 45:284–89.
———. 1981b. Nest-box and natural-cavity use in three mid-south forest habitats. J. Wildl. Manage. 45:93–101.
McKee, B. 1972. Cascadia: the geologic evolution of the Pacific Northwest. McGraw-Hill, New York. 394 pp.
McKeever, S. 1960. Food of the northern flying squirrel in northeastern California. J. Mammal. 41:270–71.
McKenzie, D. S., and R. M. Storm. 1970. Patterns of habitat selection in the clouded salamander, *Aneides ferreus* (Cope). Herptologica 26:450–54.
Meeker, J. W. 1988. Minding the Earth. The Latham Foundation, Alameda, Calif. 110 pp.
Meighan, C. W. 1967. Pacific Coast archaeology. *In* The Quaternary of the United States, edited by J. E. Wright, Jr., and D. G. Frey, 709–20. Princeton Univ. Press, Princeton, N.J.
Metter, D. E. 1964a. On breeding and sperm retention in *Ascaphus*. Copeia 1964:710–11.
———. 1964b. A morphological and ecological comparison of two populations of the tailed frog, *Ascaphus truei* Stejneger. Copeia 1964:181–95.
Miller, F. L. 1965. Behavior associated with parturition in black-tailed deer. J. Wildl. Manage. 29:629–31.
———. 1970. Distribution patterns of black-tailed deer (*Odocoileus hemionus columbianus*) in relation to environment. J. Mammal. 51:248–60.
———. 1971. Mutual grooming by black-tailed deer in northwestern Oregon. Can. Field-Nat. 85:295–301.
Miller, J. M., and K. P. Keen. 1960. Biology and control of the western pine beetle. USDA For. Serv. Mics. Publ. 800. Gov. Print. Off., Wash., D.C. 381 pp.
Minore, D. 1972. Germination and early growth of coastal tree species on organic seed beds. USDA For. Serv. Res. Pap. PNW-135. Pac. Northwest For. and Range Exp. Sta., Portland, Ore. 18 pp.
Mintzer, A. 1979. Colony foundation and pleometrosis in *Camponotus* (Hymenoptera: Formicidae). Pan-Pac. Entomol. 55:81–89.
Mitchell, R. 1987. Summary of mountain pine beetle biology. USDA For. Serv. Pac. Northw. Res. Sta., Silviculture Lab., Bend, Ore. Xerox, 2 pp.
Morgan, D. L. 1953. Jedediah Smith and the opening of the west. Univ. Neb. Press, Lincoln. 458 pp.
Morrison, P. H., and F. J. Swanson. In press. Fire history in two forest ecosystems of the central Western Cascade Range, Oregon. USDA For. Serv. Gen. Tech. Rep. Pac. Northwest Res. Sta., Portland, Ore.
Müller-Schwarze, D. 1969. Pheromone function of deer urine. Amer. Zool. 9:21.

————. 1972. Social significance of forehead rubbing in black-tailed deer (*Odocoileus hemionus columbianus*). Anim. Behav. 20:788–97.

Munford, K. 1988a. Acquisition caused stir. *Corvallis Gazette-Times*, Corvallis, Ore. February 8.

————. 1988b. War put British in control. *Corvallis Gazette-Times*, Corvallis, Ore. February 1.

————. 1988c. Waterways aided early explorers. *Corvallis Gazette-Times*, Corvallis, Ore. January 18.

Muul, I. 1969. Mating behavior, gestation period, and development of *Glaucomys sabrinus*. J. Mammal. 50:121.

Narr, K. J. 1956, Early food-producing populations. *In* Man's role in changing the face of the earth, edited by W. L. Thomas, Jr., 134–51. Univ. Chicago Press, Chicago.

Neff, J. A. 1928. A study of the economic status of the common woodpeckers in relation to Oregon horticulture. Free Press Print, Marionville, Mo. 68 pp.

Neitro, W. A., V. W. Binkley, S. P. Cline, R. W. Mannan, B. G. Marcot, D. Taylor, and F. F. Wagner. 1985. Snags (wildlife trees). *In* Management of wildlife and fish habitats in forests of western Oregon and Washington. Part 1: Chapter narratives, edited by E. R. Brown, 129–69. USDA For. Serv. Pac. Northwest. Region, Portland, Ore. Publ. Nos. R6-F & WL-192–1985.

Novakowski, N. S. 1969. The influence of vocalization on the behavior of beaver, *Castor canadensis* Kuhl. Amer. Midl. Nat. 81:198–204.

Nussbaum, R. A. 1969. Nests and eggs of the Pacific giant salamander, *Dicamptodon ensatus* (Eschscholtz). Herpetologica 25:257–62.

————. 1976. Geographic variation and systematics of salamanders of the genus *Dicamptodon* Strauch (Ambystomatidae). Misc. Publ. Mus. Zool. No. 149. Univ. Mich., Ann Arbor. 94 pp.

Nussbaum, R. A., E. D. Brodie, Jr., R. M. Storm. 1983. Amphibians and reptiles of the Pacific Northwest. Northw. Nat. Book., Univ. Press, Moscow, Idaho. 332 pp.

Nussbaum, R. A., and G. W. Clothier. 1973. Population structure, growth, and size of larval *Dicamptodon ensatus* (Eschscholtz). Northw. Sci. 47:218–27.

Nussbaum, R. A., and C. Maser. 1975. Food habits of the bobcat, *Lynx rufus*, in the Coast and Cascade Ranges of western Oregon in relation to present management policies. Northw. Sci. 49:261–66.

Okazaki, R., H. W. Smith, R. A. Gilkeson, and J. Franklin. 1972. Correlation of West Blacktail Ash with pyroclastic layer T from the 1800 A.D. eruption of Mount St. Helens. Northw. Sci. 46:77–89.

Paeth, R. C., M. E. Harward, E. G. Knox, and C. T. Dyrness. 1971. Factors affecting mass movement of four soils in the Western Cascades of Oregon. Soil Sci. Soc. Amer. Proc. 35:943–47.

Pattie, D. L. 1969. Behavior of captive marsh shrews (*Sorex bendirii*). Murrelet 50:27–32.

Perkins, J. M., and S. P. Cross. 1988. Differential use of some coniferous forest habitats by hoary and silver-haired bats in Oregon. Murrelet 69:21–24.

Péwé, T. L., D. M. Hopkins, and J. L. Giddings. 1965. The Quaternary geology and archaeology of Alaska. *In* The Quaternary of the United States, edited by J. E. Wright, Jr., and D. G. Frey, 355–74. Princeton Univ. Press, Princeton, N.J.

Pigeon, R. L., A. Bauer, A. C. Toogood, D. C. G. Dutcher, et al. 1987. 1787, the day-to-day story of the Constitutional Convention. Exeter Books, New York. 192 pp.

Pike, L. H., W. C. Denison, D. M. Tracy, M. A. Sherwood, and F. M. Rhoades. 1975. Floristic survey of epiphytic lichens and bryophytes growing on old-growth conifers in western Oregon. Bryologist 78:389–402.

Pike, L. H., R. A. Rydell, and W. C. Denison. 1977. A 400-year-old Douglas-fir tree and its epiphytes: biomass, surface area, and their distributions. Can. J. For. Res. 7:680–99.

Pirozynski, K. A., and D. W. Malloch. 1975. The origin of land plants: a matter of mycotrophism. BioSystems 6:153–64.

Placer, I. C. M. 1950. Comparative moisture regimes of humus and rotten wood. Can. Dep. Res. and Devel., For. Res. Div., Ottawa, Ontario. Silvic, Leafl. 37. 2 pp.

Poelker, R. J., and H. D. Harwell. 1973. Black bear of Washington. Wash. State Game Dep. Biol. Bull. 14:1–180.

Pricer, J. L. 1908. The life history of the carpenter ant. Biol. Bull. 14:177–218.

Pyne, S. J. 1982. Fire in America: a cultural history of wildland and rural fire. Princeton Univ. Press, Princeton, N.J. 654 pp.

Rabb, G. B. 1959. Reproductive and vocal behavior in captive pumas. J. Mammal. 40:616–17.

Rabitin, S. C., and L. H. Rhodes. 1982. *Acaulospora bireticulata* inside oribatid mites. Mycologia. 74:859–61.

Raphael, M. G, and M. White. 1984. Use of snags by cavity-nesting birds in the Sierra Nevada. Wildl. Monogr. 86:1–66.

Rausch, R. L. 1963. A review of the distribution of holarctic recent mammals. *In* Pacific Basin biogeography, edited by J. L. Gressitt, 29–43. Bishop Mus. Press, Honolulu.

Reed, C. A. 1965. North American birds eggs. Rev. ed. Dover, New York. 372 pp.

Reports of the Secretary of War. 1875–1899. Reports of the Chief of Engineers. *In* House executive documents, sessions of Congress. U.S. Gov. Print. Off., Wash., D.C. (Annual reports).

Ricek, E. W. 1967. Untersuchungen über die Vegetation auf Baumstümpfen. Teil I. Oberöesterr. Musealver. Jahrb. 112:185–252.

———. 1968. Untersuchungen über die Vegetation auf Baumstümpfen. Teil II. Oberöesterr. Musealver. Jahrb. 113:229–56.

Ritcher, P. O., and F. M. Beer. 1956. Notes on the biology of *Pleocoma dubitalis dubitalis* Davis. Pan-Pac. Entomol. 32:181–84.

Robbins, C. S., B. Bruun, and H. S. Zim. 1983. A guide to field identification of birds of North America. Golden Press, Western Publ., Racine, Wis. 360 pp.

Robinette, W. L., J. S. Gashwiler, and O. W. Morris. 1961. Notes on cougar productivity and life history. J. Mammal. 42:204–17.

Rogers, L. L. 1974. Shedding of foot pads by black bears during denning. J. Mammal. 55:672–74.

Roth, L. F. 1970. Disease in young-growth stands of Douglas-fir and western hemlock. *In* Management of young-growth Douglas-fir and western hemlock, edited by A. B. Berg, 34–38. Ore. State Univ., School of For. Pap. 666, Corvallis.

Runkle, J. R. 1982. Patterns of disturbance in some old-growth mesic forests of eastern North America. Ecology 63:1533–46.

Russell, O. 1955. Journal of a trapper: 1834–1843, edited by A. L. Haines. Univ. Neb. Press, Lincoln. 191 pp.

Sanders, C. J. 1964. The biology of carpenter ants in New Brunswick. Can. Ent. 96:894–909.

———. 1970. The distribution of carpenter ant colonies in the spruce-fir forests of northwestern Ontario. Ecology 51:865–73.

———. 1972. Seasonal and daily activity patterns of carpenter ants (*Camponotus* spp.) in northwestern Ontario (Hymenoptera: Formicidae). Can. Entomol. 104:1681–87.

Sanders, F. E., B. Mosse, and P. B. Tinker. 1975. Endomycorrhizas. Academic Press, London, England. 626 pp.

Sauer, C. O. 1952. Agricultural origins and dispersal. Amer. Geograph. Soc. 110 pp.

Scheffer, T. H. 1929. Mountain beavers in the Pacific Northwest: their habits, economic status, and control. U.S. Dep. Agricul. Farmer's Bull. 1958:1–18.

———. 1933. Breeding of the Washington varying here. Murrelet 14:77–78.

Scholar: Michelangelo had help. *Corvallis Gazette-Times*, Corvallis, Ore., 15 May 1988.

Schowalter, T. D. 1985. Adaptation of insects to disturbance. *In* The ecology of natural disturbance and patch dynamics, 235–455. Academic Press, New York.

Sealy, S. G. 1975a. Aspects of the breeding biology of the marbled murrelet in British Columbia. Bird-Banding 46:141–54.

———. 1975b. Feeding ecology of the ancient and marbled murrelets near Langara Island, British Columbia. Can. J. Zool. 53:418–33.

Seidensticker, J. C. IV, M. G. Hornocker, W. V. Wiles, and J. P. Messick. 1973. Mountain lion social organization in the Idaho Primitive Area. Wildl. Monogr. 35:1–60.

Severaid, J. H. 1942. The snowshoe hare: its life history and artificial propagation. Maine Dep. Inland Fish and Game. 95 pp.

Seward, A. C. 1941. Plant life through the ages. 2nd ed. Cambridge Univ. Press, London. 601 pp.

Shigo, A. L. 1973. A tree hurts, too. USDA For. Serv., Inf. Bull. NE-INF-16-73. Northeastern For. Exp. Sta., Broomall, Penn. 28 pp.

———. 1979. Tree decay, an expanded concept. Agricul. Inf. Bull. 419. USDA For. Serv., Wash., D.C. 72 pp.

Svihla, A., and R. D. Svihla. 1933. Notes on the jumping mouse *Zapus trinotatus trinotatus* Rhoads. J. Mammal. 14:131–34.

Shotwell, J. A. 1958. Evolution and biogeography of the aplodontid and mylagaulid rodents. Evolution 12:451–84.

Smith, C. C. 1970. The coevolution of pine squirrels (*Tamiasciurus*) and conifers. Ecol. Monog. 40:349–71.

Soldiers' remains returned after 174 years. *Corvallis Gazette-Times*, Corvallis, Ore., 1 July 1988.

Sollins, P., C. C. Grier, F. M. McCorison, K. Cromack, Jr., R. Fogel, and R. L. Fredriksen. 1980. The internal element cycles of an old-growth Douglas-fir ecosystem in western Oregon. Ecol. Monogr. 50:261–85.

Staebler, G. R. 1953. Mortality estimation in fully stocked stands of young-growth Douglas-fir. USDA For. Serv. Res. Pap. PNW-4. Pac. Northwest For. and Range Exp. Sta., Portland, Ore. 8 pp.

Stark, R. W. 1982. Generalized ecology and life cycle of bark beetles. *In* Bark beetles in North American conifers, edited by J. B. Milton and K. B. Sturgeon, 21–45. Univ. Texas Press, Austin.

Stebbins, R. C. 1954. Amphibians and reptiles of western North America. McGraw-Hill, New York. 528 pp.

———. 1985. A field guide to western reptiles and amphibians. 2d ed. Houghton Mifflin, Boston. 279 pp.

Stegner, W. 1979. The Oregon Trail . . . road to destiny. *In* Trails West, edited by R. L. Breeden, D. J. Crump, P. B. Silcott, and M. Windsor, 40–75. Special Publ. Div., Natl. Geographic Soc., Wash. D.C.

Stephens, E. P. 1956. The uprooting of trees: a forest process. Soil Sci. Soc. Proc. 113–16.

Stephenson, R. L. 1967. Quaternary human occupation of the plains. *In* The Quaternary of the United States, edited by J. E. Wright, Jr., and D. G. Frey, 685–96. Princeton Univ. Press, Princeton, N.J.

Stewart, O. C. 1956. Fire as the first great force employed by man. *In* Man's role in changing the face of the earth, edited by W. L. Thomas, Jr., 115–33. Univ. Chicago Press, Chicago.

Storm, R. M., and A. R. Aller. 1947. Food habits of *Aneides ferreus*. Herpetologica. 4:59–62.

Strickler, G. S., and P. J. Edgerton. 1976. Emergent seedlings from coniferous litter and soil in eastern Oregon. Ecology 57:801–7.

Studier, E. H. 1972. Some physical properties of the wing membranes of bats. J. Mammal. 53:623–25.

Sudworth, G. B. 1967. Forest trees of the Pacific slope. Dover, New York. 455 pp.

Swanson, F. J., and D. N. Swanston. 1977. Complex mass-movement terrains in the western Cascade Range, Oregon. Geol. Soc. Amer., Rev. Engrg. Geol. 3:113–24.

Swanston, D. N. 1971. Principal soil movement processes influenced by roadbuilding, logging and fire. *In* Forest land uses and stream environment, edited by J. T. Krygier and J. D. Hall, 29–40. For. Ext., Ore. State Univ., Corvallis.

Tabor, J. E. 1974. Productivity, survival, and population status of river otter in western Oregon. M.S. thesis. Ore. State Univ., Corvallis. 62 pp.

Tarsoff, F. J., A. Bisaillon, J. Pierard, and A. P. Whitt. 1972. Locomotory patterns and external morphology of river otter, sea otter, and harp seal (Mammalia). Can. J. Zool. 50:915–29.

Taylor, A. R. 1977. Lightning. *In* Lightning protection, vol. 2, edited by R. H. Golde, 831–49. Academic Press, London, England.

Taylor, W. P., and W. T. Shaw. 1927. Mammals and birds of Mount Rainier National Park. U.S. Gov. Print. Off., Wash., D.C. 249 pp.

Thomas, J. W., ed. 1979. Wildlife habitats in managed forests: the Blue Mountains of Oregon and Washington. USDA For. Serv. Agricul. Handb. No. 553. U.S. Gov. Print. Off., Wash., D.C. 511 pp.

Thomas, J. W., R. G. Anderson, C. Maser, and E. L. Bull. 1979. Snags. *In* Wildlife habitats in managed forests: the Blue Mountains of Oregon and Washington, edited by J. W. Thomas, 60–77. USDA For. Serv. Agricul. Handb. No. 553. U.S. Gov. Print. Off., Wash. D.C.

Thomas, J. W., H. Black, Jr., R. J. Scherzinger, and R. J. Pedersen. 1979. Deer and elk. *In* Wildlife habitats in managed forests: the Blue Mountains of Oregon and Washington, edited by J. W. Thomas, 104–27. USDA For. Serv. Agricul. Handb. No. 553. U.S. Gov. Print. Off., Wash., D.C.

Thomas, J. W., and C. Maser, eds. 1979–1985. Wildlife habitats in managed rangelands: the Great Basin of southeastern Oregon. USDA For. Serv. Pac. Northwest. For. and Range Exp. Sta., Portland. Ore. 638 pp.

Thompson, J. N. 1980. Treefalls and colonization patterns of temperate forest herbs. Amer. Midl. Nat. 104:176–84.

Toweill, D. E., and C. Maser. 1985. Food of cougars in the Cascade Range of Oregon. Great Basin Nat. 45:77–80.

Toweill, D. E., C. Maser, L. D. Bryant, and M. L. Johnson. 1988. Reproductive characteristics of eastern Oregon cougars. Northw. Sci. 62:147–50.

Toweill, D. E., C. Maser, M. L. Johnson, and L. D. Bryant. 1984. Size and reproductive characteristics of western Oregon cougars. *In* Proceedings of the Second Mountain Lion Workshop, edited by J. Roberson and F. Lindzey, 176–84. Utah Div. Wildl. Resour., Salt Lake City.

Trappe, J. M., and C. Maser. 1976. Germination of spores from *Glomus macrocarpus* (Endogonaceae) after passage through a rodent digestive tract. Mycologia 68:433–36.

———. 1978. Ectomycorrhizal fungi: interactions of mushrooms and truffles with beasts and trees. *In* Mushrooms and man: an interdisciplinary approach to mycology, edited by T. Walters, 165–79. Linn Benton Comm. Coll., Albany, Ore.

Trappe, J. M., and R. Fogel. 1978. Ecosystematic functions of mycorrhizae. *In* The belowground symposium: a synthesis of plant-associated processes, edited by J. K. Marshall, 205–14. Range Sci. Dept. Sci. Ser. 26. Colo. State Univ., Fort Collins.

Tsukada, M. 1985. *Pseudotsuga menziesii* (Mirb.) Franco: Its pollen dispersal and late Quaternary history in the Pacific Northwest. Jap. J. Ecol. 32:159–87.

Ursic, S. J., and R. J. Esher. 1988. Influence of small mammals on stormflow responses of pine-covered catchments. Water Resour. Bull. 24:133–39.

Von Haartman, L. 1968. The evaluation of resident versus migratory habits in birds: some considerations. Ornis. Fenn. 45:1–7.

Voth, E. H. 1969. Food habits of the Pacific mountain beaver, *Aplodontia rufa pacific* Merriam. Ph.D. dissertation. Ore. State Univ., Corvallis. 263 pp.

Walker, E. P., F. Warnick, S. Hamlet, K. I. Lange, M. A. Davis, H. E. Uible, and P. F. Wright. 1975. Mammals of the world, rev. for 3rd ed. by J. L. Paradiso. Johns Hopkins Univ. Press, Baltimore, Md. 1500 pp.

Wallis, G. W., and G. Reynolds. 1965. The initiation and spread of *Poria weirii* root rot of Douglas-fir. Can. J. Bot. 43:1–9.

Wargo, P. M. 1984. How stress predisposes trees to attack by *Armillaria mellea*—a hypothesis. *In* Proc. 6th IUFRO Conf. Root Butt Rots For. Trees, edited by G. A. Kile 115–22. CSIRO, Melbourne, Australia.

Waring, R. H., and J. F. Franklin. 1979. Evergreen coniferous forests of the Pacific Northwest. Science 204:1380–86.

Wells, P. V. 1970. Postglacial vegetational history of the Great Plains. Science 167:1574–82.

Wells-Gosling, N. 1985. Flying squirrels: gliders in the dark. Smithsonian Inst. Press, Wash., D.C. 128 pp.

Wernz, J. G. 1969. Spring mating of *Ascaphus*. J. Herpetol. 3:167–69.

Wernz, J. G, and R. M. Storm. 1969. Pre-hatching stages of the tailed frog, *Ascaphus truei* Stejneger. Herpetologica 25:86–93.

Whitaker, J. O., Jr., and C. Maser. 1976. Food habits of five western Oregon shrews. Northw. Sci. 50:102–7.

Whitaker, J. O., Jr., C. Maser, and L. E. Keller. 1977. Food habits of bats of western Oregon. Northw. Sci. 51:46–55.

Whitaker, J. O., Jr., C. Maser, and R. J. Pedersen. 1979. Food and ectoparasitic mites of Oregon moles. Northw. Sci. 53:268–73.

Whitaker, J. O., Jr., C. Maser, R. M. Storm, and J. J. Beatty, 1986. Food habits of clouded salamanders (*Aneides ferreus*) in Curry County, Oregon (Amphibia: Caudata: Plethodontidae). Great Basin Nat. 46:228–40.

Williams, S., and J. B. Stoltman. 1967. An outline of southeastern United States prehistory with particular emphasis on the Paleo-Indian Era. *In* The Quaternary of the United States, edited by J. E. Wright, Jr., and D. G. Frey. 669–83, Princeton Univ. Press, Princeton, N.J.

Wimsatt, W. A. 1960. An analysis of parturition in Chiroptera, including new observations on *Myotis l. lucifugus*. J. Mammal. 41:183–200.

Worster, D. 1979. Dust Bowl: the southern plains in the 1930s. Oxford Univ. Press, New York. 277 pp.

Index

❧❧❧